Late Victorian and Early Modernist Women Writers

Series Editors
Marion Thain and Kelsey Thornton

Dreams, Visions and Realities

Edited by Stephanie Forward

THE UNIVERSITY
OF BIRMINGHAM

UNIVERSITY PRESS

The Publishers gratefully acknowledge the receipt of permission to publish the following works granted by the author or her representatives:
    'The Quicksand': Reprinted by permission of the Estate of Edith Wharton and the Watkins/Loomis Agency.
    'The Storm': Reprinted by permission of the Louisiana State University Press from *The Complete Works of Kate Chopin* edited by Per Seyersted. Copyright © 1997 by Louisiana State University Press.

Every effort has been made to trace the rights-holders of copyright material used in this collection. The Publishers would be glad to hear from the representative of any author whose copyright work has been included without acknowledgement.

First published in the United Kingdom by The University of Birmingham Press, University of Birmingham, Aitchison Building, Edgbaston, Birmingham, BI5 2TT, UK.

ISBN 1 902459 27 X

British Library Cataloguing in Publication Data

A CIP catalogue record for this book is available from the British Library

Printed in Great Britain by
Lightning Source

Contents

Series Editors' Introduction

This series 'Late Victorian and Early Modernist Women Writers' owes its immediate inspiration to a casual grumble from Gail Cunningham. She was regretting that there are many splendid books by women at the turn of the nineteenth century which she would like to be able to teach, but that she was unable to put on her reading lists because her students would not be able to get hold of a copy. Anyone researching and teaching late Victorian and early modernist women writers will recognize this position: how difficult it can be to buy copies of prose texts which have changed the accepted view of literature of the period, and how frustrating that this revolution in the critical world cannot change the syllabuses we teach until good editions of these works are easily available. We decided to do something about it, and have designed a series which intends to bring back into print significant work by important and interesting women of the time, books which have been difficult to obtain but are nonetheless points of reference for those who study the period.

To establish a series of this sort is to make a clear statement about the changes taking place in our understanding of literary history and the place of women writers within it. It recognizes that a significant shift is being made in the way in which we must view not only the work produced in the late years of the nineteenth and the early years of the twentieth century but the critical position from which we understand it. We therefore thought it important to secure as editors critics and scholars whose work has figured significantly in assisting and defining this change.

Since one of the reasons for the neglect of these novels and stories is the nature of critical and social prejudices and opinions, we also thought that it was important to ask the editors to provide substantial contextualization, in introductions which should explain not only the importance of the writers for their own day but also for ours, and with substantial suggestions for further reading.

We trust that this group of books will enrich both courses in women's writing and courses on late Victorian and early modernist texts. The general reader too should find much to interest, amuse and entertain.

Marion Thain
Kelsey Thornton

Preface

"I am fond of life, and devote myself to the study of it in all its phases; and this leads to occasional adventures", Sarah Grand's Josepha nonchalantly remarks in "The Man in the Scented Coat". Whether it is Grand's New Woman writer playing at cards in a hide-out with the Prince of Wales during a fog-ridden London night, Beatrice Harraden's acclaimed pianist backpacking Switzerland in the guise of a piano tuner, Pauline Hopkins' spurned bride and abandoned wife taking male presumption for a ride, Mary Wilkins' home-loving mother putting her foot down about family accommodation, Kate Chopin's Louisiana wife spending a passionate afternoon in the arms of her lover for the immediate benefit of both their families, or Evelyn Sharp's teenage cricketer who joins the game only to change all the rules, the New Girls and rebellious Old Women in this collection appear to have a much better time of it than the prevailing image of the deadly serious and morally high-toned New Woman might lead us to expect: not for them the perils of a feminism which Elaine Showalter has recently condemned as "confining, Victorian and self-punishing" (Showalter 88).

It is certainly to the credit of this collection that the New Woman is presented in all her diversity, thematically as well as generically. As Stephanie Forward points out in her comprehensive introduction, there were many reasons why turn-of-the-century women authors were drawn to shorter forms of writing, and this is an aspect which tends to be neglected in critical appraisals of New Woman fiction. Some of the stories in this collection show an affinity with the realistic or naturalistic modes of much of the fiction of the time, while others capture the impressionistic technique of contemporary painting, or transport us to the world of dreams, the stuff of Gothic nightmares as well as of Freudian visions of the unconscious – an unconscious explored in haunting detail so that it may act on, and politicize, the reader's awareness of the condition of women in society. Thus Charlotte Mew's Poesque scenery and plot in "A White Night" intimate that live burial is the destiny of every good bride (the woman in wedding white) in the house of patriarchy: a recurrent message in *fin-de-siècle* feminist writing which is central also to Charlotte Perkins Gilman's "The Yellow Wall-paper" and Edith Wharton's "Quicksand". The eerie rituals, patterns and textual inscriptions which orchestrate female sacrifice and entombment in Mew, Gilman and Kingsford point to the irrational and arbitrary maze of male-defined structures and ideologies which entrap and paralyse women, yet as Olive Schreiner's "Dream Life and Real Life" suggests, feminists sometimes combined their attack on patriarchy with a reclamation of the concept of self-sacrifice in order to sanctify women (in Schreiner's story, black or mixed-race women) as a spiritually redemptive and morally regenerative force in society. Not all of the women presented in these stories are heroines in the conventional or even feminist sense; with its concluding tableau of cynical materialism, the ending of Ella Hepworth Dixon's "'The World's Slow Stain'", so different from the closing scene in Mabel Wotton's "The Hour of Her Life", illustrates the great variety of approaches, and it is this very hybridity and shape-shifting of the New Woman character – and writer – which make them such emblematic figures of the *fin de siècle*, an age of multiple contradictions, endings as much as beginnings, in which high realism vied with symbolist and proto-modernist literary forms and concerns, not infrequently in the work of one and the same writer. Indeed, Matthew Arnold's dictum of the "two worlds, one dead, / The other powerless to be born" (Arnold 321), is repeatedly echoed in these texts, such as when Wotton's rejected New Woman laments that she is "hanging between two worlds without belonging to either", while Caird's Old Man admits to a similar predicament, being "a sort of abortive creature, striding between two centuries".

An informed and well-balanced sense of textual hybridity is the overriding impression achieved by this collection, which brings together an exciting range of British and American writers, including a black New Woman writer, and which offers an absorbing mixture of canonical and neglected texts. The juxtaposition in particular of Gilman's famous "The Yellow Wall-paper" and Caird's little-known "The Yellow Drawing-Room" opens up a space for scrutinizing *fin-de-siècle* colour symbolism and the feminist use of metaphor, which is also of crucial significance to George Egerton's "The Mandrake Venus" and Kingsford's "The City of Blood". The introduction provides extensive contextualisations of the writers, period, and the central issues raised by their texts, teasing out the conceptual links between the stories and their thematic threads, such as the intricate way in which questions of class and racial or sexual oppression overlap and interlock. As Forward points out, many characters express a sense of alienation when they comment on events unfolding like a spectacle on the stage: ultimately, what writers sought to problematize was the performativity of gender and gender relations. That gender is a culturally constructed act (a performance) rather than an innate quality is a very modern idea which ran counter to the biological essentialism so prevalent at the turn of the century (in fact, many feminists of the time invoked biologically determinist, even eugenicist concepts in order to claim citizenship rights for women). Just as some of the writers in this collection challenged the taxonomies of late-Victorian science, so they deconstructed the masculine gaze in literature, either comically as in Caird's story, where the Old Man himself concedes the defectiveness of his vision, or dramatically as in Mew's "A White Night", which pointedly ends with the collision of female and male points of view:

> "Oh, for you", she says, and with a touch of bitterness, "it was a spectacle. The woman didn't really count."

> On looking back I see that, at the moment in my mind, the woman didn't really count. She saw herself she didn't. That's precisely what she made me see.

And this is of course precisely what the New Woman writers sought to get across to their predominantly female readership: the imperative, for women, to assert their rights, so that they would, once and for all, begin to "count": in their own as well as men's stories. As Mew's chilling introductory paragraph implies, only then would their tragedies lose their "merely accidental quality of melodrama"; would the violence they encountered cease to be perceived as "inessential" or even pleasantly "sensational"; would they rise from the shadow world of the mere "recollection ... experience ... picture", unable to "reproduce" (create) in their own right, and walk into the "radiant, bold, unapologetic, unabashed" light of Caird's sun-beamed yellow drawing-room, a vibrant symbol of the female literary imagination. I have no doubt that the reader will find much of interest and inspiration in these stories.

References

Arnold, Matthew. 'Stanzas from the Grande Chartreuse'. *Poems*. London: Dent, 1965.

Showalter, Elaine. *Inventing Herself: Claiming a Feminist Intellectual Heritage*. London: Picador, 2001.

Ann Heilmann, University of Wales Swansea

Acknowledgements

I would like to express my gratitude to Ann Heilmann for writing the preface to this anthology, and to Ann, Marion Thain and Kelsey Thornton for reading through the introduction and offering helpful advice.

Many thanks also to the courteous and efficient staff who work on the enquiry desks at Redditch Library, Worcestershire, for their assistance in tracking down the books I needed for this project.

Introduction

For much of the nineteenth century the novel was the dominant prose medium, but in the 1880s and 1890s the short story became increasingly popular. Women writers were at the heart of its development, and found it a congenial and liberating form. This anthology introduces stories written by women during the late nineteenth and early twentieth centuries, enabling modern readers to explore the themes and techniques they developed. The stories date from 1877 to 1910, and include contributions by British and American authors. The aim of the collection is to revisit their work and make it available to a wider audience. Several of the stories have not been printed since their original publication, although readers may be familiar with some of them already. Charlotte Perkins Gilman's "The Yellow Wall-paper", for example, has appeared in other anthologies. It merits inclusion here because it can be discussed alongside Mona Caird's little-known tale "The Yellow Drawing-Room".

The era covered was a very significant one for women, as they questioned their restricted position in society. Throughout this vibrant period of transition there were campaigns for reform in many different areas of their lives. They were seeking enhanced opportunities for education and employment, and hoped for professional recognition. There were demands for political enfranchisement and emancipation. Changes were requested in the laws pertaining to marriage, divorce and custody rights, and anxieties were voiced about the controversial subjects of prostitution and the dangers of sexually transmitted diseases. Women often espoused causes such as animal rights and vegetarianism, and some were attracted to spiritualism.

Critics have been drawn to the fascinating figure of the New Woman of the *fin de siècle*, who was mercilessly lampooned in her own day in the pages of *Punch*. However a recent volume of essays stresses the fact that The New Woman did not exist, and Lyn Pykett has suggested that the phrase is "a shifting and contested term" (Pykett, p. xi). Certainly it would be misleading to suggest that women all wanted the same things, and that they all worked together with specific hopes and dreams in common. Nevertheless, "dreaming" is a repeated idea in their writing and the stories in this volume tend to share some powerful imagery and themes. The anthology has not been arranged chronologically; rather it begins with a startling treatment of a controversial subject, which leads into another writer's attempt to address a related topic. Each story is linked to the next, as a number of interlocking issues are introduced in the book as a whole.

The term "Short-story" was first used to define a specific literary form by the American critic Brander Matthews, in an article in the *Saturday Review*, July 1884. Peter Keating has pointed out that Nathaniel Hawthorne and Edgar Allan Poe had called their work "tales" (Keating, p. 39). The short story liberated authors from some of the constraints imposed by novels: they could make a point very quickly, without needing to set scenes in minute detail, and without tracing intricate patterns of cause and effect. The three-decker novel had tended to follow particular plot conventions, and to conclude with either marriage or death; but in short stories authors found flexibility. They could focus on specific episodes, encounters and impressions, analysing psychological responses to those moments, and it was acceptable for the ending to remain open.

During the course of the nineteenth-century, British writers were influenced by a number of major literary trends from other countries and cultures. They encountered the realism of Flaubert, Maupassant, Dostoevsky, Tolstoy and Turgenev; the naturalism of Zola, Ibsen, Hamsun and Strindberg; and the symbolism of French writers, including Huysmans, Rimbaud and Verlaine. The short story form was mastered by American, French and Russian authors before having an impact in Britain. Many British authors were "disciples" of authors from abroad: for example, Ella D'Arcy admired the writings of Guy de Maupassant.

Contemporary periodicals and newspapers often contained fiction, and there was an ever-increasing demand for short stories. Keating has noted some illuminating statistics demonstrating the popularity of periodicals in the late nineteenth and the early twentieth centuries. In 1875 the *Newspaper Press Directory* listed 643 weekly, monthly and quarterly magazines; the number cited for 1885 was 1,298, rising to 2,081 in 1895 and 2,531 in 1903. Keating comments that these figures are not complete, but certainly indicate trends (Keating, p. 34). Holbrook Jackson, in his retrospective study of the 1890s, claimed that these publications "represented the unique qualities in the literature and art of the decade; they were bone of its bone and flesh of its flesh" (Holbrook Jackson, p. 41). The titles themselves convey something of the dandyish and playful flavour of the time. They included: the *Butterfly*, the *Chameleon*, the *Dome*, *Eureka*, the *Evergreen*, the *Hobby Horse*, the *Idler*, the *Pageant*, the *Pall Mall*, the *Parade*, *Pick-me-up*, the *Poster*, the *Quarto*, the *Rose Leaf*, the *Savoy*, the *Studio*, the *Temple*, *To-Day*, *To-Morrow*, the *Windsor* and the notorious *Yellow Book*. Some authors built their whole literary careers by producing short stories. The form proved ideal for adventure tales and ghost stories, for fantasies and utopian dream sequences. One of the major attractions of the short story was its versatility.

The short story had a fluidity of form, which was a feature of other branches of the arts. Jackson observed that during the 1890s striking effects were created by transposing terms from one set of artistic ideas to another, in the manner of Baudelaire's theory of correspondences. Thus Whistler gave pictures musical titles, for example "Symphonies" and "Harmonies", and W. E. Henley used musical terms for his poems, such as "Scherzando" and "Largo e Mesto" (Jackson, p. 173). Ella D'Arcy entitled her first anthology of short stories *Monochromes*. George Egerton's short stories of the eighteen nineties were published in volumes with titles suggesting musical pieces: *Keynotes*, *Discords*, *Symphonies* and *Fantasias*.

The rapidly expanding market for fiction offered opportunities to enterprising women writers like Egerton, and it is easy to see why the short story was particularly appealing to them. There were financial rewards: generally authors would receive the bulk of their payment for the initial periodical publication of a short story, but anthologies secured an additional sum. Women who could grasp only occasional moments to write, in between their other commitments, found the short story a very convenient medium. Furthermore, they could explore issues which genuinely concerned them, and attempt a range of writing styles.

The first story in this collection, George Egerton's "The Mandrake Venus", deals with prostitution. Egerton experimented with new modes of expression to describe innermost feelings and sexual desires, and her writing deserves our attention because of its provocative content, innovative techniques and perceptive psychological analysis. She derived her method of describing fleeting states of mind from some of the Scandinavian writers she admired, particularly Knut Hamsun. Her first book, *Keynotes* (1893), made a considerable contribution to women's literature of the *fin de siècle* and anticipated modernist writing. Its critics associated the publisher, John Lane, with the "feminisation" of fiction. They condemned the egotistical, introspective nature of the writing, and its "morbid" preoccupation with sexuality (Miller, pp. 25–6)

The theme of prostitution features in a number of Egerton's stories. *Discords* (1894) contains powerful indictments of society's attitudes in "Gone Under" and "Virgin Soil". The 1905 volume *Flies in Amber* includes "Mammy", about a young harlot dying of consumption in a London brothel (Forward, "Attitudes to Marriage and Prostitution", pp. 71–2). Lynda Nead has observed that nineteenth-century definitions of the prostitute were "multiple, fragmented and frequently contradictory". She could be viewed as an independent woman earning a living, or as a once-respectable person who had been reduced to selling herself; she might be seen as diseased and disruptive, or she could be sentimentalised as a victim. Definitions of the prostitute "were not discrete constructions but were constantly competing and working across each other" (Nead, pp. 91, 127).

In the summer of 1885, W. T. Stead, editor of the *Pall Mall Gazette*, published a series of articles about prostitution in London. "The Maiden Tribute of Modern Babylon" described the perils facing vulnerable young girls. The title was inspired by an ancient Greek myth, which described how the monstrous Minotaur was given seven boys and seven girls every nine years by the people of Athens. Stead's findings generated an immediate and far-reaching response. The Government raised the age of consent from thirteen to sixteen, under the Criminal Law Amendment Act of 1885, and the police were given increased authority to deal with prostitutes. In *City of Dreadful Delight*, Judith R. Walkowitz has explained how the prostitutes Stead was claiming to help actually became victims of police purges and public persecution (Walkowitz, pp. 85, 95).

Egerton's allegory "The Mandrake Venus", from *Fantasias* (1898), is her most harrowing account of prostitution. The very title is weird: the mandrake is a plant with a forked root, thought to resemble the human form. It was fabled to utter a deadly shriek when plucked from the ground, and was used in witchcraft or as a narcotic. In the story a pilgrim observes young men who are being led to a city, where they pay homage to "the World Harlot, the Mandrake Venus, the Arch-wife, the Ever-existing". Her throne is fashioned from men's bones, encrusted with golden coins, but, although she is extremely beautiful, passionate and sensual, she is "loathsome as a leper". Egerton describes an erotic scene in which women advance, "clad in garments of cobweb tissue". The use of sibilance accentuates the serpentine imagery, with its connotations of temptation and evil: "They swept on in sinuous lines, swaying, swinging, interlacing, in maddening intricacies; scattering scarlet blossoms as they danced, until their little white feet seemed to dip into a sea of blood." The men are drawn to the girls, as if by invisible magnets, but the pilgrim hears terrible screams: "the cry of the maid as she is torn from innocence and womanhood to minister to the service of the great Harlot mother, even as the mandrake cries as it is torn from its roots". The chilling message is that: "Nations change, creeds arise and die; the house of the Mandrake Venus is alone invincible."

Egerton's graphic imagery suggests sacrifice, and recalls Stead's articles on "The Maiden Tribute of Modern Babylon"; however, her Venus figure is an extraordinary mass of contradictions. She is delineated with images of power, mystery and voluptuousness; yet along with the magnificence there is cruelty and foulness. This provocative story highlights the sheer variety of discourses about sexuality in Victorian times, and raises interesting questions. Was the prostitute a deprived creature who deserved sympathy, or a depraved creature with animalistic sexual instincts? Was woman at once "angel and demon", "a figure of radical instability" (Shuttleworth, ch. 3, especially p. 55)?

A strange procession and images of sacrifice also feature in the second story, Charlotte Mew's macabre "A White Night", set in Spain in 1876.

A man named Cameron has been working there, and is joined by his sister, Ella, and brother-in-law, King. After getting locked into a church, they prepare to spend the night there. Fifty to sixty monks arrive with an enigmatic woman. She seems to acquiesce in a lengthy ritual, which culminates in her being buried alive. Cameron is adamant that they should not reveal themselves or intervene in the ceremony, and no white (k)night emerges to rescue the woman.

The notion of live burial imbues the story with a distinctly Gothic atmosphere. Enclosure, imprisonment, literal and figurative confinement: these images are pervasive in nineteenth-century women's writing (Gilbert and Gubar, p. 83). Much of Mew's work reflects the constraints placed upon women, and their habitual renunciation. In "A White Night" the victim is dressed from head to foot in white linen, connoting purity and innocence. She seems to be a representative figure of indeterminate age, acting out a role mechanically. Mew repeatedly uses vocabulary suggesting a theatrical spectacle. Cameron points out the incident's "merely accidental quality of melodrama". He observes that the woman plays her part "with superb effect", and he relates the story as though watching the staging of a drama. She detaches herself from "the living actors in the solemn farce". When Cameron realises that his sister is profoundly disturbed by what they are witnessing, he notes that the performance is "not a woman's comedy". The monks proceed with their ceremony, and Cameron feels he has been manipulated: "They managed the illusion for themselves and me magnificently." Afterwards Ella is haunted: "She refuses to admit that, after all, what one is pleased to call reality is merely the intensity of one's illusion."

"The Mandrake Venus" and "A White Night" both suggest that men and women are carried along by an incomprehensible force greater than themselves. In her opening paragraph Egerton speaks of "a cinématographe of the universe from time primeval". A tinker tells the pilgrim: "we have all been some one else; we are only going on over and over again". The train of men and boys on the pilgrimage dance "as if obsessed", and the women "as if bitten by a tarantula". Each night brings a victim to the great Harlot mother, because the mandrake poison "is carried from generation to generation". In Mew's story the faces of the monks "seemed to merge into one face – the face of nothing human – of a system, of a rule. It framed the woman's and one felt the force of it: she wasn't in the hands of men."

Women writers frequently used images of sacrifice, and suggested comparisons between the suffering endured by women and the treatment of animals. During the second half of the nineteenth century, campaigners in North America and Europe condemned vivisection. Surgical techniques were improving and major advances were being made in the understanding of human physiology, but animal sympathisers felt that these gains were often the result of experiments conducted upon helpless, conscious creatures without the use of anaesthetics. A number of late-Victorian authors criticised such experiments: for example, the heroine of Sarah Grand's novel *The Beth Book* (1897) is devastated to discover that her husband is a practising vivisectionist, and she debates the subject with him (Grand, *The Beth Book*, ch. 46). It is significant that their discussion leads into a heated altercation about the treatment of prostitutes, because reformers often drew links between the abuse of defenceless creatures and the repression of women by the medical profession and by men generally. Another leading feminist writer, Mona Caird, became President of the Independent Anti-Vivisection League, and published on animal rights.

Anna Kingsford was a high-profile campaigner against vivisection, and this concern is reflected in her graphic story "The City of Blood". She and Frances Power Cobbe became the most active British vivisectionists internationally. Kingsford wrote many articles about animal experimentation, and lectured widely in Europe. Her efforts were strengthened by the fact that she was one of the few female crusaders to be a qualified doctor. Indeed, as a medical student in Paris in the 1870s she offered herself as a subject for vivisection. She cursed opponents, claiming responsibility for the deaths of the French physiologist Claude Bernard in 1878 and Paul Bert in 1886. Her friends thought of her as a reincarnation of the goddess Isis (Meade, p. 277).

Kingsford lived with Edward Maitland. They were both theosophists and believed that truths were relayed through them during special dreams. The allegories in Kingsford's volume *Dreams and Dream Stories* are steeped in theosophical imagery. In "The City of Blood" the narrator dreams of a desolate street filled with buildings resembling a prison. She becomes aware of strange sounds of suffering, then blood oozes from a house which is actually the laboratory of a vivisectionist. However the dream extends in scope, because the various houses are the settings for a range of abuses on both animals and humans. Maitland said that he was profoundly impressed by the relation of the dream, as well as being apprehensive about its effects upon Anna Kingsford, "by reason of its tendency to confirm and aggravate her already strong tendency to pessimism". Soon afterwards, when he was "between waking and sleeping", he was "given" a sequel, in which he learned that there was *one* way of escaping from the dreadful City – by ascending to heaven. He and Kingsford came to recognise the dream as:

> an exquisite and prophetic allegory of the state to which the world has become reduced under a priest-constructed religion and a civilisation wholly materialistic, and of the way in which our own and all other redemptive work must be done, in that only they who have first ascended in themselves can – returning – enable others also to ascend and accomplish their needed salvation (Maitland, vol. 1, pp. 160–62).

Olive Schreiner also wrote many allegorical dream sequences, which were very popular in her own day and were a source of inspiration to the suffragettes (Forward, "The Dreams of Olive Schreiner"). It is not surprising that this form appealed to her: she was raised in South Africa, where her parents were missionaries; throughout her childhood she was immersed in biblical teachings, and would appreciate the power of parables. Although she lost her faith and became a freethinker at an extraordinarily young age, the influence of biblical phrasing, rhythms and imagery is apparent in her writing.

When Schreiner published her volume *Dreams* (1890) the reviewer in the *Athenaeum* compared the dream sequences to the painted allegories of Watts, and the *Daily Chronicle* described the author as a "poet-painter". Contemporary critics also praised the volume's lyrical qualities. The short story has an affinity with poetry, and in the 1890s critics enthused about the virtually seamless blending of the two genres. The *Athenaeum* review said of Schreiner's dreams: "Written in exquisite prose they have the essential qualities of poetry, and are, indeed, poems in English." In the *Northern Daily News* they were referred to as "veritable prose poems" (Schreiner, pp. 5, 6).

The creation of dream sequences was therapeutic, enabling Schreiner to withdraw from her anxieties and to sublimate her desires by envisaging a utopian world and the melioration of the human race. For many contemporary women, dreams were a means of escape. Schreiner's vision extended beyond escapism, however, for she hoped to motivate her readers through idealism and optimism to regenerate society: "to carry the dreams and ideals we have formed out into the world, and incarnate them quietly and simply day by day in action" (Letter to Karl Pearson, 23 October 1886. Rive, pp. 108–11).

Dreams feature prominently in one of Schreiner's early tales, "Dream Life and Real Life: a Little African Story", which first appeared in *The New College Magazine* in 1881. Her brother Fred was headmaster of New College School, in Eastbourne, and she stayed with him when she first came to England. The story concerns Jannita, an indentured orphan employed as a goatherd by a cruel Boer family. In her "dream life" the farm is transformed into a pretty, welcoming place; her abusive employers are kind; and, best of all, her father arrives to carry her back to Denmark. Dreaming helps Jannita to cope with her wretched existence; unfortunately there is a sharp contrast between "dream life" and "real life". When Jannita overhears three men plotting to set fire to the farm and to rob the owner, she calls out a warning to her employer. The men murder her and bury her beside her stone "home".

Ann Heilmann has suggested that "with her central Christian metaphor of self-sacrifice Schreiner tapped into the feminist unconscious of the time" (Heilmann, "Dreams in Black and White", pp. 181–2). Jannita is a Christ-like figure. Her racial identity is unclear, because we cannot tell whether she is white, black or of mixed race. Her self-sacrifice may imply that, together, and irrespective of their ethnic backgrounds, women can bring about the regeneration of the human race.

Ella D'Arcy's story, "An Engagement", introduces a different kind of oppression. The heroine dies in less gruesome circumstances; nevertheless, she is clearly a victim. Having invested in a medical practice at Jacques-le-Port, Dr. Jack Owen courts Agnes Allez, believing her to be worth ten thousand pounds. The unscrupulous Owen easily wins the poor girl. She is only seventeen: an inexperienced child who is living a cloistered existence with her grandmother and her mentally retarded brother. Following their engagement, Owen learns that her cash is likely to be tied up, and he is mortified to discover that her family's money has been accumulated from a drapery business. Agnes is devastated by his decision to cancel the engagement.

Despite repeated rebuffs she persists in making excuses for him: this is "the eternal rehabilitative process, in which every woman shows herself such an adept in relation to the man she loves". As the months pass her love remains constant, until one day Owen cuts her dead in public. Her interminable journey home under the blazing, inexorable sun is too much for her and she dies. Agnes is a victim in so many ways. Her upbringing restricts her, leaving her vulnerable; Owen exploits her with cynical ruthlessness; he, in turn, is influenced by the rigid class structure on the Islands. Agnes is reminiscent of some of the doomed heroines of French fiction. D'Arcy traces her decline graphically: a decline that is both emotional and physical.

Mabel E. Wotton's story, "The Hour of her Life", is also about class differences. Annette Browning's father was an officer and gentleman, but married beneath him. She has established a successful business, running an exclusive flower-shop "in the heart of Clubland", and is adored by eligible bachelor Freddy Calvin – the heir to a Lord. Although Annette is an independent, professional woman, it is not possible for her to cross the class divide. She elects to make a dignified exit and, in so doing, she shows herself to be a better person than those who are, ostensibly, her superiors. Wotton highlights the difficulties facing women who were placed awkwardly in the social hierarchy.

In 1894 Ella Hepworth Dixon published her novel *The Story of a Modern Woman*, a *Bildungsroman* describing Mary Erle's efforts to survive after the death of her father. Dixon's text can be read alongside the 1888 novel *Out of Work* by "John Law" (Margaret Harkness) and Mary Cholmondeley's *Red Pottage* (1899), as all three authors produced realist fiction. *The Story of a Modern Woman* is a plea for sisterhood; for what Dixon called "a kind of moral and social trades-unionism among women" (Dixon, "The Book of the Month", p. 71). Interestingly there is an Oscar Wilde figure, called Mr Beaufort Flower, and Wilde is parodied again in Dixon's short story "'The World's Slow Stain'". In a sense, Wilde was fair game. Male writers like Henry James and Wilde satirised other authors, so perhaps Dixon did not need to feel any qualms about returning the gesture. Having said that, Wilde had helped to further her literary aspirations by publishing some of her work in *The Woman's World* during his editorship from November 1887 to October 1889.

Cynicism and weariness pervade "'The World's Slow Stain'". The title of the story is a quotation from Shelley's *Adonais*: "From the contagion of the world's slow stain / He is secure" (XL). Adela Buller has made up her mind to contract a marriage of convenience with Anthony Mellingham, despite the fact that he jilted her ten years earlier. Throughout the tale she is shown to be conscious of her image and her role in society, and assumes poses as and when necessary. Adela views life as a card game, in which the male players are inveterate gamblers and the women have never had the rules explained to them properly.

The odious Gilbert Vincent is heavily based on Wilde. Dixon repeatedly emphasises his fat face and feminine hands; his "uncanny" pallor; his languid demeanour; his "curious", "dubious" and "singularly unpleasant" smile. Both of the male characters in the plot are unscrupulous. Adela visibly ages at the end of the story, but she is determined to see the "game" through. She is a participant, coping as best she can when the odds seem stacked against her. "'The World's Slow Stain'" is an example of naturalist writing, in that we see Adela struggling to adapt to her environment.

Dixon was regarded as part of the *Yellow Book* circle; however she was critical of *fin-de-siècle* society, and was displeased when a friend spoke of her as a "new woman" (Dixon, *As I Knew Them*, p. 41). Her story engages with the contemporary debate about the characteristics of the "modern" woman. Gilbert Vincent regards Adela as "curious" and "one of a new species": "She calls it 'dull' of a woman not to have had emotional experiences, and wouldn't thank you if you altered your conversation to spare her blushes....Yet she can be very sweet, very attractive; and she is curiously feminine – for a modern type."

"'The World's Slow Stain'" was published in 1904. Edith Wharton's story of the same year, "The Quicksand", also explores the individual's relationship to the environment. Hope Fenno falls in love with Alan Quentin, yet feels she cannot marry him because of her moral objections to the newspaper he owns. His mother advises her: "Life is made up of compromises: that is what youth refuses to understand. I've lived long enough to doubt whether any real good ever came of sacrificing beautiful facts to even more beautiful theories."

Hope decides to remain faithful to her beliefs, but six months later the girl has visibly wilted. Her sacrifice of love has proved to be painful, and she tells Mrs. Quentin that she has come round to her way of thinking. At this point, however, the older woman interrupts her and insists that Hope was in the right after all. Now they face each other, woman to woman, soul to soul. It transpires that Hope's position mirrored that of

Mrs. Quentin many years earlier, when she had been unhappy about the newspaper. She had tried to ignore it, and its hateful contents, but she can see that Alan's work "is a kind of hideous idol to which he would make human sacrifices!" She tells Hope: "It's because I see you're alive, as I was, tingling with beliefs, ambitions, energies, as I was – that I can't see you walled up alive, as I was, without stretching out a hand to save you!"

The word "sacrifice" features repeatedly in Wharton's story, and the reference to being "walled up", or buried alive, provides an interesting starting point for linking "The Quicksand" with Mew's "A White Night" and, as we shall see, with Ménie Muriel Dowie's "A Cowl in Cracow". The story is left open, as Hope reflects upon her future course of action. There is an illuminating introduction to Wharton's fiction in Katherine Joslin's study of the writer and her work. She observes that Wharton's fictive world "is peopled with both men and women, who must struggle for selfhood within the social context; she insistently and, many critics have claimed, even perversely avoids the easy, happy ending" (Joslin, p. 35, also ch. 2).

Mrs. Quentin's initial advice to Hope accords with the experience of Justine Brent in Wharton's novel *The Fruit of the Tree* (1907), in which she learns that life is "a succession of pitiful compromises with fate, of concessions to old traditions, old beliefs, old charities and frailties" (Wharton, p. 624). Joslin notes Wharton's keen interest in Darwin's *On the Origin of Species* and suggests that in her fiction the survivor is the person who is best able to conform or fit with the social structure. Thus survival depends upon one's ability to compromise. Darwin also published his *Descent of Man* in 1871, and in fact Wharton's "The Quicksand" is from a volume entitled *"The Descent of Man" and Other Stories* (1904).

Concepts of compromise and conformity were challenged by women who wanted to experience more freedom from restrictive life-styles and mundane responsibilities. Sarah Grand's story "The Man in the Scented Coat" describes a New Woman venturing out in London. A number of critics have outlined how women negotiated their place in the city in late Victorian times, contesting masculine domination of the terrain and challenging gender boundaries (Nord, Parsons, Walkowitz, *City of Dreadful Delight*, chs. 1 and 2, Wilson). Improved transport networks facilitated travel, enabling women to encroach upon traditional male areas. Josepha, the woman in Grand's story, intends to walk to the station and catch a train, after visiting her friend. Increased mobility could, however, lead women into precarious situations: a woman on her own might be mistaken for a prostitute; also "roughs" might be encountered (Grand's heroine meets a gang). The Jack the Ripper murders had taken place in Whitechapel in 1888, so they would still be relatively fresh in the minds of readers. The big city was a seductive, challenging place for females, with the prospect of adventure but also the possibility of danger.

Grand left her husband in 1890, and moved to London in 1891. During her early years there she wrote a number of stories which were published later, in 1908, in the volume *Emotional Moments*. In the preface she explains that her prior knowledge of London had been gained during visits, when she viewed the city as "a pleasant dream-region, delicately tinted in healthy colours, with every beauty accentuated, and all the ugliness successfully concealed; the goodness was made apparent; the underlying misery, the cruelty, the evil, little suspected". Having settled there, she was shocked: "As from the centre of a circle I saw Society, at that time, all about me, piled up into a dense mass – a mass in which the more attractive attributes of human nature were obliterated, the more repulsive features forced into prominence." She lamented that avaricious, influential people were "lowering the standard" (Grand, *Emotional Moments*, pp. xi, xv).

In "The Man in the Scented Coat" Josepha finds herself caught up in a fracas between two gentlemen and a gang of ruffians. The perfumed man is short and stout, with a muffler concealing the lower part of his face; nevertheless the "roughs" recognise him. One of them declares: "We don't want to support no more blamed expensive royal aristocrats, we don't." Subsequently Josepha follows the gentlemen. She is clearly an advanced young lady, as she accepts a cigarette and converses with ease. Josepha plays cards with the man in the scented coat, but cannot help thinking "of the part such a man might play in life if only he devoted himself with the same conscientious intelligence to nobler pursuits". Before parting from her, the man makes it clear that her silence would be appreciated. Some months later she receives a gift, but rejects it contemptuously, with "royal scorn", because she "should have been trusted, not tried".

It seems likely that the mysterious man is supposed to be the Prince of Wales, who lived a notoriously profligate life-style and was a keen gambler. Here the portrait is of a self-indulgent idler, absorbed in trivial amusements. Josepha is depicted as being superior to him, because of her greater integrity. In this respect, she can be compared to Wotton's heroine Annette Browning.

Many of Grand's female characters revel in being outdoors; for example, Adalesa in "The Yellow Leaf" and Eugenia in "Eugenia: A Modern Maiden and a Man Amazed" (Grand, *Our Manifold Nature*). In Grand's novels a number of her heroines seek excitement by venturing out at night: Angelica in *The Heavenly Twins* (1893), Beth in *The Beth Book* (1897) and Babs in *Babs the Impossible* (1901). They feel confined and frustrated with their lives and enjoy the thrill of rebellion. Grand must have been fond of the character Josepha, because she features again in later stories. In *Variety* (1922) she appears in "I Can't Explain It" and in "Josepha Recounts a Remarkable Experience".

In Ménie Muriel Dowie's "A Cowl in Cracow" the narrator roams about in the town, without supervision. Like Josepha in Sarah Grand's story, the woman negotiates the terrain on her own terms. A mysterious atmosphere is evoked when the heroine arrives at a strange, silent building. In the tale that unfolds, there are some striking affinities with Charlotte Mew's "A White Night".

The three explorers in Mew's story feel like intruders as they observe the ghastly immolation of the young woman. In Dowie's story the narrator feels that she is intruding when she enters the building, which resembles a nunnery. To her astonishment, she disturbs a young man attired in an unusual garment similar to a monk's. In both tales there is a distancing effect as the episodes are described as being like scenes in a play. Mew's spectators feel that they are watching a performance, and cannot intervene. Dowie's heroine states: "To me, he appeared a creature in a front scene, I one of the audience, of whom nothing but attention was expected." The young man, a Pole, explains that he was devoted to a cause but was reprimanded by his father; now he is cloistered away from society.

In both stories people are buried alive, and the narratives can be explored as metaphors for the human condition. Readers of Mew's account may well feel that her story says something about the restricting bonds of patriarchy, as the young woman resigns herself to her fate. In Dowie's story, however, it is the woman who walks out free into the sunshine. The young man is the sacrifice, handed over to the Church by his own father. He feels morally obliged to remain there, having made a promise.

Charlotte Perkins Gilman and Mona Caird both wrote stories about women who feel "buried" and constrained by men. Gilman's famous short story "The Yellow Wall-paper" (1892) is widely acknowledged to be a feminist classic. However before her tale was published, the British writer Mona Caird independently wrote her own study in yellow called "The Yellow Drawing-Room". Gilman's story was written in 1890, but was not published until 1892. In 1891 Caird published a volume called *A Romance of the Moors*, which contained "The Yellow Drawing-Room". The two stories merit examination alongside each other, because both are studies of confinement, hysteria and obsession and their authors had shared concerns and aims. There were wide-spread fears that social degeneration would result if women rejected their traditional roles as wives and mothers. Caird and Gilman describe the psychological pressures for women living in a patriarchal society.

Gilman's story was written after she underwent treatment for depression, following the birth of her only child. The "rest cure", prescribed by the eminent neurologist Silas Weir Mitchell, almost drove her insane (Showalter, *The Female Malady*, pp. 138–44, 158, 181). Patients were isolated and encouraged to consume large quantities of food; were forbidden to indulge in intellectual activities, and were subjected to passive exercise by means of massage. The intention was to make them become childlike, submissive and heavily dependent upon their doctors. For a woman like Gilman, an intellectual who revelled in exercising both her mind and her body, the "cure" was tantamount to torture.

The narrator of the story is confined in a room with yellow wallpaper, which she finds increasingly oppressive. She is driven into madness by a complex fusion of desires, frustrations and guilt: whilst yearning to escape, she knows that she is evading her duties and responsibilities. Having discerned a face in the wallpaper she believes that a woman is creeping about behind it; indeed, sometimes many women seem to be trapped. Eventually she peels off the paper to release the figure, and believes that she herself has emerged. Triumphantly she informs her husband that he cannot put her back, but the reader is conscious that her "victory" will be a very limited and hollow one.

"The Yellow Wall-paper" has attracted a great deal of critical attention, and has been analysed from many different angles (e.g., see Bauer, Erskine and Richards, Golden, Golden and Zangrando, Gough and Rudd, and Lane). The story can be read as an attack upon marriage and motherhood, and an appeal for women to have more choices about their lives. Gilman hints that creative women are stifled, highlighting one of the problems facing female artists. The story is also an indictment of the medical profession's attitude to female patients, with its harrowing account of the methods used to control the "hysteric". Another thought-provoking issue is Gilman's response to decadence and aestheticism (Heilmann, "Overwriting Decadence", pp. 175–88).

Caird's "The Yellow Drawing-Room" is archetypal of the 1890s, reflecting the author's awareness of living through a period of transition (Forward, "A Study in Yellow", Heilmann, "Mona Caird"). The male narrator, Mr. St. Vincent, analyses an episode in his life which has "unhinged" him. His distress is due to the power exerted over him by Vanora Haydon. Having been given permission to decorate and furnish a drawing-room, Vanora's colour choice is a brilliant yellow. She has made her mark upon the drawing-room: in effect it is a room of her own, something denied to so many women at that time. St. Vincent cannot cope with this colour scheme, because it is a manifestation of Vanora's unpredictability and her refusal to submit to male domination. She has no intention of changing the colour to suit him; but, ironically, and to her chagrin, Vanora is enthralled by him. Another of her admirers, George Inglis, observes that the strange relationship between St. Vincent and Vanora is a kind of contest: "if one could imagine the Eighteenth Century as a lover wooing the Nineteenth Century, this is the sort of angular labyrinthine courtship we should have". Whilst Inglis speaks in terms of the eighteenth and nineteenth centuries, Caird actually conveys the difficulties of living through the period of transition at the end of the nineteenth century. The implication is that the same problems will persist into the twentieth century. St. Vincent and Vanora are drawn to each other, but cannot compromise: both fear becoming "unhinged".

The references to "yellow" are charged with significance, in view of the colour's associations in the late nineteenth century. James McNeill Whistler popularised egg-yolk yellow; it became the fashionable shade for interior decoration, and was regarded later as the colour which best represented the art of the 1890s. Holbrook Jackson referred to yellow as "the colour of the hour, the symbol of the time spirit. It was associated with all that was *bizarre* and queer in art and life, with all that was outrageously modern" (Jackson, p. 54). Katherine Lyon Mix has noted that yellow breakfasts were given by Sir Richard Burton; and that yellow sunflowers were painted by William Morris on the walls of the Oxford Union, becoming "the symbol of aestheticism in the hand of Oscar Wilde". She also mentioned that "Mona Caird had her drawing room done with yellow curtains and carpet" (ch. 1). The first quarterly volume of *The Yellow Book* appeared in 1894: "a youthful and vigorous attempt to make a beginning, to break new ground, to clear the air.....The very colour chosen was that of the notoriously immoral French novel" (Denny, p. 9). Richard Le Gallienne's *The Boom in Yellow* highlighted the popularity of the colour, and he suggested that the success of Iota's *The Yellow Aster* (1894) was largely due to its title. In his *Prose Fancies* he declared: "the triumph of yellow is imminent" (Jackson, pp. 54–5). A critic of New Woman literature, Hugh E. M. Stutfield, spoke out against "the yellow lady novelists". Their work was full of morbid self-analysis, and was symptomatic of the degeneration rife in society ("Tommyrotics" and "The Psychology of Feminism"). As Caird's story was published in 1891, she was clearly a herald of what was to come.

Colour in a different sense inspired a special genre which emerged in nineteenth century America, based upon particular locales and communities. Prose fiction was the medium used for most "local color" writing, although poetry and non-fiction were also employed for regionalist works. Authors tried to capture the distinctive features of an area: the vocabulary and dialect, the landscape, the subject matter, customs and characters reflecting the qualities and concerns of the region. Americans were keen to establish a literature of their own, distinct from other traditional forms.

The "local color" stories of Mary E. Wilkins have been praised for their realism. She married a Mr. Freeman in 1902 and so is often referred to as Mary E. Wilkins Freeman. Her characters are beautifully drawn, and she evokes the rural New England community with great sensitivity and perceptiveness. In "The Revolt of 'Mother'" Sarah Penn is an oppressed wife, small in stature, with a look of mildness, benevolence and meekness; but, ultimately, she asserts herself and achieves a memorable victory. Many of Wilkins's stories hint at the potential for revolt that simmers within people who lead humdrum lives. Some local colorists tended to produce caricatures, but Wilkins clearly empathises with many of her figures, respecting their stoical courage in conditions of poverty and hardship.

Kate Chopin also wrote "local color" stories, using a Louisiana setting. She was, however, influenced by a number of important European writers: notably by Daudet, Maupassant, Molière and Flaubert. Willa Cather was the first critic to call Chopin's novel *The Awakening* "a Creole *Bovary*" (Toth, p. 352). The transgressive plot of *The Awakening* certainly has much in common with *Madame Bovary*: both Emma Bovary and Edna Pontellier struggle to transcend the restrictions of marriage and motherhood, and what they yearn for is always out of reach. Flaubert and Chopin explore a woman's dilemma as she confronts passion, and both authors were vilified by critics.

Maupassant was an even greater source of inspiration. Chopin explained:

> I read his stories and marvelled at them. Here was life, not fiction; for where were the plots, the old fashioned mechanism and stage trapping that in a vague, unthinking way I had fancied were essential to the art of story making. Here was a man who had escaped from tradition and authority, who had entered into himself and looked out upon life through his own being and with his own eyes; and who, in a direct and simple way, told us what he saw. When a man does this, he gives us the best that he can; something valuable for it is genuine and spontaneous. (Toth, p. 205)

Maupassant died of syphilis in 1893. From 1894 onwards Chopin translated his stories, and her own volume of short stories, *Bayou Folk* (also 1894), emulates Maupassant's style. Often in her work she evokes a haunting atmosphere, broaching the subject of sexual desire with erotic, sensual language. Many of her heroines are passionate and frustrated, longing to spread their wings, and Chopin captures their cynicism and isolation.

"The Storm" was written in 1898, after Chopin had become famous, but she did not consider publishing it because she knew that its explicit treatment of sexual longing would be condemned (Toth, p. 320). She had been very sympathetic when Mary E. Wilkins's novel *Pembroke* (1894) was criticised for being unwholesome. Eventually "The Storm" was printed in *The Complete Works of Kate Chopin* in 1969. It was actually a sequel to an earlier tale, called "At the 'Cadian Ball". In the first story Chopin had introduced the characters Alcée, Bobinôt, Clarisse and Calixta.

In real life Chopin had an affair with a man called Albert Sampite, when she was living in Cloutierville. We do not know whether the clandest-ine relationship began before or after the death of her husband, Oscar. Chopin lived in a society where women were expected to conform to a domestic ideal; however she knew that this could be stultifying and, ultimately, destructive. Sampite is depicted in "The Storm" as the planter Alcée Laballière. He is married to Clarisse, and Calixta's husband is Bobinôt.

Calixta is at home sewing. The sewing symbolises acceptance of the domestic round, but her task is set aside when Alcée seeks refuge from the storm and reminds her of a time when they kissed passionately. Now they consummate their passion, actually within Calixta's marital home, whilst the storm rages outside. Afterwards Calixta welcomes home her husband and child and Alcée writes an affectionate letter to his wife, who is away with their children. The concluding sentence is striking: "So the storm passed and everyone was happy." In *The Awakening* the frustrated heroine, Edna Pontellier, resorts to suicide, but in "The Storm" Chopin permits Calixta to follow "nature" freely and to enjoy her sexual fling. This involves transgression against society's accepted code of behaviour. Chopin might be implying that if individuals deny their longings, their respectable response might ultimately be more destructive for themselves and for society as a whole. As Ann Heilmann has pointed out to me, in Ella D'Arcy's "An Engagement" the stark alternative to sexual fulfilment is death. It is not really surprising that Chopin's provocative story did not appear in print in its own day.

Chopin was a prolific writer, supporting her six children after she was widowed. The public's interest in short stories enabled women from a variety of backgrounds to earn a living. Many minority magazines were established at the turn of the century in America, providing ethnic authors with an outlet for their work. Carmen Birkle has made the point that the women's movement was not just a white middle-class affair, and she has explored depictions of the New Woman in stories by the Native American Zitkala–Ša (1876–1938), the Chinese American Sui Sin Far (1865–1914), the Mexican American María Cristina Mena (1893–1965) and the German American Helen Reimensnyder Martin (1868–1939) (Heilmann, *Feminist Forerunners*). These writers responded to the public's interest in short stories, seizing the opportunity to address contemporary race and gender issues.

The African-American Pauline E. Hopkins had her writing published by the Colored Cooperative Publishing Company, both in the *Colored American Magazine* and in book form (See Bair, Bergman, Garvey and Matter-Seibel in Heilmann, *Feminist Forerunners*, Busby, Shockley and Washington). Her first novel, *Contending Forces* (1900), addresses race and gender issues. In the preface Hopkins highlights the importance of fiction for her people: "It is a record of growth and development from generation to generation. No one will do this for us: we must ourselves develop the men and women who will faithfully portray the innermost thoughts and feelings of the Negro with all the fire and romance which lie dormant in our history."

Hopkins's story "Bro'r Abr'm Jimson's Wedding: A Christmas Story" came out in 1901. Like Mary E. Wilkins, she sets her tale in New England; however, she describes a different section of the community. The people are well-to-do Afro-Americans, with a Church described as "the richest plum in the ecclesiastical pudding". During the course of this lively romp, Brother Jimson gets his just des(s)erts.

Needless to say, where there are winners there are also losers. Ella Hepworth Dixon's heroine Adela thinks of life as a card game – one that women are unlikely to win. The other games people play include that fine British institution, cricket, which is taken by Evelyn Sharp as the ostensible subject of one of her tales in *Rebel Women*. The ramifications of the story's actual theme are profound. "The Game that wasn't Cricket" is written in the first person, with a conversational style enhanced by delightful touches of humour; yet Sharp addresses a serious issue. The story is about gender expectations: parents foster sex antagonism by separating their boys and girls when they play, assigning them "appropriate" activities.

The characters in the story are not given names, because they are representative figures. The narrator describes an incident where role reversal takes place. A girl is always left holding the baby while her brother enjoys a game of cricket; but one evening she seizes the opportunity to participate in the game, despite protests from the outraged boys. Indeed, she does not simply play the game; she transforms it. Ultimately the boys regain control of the game and the girl returns, weeping, to her designated role as babyminder. However, the narrator notes wryly that the girl's innovative tactics are adopted by the regular team.

In Beatrice Harraden's "A Bird on its Journey" the young heroine is more successful in her attempts to be taken seriously. Harraden's 1893 novel *Ships that Pass in the Night* incorporated allegories, as did Olive Schreiner's *The Story of an African Farm* (1883), and, like Schreiner, she also wrote individual allegories. In "A Bird on its Journey" the guests at a hotel in Switzerland fail to recognise the talented musician Thyra Flowerdew, mistaking her for a piano tuner. Oswald Everard decides she is "what the novels call an advanced young woman". He is attracted to this "wild little bird", and hopes to tame her. Thyra, however, regards herself as "a bird of passage", and has no intention of renouncing her freedom. Her ambition is to rise to the very top of her profession.

Female writers in the nineteenth century frequently compared women to birds trapped in cages, or to birds with clipped wings, yearning to fly freely. Many Victorian women felt frustrated by the sheer repetitiveness of their daily routine. Florence Nightingale criticised the grinding monotony of the domestic sphere, and memorably likened women to the Archangel Michael upon Saint Angelo in Rome, having enormous wings, but being unable to fly (Nightingale, 228). Harraden's story is interesting because her heroine has managed to escape from the traditional woman's sphere and to triumph in her chosen career.

Dreams, Visions and Realities demonstrates that a number of key images appeared time after time as female authors used short stories to reflect upon the experiences of their age. It would be a sheer impossibility in a book of this length to cover the whole range of women's writing in the late nineteenth and early twentieth centuries; besides, any anthology inevitably reflects the interests and predilections of its editor. Nevertheless, I hope that this collection will illustrate the range of subject and style which women explored in this new genre; that it will prove useful to those who are studying the period, and that it will whet the appetite of the casual browser.

Works cited and suggested further reading

Alexander, Sally. *Becoming a Woman and Other Essays in 19ᵗʰ and 20ᵗʰ Century Feminist History*. London: Virago, 1994.

Bauer, Dale M., ed. *Charlotte Perkins Gilman: The Yellow Wall-paper*. Boston: Bedford Books, 1998.

Bennett, Bridget, ed. *Ripples of Dissent: Women's Stories of Marriage from the 1890s*. London: J. M. Dent and Sons, 1996.

Birkle, Carmen. "Multiculturalism and the New Woman in Early Twentieth-Century America". *Feminist Forerunners: (New) Womanism and Feminism in the Early Twentieth Century*. Ed. Ann Heilmann. London: Pandora, 2001.

Bland, Lucy. *Banishing the Beast: English Feminism and Sexual Morality 1885–1914*. Harmondsworth: Penguin Books, 1995.

Brown, Heloise, Madi Gilkes, and Ann Kaloski-Naylor, eds. *White?Women: Critical perspectives on race and gender*. York: Raw Nerve Books, 1999.

Busby, Margaret, ed. *Daughters of Africa*. London: Vintage, 1993.

Caird, Mona. *A Sentimental View of Vivisection*. London: W. Reeves, 1895.

—— *Beyond the Pale, an Appeal on Behalf of the Victims of Vivisection*. London: W. Reeves, 1896.

—— *Some Truths About Vivisection*. London: Victoria Street Society, 1894.

Denny, Norman, ed. *The Yellow Book, a Selection*. London: The Bodley Head, 1949.

Dixon, Ella Hepworth. *The Story of a Modern Woman* reviewed in "The Book of the Month. The Novel of the Modern Woman". *Review of Reviews* X (1894): 71.

—— *As I Knew Them: Sketches of People I Have Met Along the Way*. London: Hutchinson, 1930.

Dowling, Linda. "The Decadent and the New Woman in the 1890s". *Nineteenth Century Fiction* 33:4 (1979): 434–53.

Egerton, George. *Fantasias*. London: John Lane, 1898.

—— *Flies in Amber*. London: Hutchinson, 1905.

—— *Keynotes* and *Discords*. University of Birmingham Press, 2003 reprint. The volumes were originally published separately, in 1893 and 1894 respectively.

—— *Symphonies*. London: John Lane, 1897.

First, Ruth and Ann Scott. *Olive Schreiner: A Biography* [New York, 1980]. Reprinted New Brunswick, New Jersey: Rutgers University Press, 1990.

Forward, Stephanie. "A Study in Yellow: Mona Caird's 'The Yellow Drawing-Room'". *Women's Writing* 7.2 (2000): 295–307.

—— "Attitudes to Marriage and Prostitution in the Writings of Olive Schreiner, Mona Caird, Sarah Grand and George Egerton". *Women's History Review* 8.1 (1999): 53–80.

—— "The Dreams of Olive Schreiner". *Irish Journal of Feminist Studies* 3.1 (Autumn 1998): 61–74.

Gardiner, Juliet, ed. *The New Woman: Women's Voices 1880–1918*. London: Collins and Brown Limited, 1993.

Gilbert, Sandra M. and Susan Gubar. *The Madwoman in the Attic: the Woman Writer and the Nineteenth-Century Literary Imagination*. New Haven and London: Yale University Press, 1979.

Gilman, Charlotte Perkins. *The Yellow Wallpaper*. Eds. Thomas L. Erskine and Connie L. Richards. New Brunswick, New Jersey: Rutgers University Press, 1993.

Glasser, Leah Blatt. *In a Closet Hidden: The Life and Work of Mary E. Wilkins Freeman*. University of Massachusetts Press, 1996.

Golden, Catherine, ed. *The Captive Imagination: A Casebook on 'The Yellow Wall-paper'*. New York: The Feminist Press, 1992.

Golden, Catherine, and Joanna Schneider Zangrando, eds. *The Mixed Legacy of Charlotte Perkins Gilman*. Newark, University of Delaware Press, 2000.

Gough, Val and Jill Rudd, eds. *A Very Different Story: Studies on the Fiction of Charlotte Perkins Gilman*. Liverpool: Liverpool University Press, 1998.

Grand, Sarah. *Emotional Moments*. London: Hurst and Blackett, 1908.

—— *Our Manifold Nature*. London: William Heinemann, 1894.

—— *The Beth Book* [1897]. Reprinted Bristol: Thoemmes Press, 1994.

Gruesser, John Cullen, ed. *The Unruly Voice: Rediscovering Pauline Elizabeth Hopkins*. University of Illinois, 1996.

Heilmann, Ann and Stephanie Forward, eds. *Sex, Social Purity and Sarah Grand*. London and New York: Routledge, 2000.

Heilmann, Ann. "Dreams in Black and White: Women, Race and Self-Sacrifice in Olive Schreiner's Allegorical Writings". *White?Women: Critical perspectives on race and gender*. Eds. Heloise Brown, Madi Gilkes and Ann Kaloski-Naylor.

——, ed. *Feminist Forerunners: (New) Womanism and Feminism in the Early Twentieth Century*. London: Pandora, 2001.

—— "Mona Caird (1854–1932): Wild Woman, New Woman, and Early Radical Feminist Critic of Marriage and Motherhood". *Women's*

History Review 5 (1996): 67–97.

—— "Overwriting Decadence: Charlotte Perkins Gilman, Oscar Wilde, and the Feminization of Art in 'The Yellow Wall-Paper'". *The Mixed Legacy of Charlotte Perkins Gilman*. Eds. Golden and Zangrando. 175–88.

Holcombe, Lee. *Wives and Property: Reform of the Married Women's Property Law in Nineteenth-Century England*. University of Toronto Press, 1983.

Hopkins, Pauline E. *Contending Forces: A Romance Illustrative of Negro Life North and South*. Boston: Colored Cooperative Publishing, 1900.

Jackson, Holbrook. *The Eighteen Nineties: a Review of Art and Ideas at the Close of the Nineteenth Century* [1913]. London: The Cresset Library, 1988.

Joslin, Katherine. *Edith Wharton*. Basingstoke and London: Macmillan, 1991.

Keating, Peter. *The Haunted Study: a Social History of the English Novel 1875–1914*. London: Fontana Press, 1991.

Kersley, Gillian. *Darling Madame: Sarah Grand and Devoted Friend*. London: Virago, 1983.

Kingsford, Anna. "The Uselessness of Vivisection". *Nineteenth Century* 11 (1882): 171–83.

Lane, A. J., ed. *The Charlotte Perkins Gilman Reader*. London: The Women's Press, 1981.

Ledger, Sally and Scott McCracken, eds. *Cultural Politics at the Fin de Siècle*. Cambridge: Cambridge University Press, 1995.

Ledger, Sally. *The New Woman: Fiction and feminism at the fin de siècle*. Manchester; Manchester University Press, 1997.

—— *Women's Writing at the Fin de Siècle*. Special edition of *Women's Writing* 3.3 (1996).

Maitland, Edward. *A. Kingsford, Her Life, Letters, Diary and Work*, 2 volumes. London: Watkins, 1896.

Meade, Marion. *Madame Blavatsky: The Woman Behind the Myth*. New York: G. P. Putnam's Sons, 1980.

Miller, Jane Eldridge. *Rebel Women: Feminism, Modernism and the Edwardian Novel*. London: Virago Press Limited, 1994.

Mix, Katherine Lyon. *A Study in Yellow*. London: Constable & Co. Ltd., 1960.

Nead, Lynda. *Myths of Sexuality: representations of women in Victorian Britain*. Oxford: Basil Blackwell, 1988.

Nightingale, Florence. *Cassandra and other selections from Suggestions for Thought* [1852]. Ed. Mary Poovey. London: Pickering and Chatto, 1991.

Nord, Deborah Epstein. *Walking the Victorian Streets: Women, Representation and the City*. Ithaca and London: Cornell University Press, 1995.

Parsons, Deborah. *Streetwalking the Metropolis: Women, the City and Modernity*. Oxford: Oxford University Press, 2000.

Pykett, Lyn, "Foreword". *The New Woman in Fiction and in Fact: Fin-de-Siècle Feminisms*. Eds. Angelique Richardson and Chris Willis. Basingstoke and New York: Palgrave Publishers Ltd., 2001.

Rive, Richard, ed. *Olive Schreiner: Letters. Volume I: 1871–1899*. Oxford: Oxford University Press, 1988.

Rudd, Jill and Val Gough, eds. *Charlotte Perkins Gilman: Optimist Reformer*. Iowa: University of Iowa Press, 1999.

Rupke, Nicolaas A., ed. *Vivisection in Historical Perspective*. London and New York: Routledge, 1990.

Schreiner, Olive ('Ralph Iron'). "By the Same Author". *Dream Life and Real Life*. London: T. Fisher Unwin, Pseudonym Library, 1893.

Shanley, Mary Lyndon. *Feminism, Marriage and the Law in Victorian England, 1850–1895*. London: I. B. Tauris, 1989.

Shockley, Ann Allen, ed. *Afro-American Women Writers 1746–1933: An Anthology and Critical Guide*. Boston: G. K. Hall and Co., 1988.

Showalter, Elaine. *A Literature of Their Own: from Charlotte Brontë to Doris Lessing*. London: Virago, 1978.

——, ed. *Daughters of Decadence: Women Writers of the Fin-de-Siècle*. London: Virago, 1993.

—— *The Female Malady: Women, Madness and English Culture, 1830–1930*. London: Virago, 1987.

—— *Sexual Anarchy: Gender and Culture at the Fin de Siècle*. London: Bloomsbury, 1991.

Shuttleworth, Sally. "Female circulation: medical discourse and popular advertising in the mid-Victorian era". *Body/Politics. Women and the Discourses of Science*. Eds. Mary Jacobus, Evelyn Fox Keller and Sally Shuttleworth. New York and London: Routledge, 1990.

Smith, Joan, ed. *Femmes de Siècle. Stories from the '90s: Women Writing at the End of Two Centuries*. London: Chatto and Windus, 1992.

Stead, W. T. "The Maiden Tribute of Modern Babylon". *Pall Mall Gazette* (6–10 July 1885).

Stetz, Margaret. "Turning Points: Mabel E. Wotton". *Turn-of-the-Century Women* 3 (Winter 1986).

Stutfield, Hugh E. M. "Tommyrotics". *Blackwood's Magazine* (June 1895): 833–45.

—— "The Psychology of Feminism". *Blackwood's Magazine* (January 1897): 104–17.

Toth, Emily. *Kate Chopin*. London: Century, 1990.

Vicinus, Martha. *Independent Women: Work and Community for Single Women 1850–1920*. London: Virago, 1985.

Walkowitz, Judith R. *City of Dreadful Delight: narratives of sexual danger in late-Victorian London*. London: Virago Press, 1992.

—— *Prostitution and Victorian Society: Women, Class and the State*. Cambridge: Cambridge University Press, 1980.

Washington, Mary Helen, ed. *Invented Lives: Narratives of Black Women 1860–1960*. London: Virago, 1989.

Wharton, Edith. *The Fruit of the Tree*. New York: Scribner's, 1907.

White, Terence de Vere, ed. *A Leaf from the Yellow Book: The Correspondence of George Egerton*. London: The Richards Press, 1958.

Wilson, Elizabeth, *The Sphinx in the City: Urban Life, the Control of Disorder, and Women*. London: Virago, 1991.

The Mandrake Venus
by George Egerton

A pilgrim, born of investigation by truth, was travelling along the highway of the world. It was a great wide road trodden bare by the never-ceasing footsteps of the children of man; and if any one possessed, as did this poor pilgrim, the inner ear of which the hearing is so fine that it registers the continuance of all the air waves – called, for convenience, sound – of every vibration since the beginning of the world; and the vision, which is the past sight of all humanity, he would have found in himself a cinématographe of the universe from time primeval. To him the highway was such, for the great dead still walked it in company with the living.

Many by-roads led from the great road to the cities of the world, only the mile-stones registered cycles instead of ordinary miles. Sometimes the pilgrim grew very weary; for the ceaseless beat of the marching feet, the tramp of armies, dull tread of the labourers, gliding steps of the women, and the tripple of the little children, following their invisible pied piper, gave him no rest.

Many things puzzled him. The eyes, in particular, wearied him; for he saw the *same* eyes peering at him from between the long slit lids of some snake-crowned Egyptian courtesan, the hollow sockets of a peasant woman straining her back to her burden, the meek eyelids of some penitent nun. Once when he seated himself near a spring to rest, he spoke of this haunting idea to a tinker who was mending a kettle merrily. He was a tinker by choice, having failed to make the world accept him as a critic.

"I have a theory about that," said the tinker.

"Yes?" cried the pilgrim, eagerly, for indeed these ghost eyes puzzled him sorely.

"Of course I don't see the eyes in divers settings as you do, and, as a critic, if I ever hope to get anything to do in the conventional schools, I am bound to discourage the use of the historic present, much less a vision that might add the historic future. I am inclined to think that there never have been any more people than there are now. What I mean is, we have all been some one else; we are only going on over and over again."

"Hum," sighed the pilgrim, dubiously; "but we started with two —"

"Oh, of course, if you are a believer in the apple myth! But even so," jauntily, "I am not prepared to say at what stage in evolution the creation of psychical atoms ceased, to be replaced by reincarnations in successive physical envelopes — perhaps with the birth of conscience and moral responsibility. In any case why trouble? What has logical reasoning to do with speculative philosophy? The intuitive discovery of to-morrow *always* upsets the logical conclusion of yesterday!" admiring a patch he had put on the kettle, with his head aslant.

The pilgrim bade him adieu, and journeyed anew until he came to the widest of all the side roads. It was a tremendous wide road along which youths of every year danced recklessly, — ghost lads with sandalled feet, flower crowned and hyacinthine locked, as well as the youths of the present day. Here and there on his way he noticed a mother stoop to her lad as she kissed him with tears on the threshold of home, and fastened the cockle-shell of pilgrimage to his hat; had noted how she told him with lowered lids and a maid blush on her matron cheek, in clean, plain words of the way *this* road led, and implored him to avoid it. 'Tis true they had not been many: most of the mothers had closed the door as their lad bounded forth on the path of Youth's venture, in ignorance of its dangers; and seated themselves by the fire to enjoy a good cry, a cup of tea, and a roseate romance with none of the unpleasant facts of life in it.

Thus it happened that most of the youths, when they came to the turn of the road and saw the procession of lads, hesitated. A few, still feeling the mother's words in their ears, hurried along the highroad, but the greater number joined the throng recklessly; for a gorgeous magic bird with glowing plumage soared and fell, dropping notes of golden music in a witch melody that thrilled in their blood as fire boils water, and whispered in their senses and roused the infinite yearnings of youth that are a torture and delight. It sang of woman, the other part of him, in her beauty and sorcery; and the lads, following the fatal lure with dazed eyes, never saw that the bird was stabbed in the breast by a giant thorn; that its song was the quintessence of pain which borders ever on a delirious joy; and that a trickle of blood ran as it soared.

"Whither are we going?" they shouted to an old man cowering at the roadside.

"To the city of many names, — the Kingdom of the Mandrake Venus, Man's Desire; where the meads are ablaze with passion flowers and poppies, and the fountains are fed with good women's tears!"

As they neared it, they broke into a wild irregular dance, for the song of the bird was throbbing in their blood now, and in this manner they reached the gate of the city. They were forced to halt at the brazen portal with its curious tracery of serpents and flowers, for it was closed.

"It is the hour of sleep!" said the beldame, sitting on her hams inside the bars; "when the dusk falls, you can enter."

So they sat down and chanted the song of the bird to beguile the time away; and when the brooding dusk swooped swiftly and silently down, shrouding her face in a mantle of shadows, there was a great movement inside the portal as when an army awakes, and the wide streets and narrow alleys became suddenly flooded with electric light, the gates swung open, and the men darted through and stood in bewilderment inside. The houses were many, all with open windows and doors. There was a flutter and a flimmer of drapery, a sound of tripping feet, a rill of perfume that crushed back the cool breath of the earth, and the delicate exhalations of its night blooms, as the breath of a drunkard might absorb that of a child.

"Where do we go now?" the pilgrim asked of a man with hollow, fevered eyes, who seemed to know the way.

"To pay homage to the World Harlot, the Mandrake Venus, the Arch-wife, the Ever-existing, who has been, is, and will be. The only ruler whose dynasty has endured unbroken through all the phases of time. If you know her not, turn back ...."

The train of men and youths danced as if obsessed until they came to a great marble palace. Entering, they found themselves in an ante-room. The white marble floor was inlaid with a mosaic device of serpents and flowers. They passed through to an immense hall; plashing fountains of enervating perfume played in each corner, and a music that seemed born of madness, and the ecstasy of pain rang from a hidden orchestra.

A gigantic throne was placed at the end of the hall. It was fashioned couch-form of bones, — men's bones, the pilgrim thought with a shudder, — gleaming ivory white as if bleached by rain in moonlight; polished with their marrow until they shone like mirrors, thickly encrusted at intervals with golden coins. Superb cushions of a costly silken web flashing crimson in its purples were laid upon it. These details did not strike him until afterwards. His eyes were held by the gigantic female, couchant amidst the changeful drapery. Fascinated, repelled, he felt as a frog in the cage of a snake, for she was splendid in her audacity; surpassing in her beauty; white with a flabby softness of flesh, and a vileness of expression that made her loathsome as a leper.

She lay supinely, darting keen though languid glances through her heavy lids, from eyes that burnt with sombre fire, and lured as a serpent; blazed with passion and yet were cold; her full lips curved sensually, her hair — strange hair, black yet gold in its lights, so that no man knew its real colour — was crowned with scarlet flowers; a long scarf or mantle of the thinnest tissue, saffron in hue, shot with carmine, richly broidered with gold, hung from her shoulders; it was caught at the hollow of her throat by a clasp of a myriad shining gems. A flexible serpent, the lamellæ of virgin gold, a triumph of the goldsmith art, encircled her loins: so cunningly were the diamond eyes set in the jewelled head that they seemed quick with an evil lustre. She held an iron thyrsus entwined with fresh bindweed, and the blooms of the enchantress nightshade in her hand.

The eyes of all those who had entered the hall were fixed upon her, and she held them with her basilisk gaze.

There was a crash of music, and the lure-song of the bird that thrilled in the blood, burst from a thousand throats; and from each aisle women advanced, clad in garments of cobweb tissue that clung to their swaying limbs, and parted airily to the rhythm of their steps — fluttering, trembling into ever-changing hues. They swept on in sinuous lines, swaying, swinging, interlacing in maddening intricacies; scattering scarlet blossoms as they danced, until their little white feet seemed to dip into a sea of blood. Some had passion flowers twined in their hair, some roses, some jewels, others were clad simply in the marvellous mantle of their hair. Eyes blue as brook-lime, dark as storm nights, changeful as opals, innocent, reckless, tragic, glad, peered from their many-typed faces. Sometimes the rattle of their anklets and bangles made a clirring accompaniment to the melody, sometimes the lights dimmed, and they danced in silent steps until their movements became shadow-fine as the sensuous whispering of a tropical night. The men nodded to the melody until they stood, with their breasts thrust forward, as if drawn by invisible magnets held in the feet of the dancing jades.

The pilgrim noted that many of the women were old, some barely reached girl-hood, but they all danced as if bitten by a tarantula, until the vast hall was as one gleaming, glittering, intoxicating intermingling of rhythmic movement and rainbow play.

The music died away in a sob; the Mandrake Venus rose to her feet and waved her thyrsus, the mantle fell back, revealing her voluptuous, leprous, white body, from her powerful breast to her slim strong ankles. The throng pressed forward as one man to pay her homage and lay their offerings at her feet. Many just bowed before her throne, and darted towards the crimson hangings behind it. To those she nodded indifferently; but as each novice stepped forward, she bent and smiled as she snatched the white flower of virgin youth that adorned his brow, though he knew it not, and stuck it in her girdle.

As the last man passed, the music pealed riotously forth in ever madder strains, and slaves bearing crystal goblets of frothing wine drugged with the juice of white poppies and black henbane, filed through the hall.

She sank back into her erstwhile position, with her chin held in the cup of her cruel hand, her eyes gazing enigmatically forth — superb in her isolation. The pilgrim stole softly out, and sauntered into one of the many galleries that led from the throne-room. Some hours later he emerged into the close night, with eyes heavy with the pain of what he had seen.

Ever and again a wail penetrated to his ear; he leant and touched a crone, as he thought, on the shoulder. A woman looked up, and the depths of despair in her eyes made him shiver as the feel of the unseen about one in certain rooms. She was young in years, but the youth in her face was seared to age by pain. A glimpse of her mouth would have paralysed a tender heart: she rose to her feet and walked with him.

"What is that wail ever and again?" asked he.

She laughed bitterly.

"That is the cry of the maid as she is torn from innocence and womanhood to minister to the service of the great Harlot mother, even as the mandrake cries as it is torn from its roots. Each night brings a victim —"

They walked on in silence until they came to a lazaretto. A tumbril was drawn up at the entrance; prostrate forms, some silent, some laughing in blasphemous jest at their own plight, were being hoisted into it; it rattled down the white street towards the great highway of the world.

The pilgrim — for the faces he had seen had frightened him — looked with questioning eyes at the mask-like face at his side. She answered his mute query:–

"Those are the victims of the mandrake poison, the evil virus, that works in humanity to the downfall of nations, and is carried from generation to generation; they are bound to the lazar houses of the great city!"

"And then?"

"Then? Then they are free to seek the camps, and streets, and houses of the land, and mingle once more with the sons of men—"

"God!" cried the pilgrim, "and I might have a son—"

"Well, it's all in the interests of morality!" laughed the woman; "at least, that is what we hear they say out there in the pulpits of the preaching houses and the firesides of the homes. Nations change, creeds arise and die; the house of the Mandrake Venus is alone invincible. It has been so as far back as the annals of men date. No power has yet been strong enough to break our reign; we are the great world sore, the serpent coiled round the homesteads of men. Your wise men say we are the victims necessary to your perfected system of human relationship. I know not; I only suffer, and sow the flower of revenge, and death, and downfall in the youth of mankind. Your white Christ pointed a way by eating and drinking with one of us, and cast a crumb of comfort amongst us in olden days; his followers have never added enough crumbs to make a loaf. Good-night, good-bye!"

The pilgrim dragged himself wearily through the gate of exit, and came to a cross-road in the world's highway, where a gigantic mission cross cast its shadow on the roadside. He sat and looked at the Christ, and a great cry rent his heart as he thought of the scenes he had witnessed; for the Christ hung limply in the moonlight, and his followers blinded their eyes voluntarily to the facts of life, and raised mortgages for the erection of splendid cathedrals to their particular form of idolatry, caskets to confine their sympathies, stone pix in which to isolate their souls; and the pilgrim wept at the feet of the dead wooden Christ with the poor features mutilated by stress of time, who gave no answer to his agonised prayer: *When will the dynasty of the Mandrake Venus cease to govern amidst the sons of men?*

A White Night
by Charlotte Mew

"The incident", said Cameron, "is spoiled inevitably in the telling, by its merely accidental quality of melodrama, its sensational machinery, which, to the view of anyone who didn't witness it, is apt to blur the finer outlines of the scene. The subtlety, or call it the significance, is missed, and unavoidably, as one attempts to put the thing before you, in a certain casual crudity, and inessential violence of fact. Make it a mediæval matter — put it back some centuries — and the affair takes on its proper tone immediately, is tinctured with the sinister solemnity which actually enveloped it. But as it stands, a recollection, an experience, a picture, well, it doesn't reproduce; one must have the original if one is going to hang it on one's wall."

In spite of which I took it down the night he told it and, thanks to a trick of accuracy, I believe you have the story as I heard it, almost word for word.

It was in the spring of 1876, a rainless spring, as I remember it, of white roads and brown crops and steely skies.

Sent out the year before on mining business, I had been then some eighteen months in Spain. My job was finished; I was leaving the Black Country, planning a vague look round, perhaps a little sport among the mountains, when a letter from my sister Ella laid the dust of doubtful schemes.

She was on a discursive honeymoon. They had come on from Florence to Madrid, and disappointed with the rank modernity of their last halt, wished to explore some of the least known towns of the interior: "Something unique, untrodden, and uncivilised," she indicated modestly. Further, if I were free and amiable, and so on, they would join me anywhere in Andalusia. I was in fact to show them round.

I did "my possible"; we roughed it pretty thoroughly, .but the young person's passion for the strange bore her robustly through the risk and discomforts of those wilder districts which at best, perhaps, are hardly woman's ground.

King, on occasion nursed anxiety, and mourned his little luxuries; Ella accepted anything that befel, from dirt to danger, with a humorous composure dating back to nursery days – she had the instincts and the physique of a traveller, with a brilliancy of touch and a decision of attack on.human instruments which told. She took our mule-drivers in hand with some success. Later, no doubt, their wretched beasts were made to smart for it, in the reaction from a lull in that habitual brutality which makes the animals of Spain a real blot upon the gay indifferentism of its people.

It pleased her to devise a lurid Dies Irae for these affable barbarians, a special process of re-incarnation for the Spaniard generally, whereby the space of one dog's life at least should be ensured to him.

And on the day I'm coming to, a tedious, dislocating journey in a springless cart had brought her to the verge of quite unusual weariness, a weariness of spirit only, she protested, waving a hand toward our man who lashed and sang alternately, fetching at intervals a sunny smile for the poor lady's vain remonstrances before he lashed again.

The details of that day – our setting forth, our ride, and our arrival – all the minor episodes stand out with singular distinctness, forming a background in one's memory to the eventual, central scene.

We left our inn – a rough posada – about sunrise, and our road, washed to a track by winter rains, lay first through wide half-cultivated slopes, capped everywhere with orange trees and palm and olive patches, curiously bare of farms or villages, till one recalls the lawless state of those outlying regions and the absence of communication between them and town.

Abruptly, blotted in blue mist, vineyards and olives, with the groups of aloes marking off field boundaries, disappeared. We entered on a land of naked rock, peak after peak of it, cutting a jagged line against the clear intensity of the sky.

This passed again, with early afternoon our straight, white road grew featureless, a dusty stretch, save far ahead the sun-tipped ridge of a sierra, and the silver ribbon of the river twisting among the barren hills. Toward the end we passed one of the wooden crosses set up on these roads to mark some spot of violence or disaster. These are the only sign-posts one encounters, and as we came up with it, our beasts were goaded for the last ascent.

Irregular grey walls came into view; we skirted them and turned in through a Roman gateway and across a bridge into a maze of narrow stone-pitched streets, spanned here and there by Moorish arches, and execrably rough to rattle over.

A strong.illusion of the Orient, extreme antiquity and dreamlike stillness marked the place.

Crossing the grey arcaded Plaza, just beginning at that hour to be splashed with blots of gaudy colour moving to the tinkling of the mule-bells, we were soon upon the outskirts of the town – the most untouched, remote and, I believe, the most remarkable that we had dropped upon.

In its neglect and singularity, it made a claim to something like supremacy of charm. There was the quality of diffidence belonging to unrecognised abandoned personalities in that appeal.

That's how it's docketed in memory – a city with a claim, which, as it happened, I was not to weigh.

Our inn, a long, one-storeyed building with caged windows, most of them unglazed, had been an old palacio; its broken fortunes hadn't robbed it of its character, its air.

The spacious place was practically empty, and the shuttered rooms, stone-flagged and cool, after our shadeless ride, invited one to a prolonged siesta; but Ella wasn't friendly to a pause. Her buoyancy survived our meal. She seemed even to face the morrow's repetition of that indescribable experience with serenity. We found her in the small paved garden, sipping chocolate and airing Spanish with our host, a man of some distinction, possibly of broken fortunes too.

The conversation, delicately edged with compliment on his side, was on hers a little blunted by a limited vocabulary, and left us both presumably a margin for imagination.

Sí, la Señora, he explained as we came up, knew absolutely nothing of fatigue, and the impetuosity of the Señora, this attractive eagerness to make acquaintance with it, did great honour to his much forgotten, much neglected town. He spoke of it with rather touching ardour, as a place unvisited, but "digno de renombre illustre", worthy of high fame.

It has stood still, it was perhaps too stationary; innovation was repellent to the Spaniard, yet this conservatism, lack of enterprise, the virtue or the failing of his country – as we pleased – had its aesthetic value. Was there not, he would appeal to the Señora, "una belleza de reposo", a beauty of quiescence, a dignity above prosperity? "Muy bien." Let the Señora judge, you had it there!

We struck out from the town, perhaps insensibly toward the landmark of a Calvary, planted a mile or so beyond the walls, its three black shafts above the mass of roofs and pinnacles, in sharp relief against the sky, against which suddenly a flock of vultures threw the first white cloud. With the descending sun, the clear persistence of the blue was losing permanence, a breeze sprang up and birds began to call.

The Spanish evening has unique effects and exquisite exhilarations: this one led us on some distance past the Calvary and the last group of scattered houses – many in complete decay – which straggle, thinning outwards from the city boundaries into the campo.

Standing alone, after a stretch of crumbling wall, a wretched little venta, like a stop to some meandering sentence, closed the broken line.

The place was windowless, but through the open door an oath or two – the common blend of sacrilege and vileness – with a smell of charcoal, frying oil-cakes and an odour of the stable, drifted out into the freshness of the evening air.

Immediately before us lay a dim expanse of treeless plain: behind, clear cut against a smokeless sky, the flat roof lines and towers of the city, seeming, as we looked back on them, less distant than in fact they were.

We took a road which finally confronted us with a huge block of buildings, an old church and convent, massed in the shadow of a hill and standing at the entrance to three cross-roads.

The convent, one of the few remaining in the south, not fallen into ruin, nor yet put, as far as one could judge, to worldly uses, was exceptionally large. We counted over thirty windows in a line upon the western side below the central tower with its pointed turret; the eastern wing, an evidently older part, was cut irregularly with a few square gratings.

The big, grey structure was impressive in its loneliness, its blank negation of the outside world, its stark expressionless detachment.

The church, of darker stone, was massive too; its only noticeable feature a small cloister with Romanesque arcades joining the nave on its south-western wall.

A group of peasant women coming out from vespers passed us and went chattering up the road, the last, an aged creature shuffling painfully some yards behind the rest still muttering her

> 'Madre purisima,
> Madre castisima,
> Ruega por nosostros,'

in a kind of automatic drone.

We looked in, as one does instinctively: the altar lights which hang like sickly stars in the profound obscurity of Spanish churches were being quickly blotted out.

We didn't enter then, but turned back to the convent gate, which stood half open, showing a side of the uncorniced cloisters, and a crowd of flowers, touched to an intensity of brilliance and fragrance by the twilight. Six or seven dogs, the sandy-coloured lurchers of the country, lean and wolfish-looking hounds, were sprawling round the gateway; save for this dejected crew, the place seemed resolutely lifeless; and this absence of a human note was just. One didn't want its solitude or silence touched, its really fine impersonality destroyed.

We hadn't meant – there wasn't light enough – to try the church again, but as we passed it, we turned into the small cloister. King, who had come to his last match, was seeking shelter from the breeze which had considerably freshened, and at the far end we came upon a little door, unlocked. I don't know why we tried it, but mechanically, as the conscientious tourist will, we drifted in and groped round. Only the vaguest outlines were discernible; the lancets of the lantern at the transept crossing, and a large rose window at the western end seemed, at a glance, the only means of light, and this was failing, leaving fast the fading panes.

One half-detected, almost guessed, the blind triforium, but the enormous width of the great building made immediate mark. The darkness, masking as it did distinctive features, emphasised the sense of space, which, like the spirit of a shrouded form, gained force, intensity, from its material disguise.

We stayed not more than a few minutes, but on reaching the small door again we found it fast; bolted or locked undoubtedly in the short interval. Of course we put our backs to it and made a pretty violent outcry, hoping the worthy sacristan was hanging round or somewhere within call. Of course he wasn't. We tried two other doors; both barred, and there was nothing left for it but noise. We shouted, I suppose; for half an hour, intermittently, and King persisted hoarsely after I had given out.

The echo of the vast, dark, empty place caught up our cries, seeming to hold them in suspension for a second in the void invisibility of roof and arches, then to fling them down in hollow repetition with an accent of unearthly mimicry which struck a little grimly on one's ear; and when we paused the silence seemed alert, expectant, ready to repel the first recurrence of unholy clamour. Finally, we gave it up; the hope of a release before the dawn, at earliest, was too forlorn. King, explosive and solicitous was solemnly perturbed, but Ella faced the situation with an admirable tranquillity. Some chocolate and a muff would certainly, for her, she said, have made it more engaging, but poor dear men, the really tragic element resolved itself into – No matches, no cigar!

Unluckily we hadn't even this poor means of temporary light. Our steps and voices sounded loud, almost aggressive, as we groped about; the darkness then was shutting down and shortly it grew absolute. We camped eventually in one of the side chapels on the south side of the chancel, and kept a conversation going for a time, but gradually it dropped. The temperature, the fixed obscurity, and possibly a curious oppression in the spiritual atmosphere relaxed and forced it down.

The scent of incense clung about; a biting chillness crept up through the aisles; it got intensely cold. The stillness too became insistent; it was literally deathlike, rigid, exclusive, even awfully remote. It shut us out and held aloof; our passive presences, our mere vitality, seemed almost a disturbance of it; quiet as we were, we breathed, but it was breathless, and as time went on, one's impulse was to fight the sort of shapeless personality it presently assumed, to talk, to walk about and make a definite attack on it. Its influence on the others was presumably more soothing, obviously they weren't that way inclined.

Five or six hours must have passed. Nothing had marked them, and they hadn't seemed to move. The darkness seemed to thicken, in a way, to muddle thought and filter through into one's brain, and waiting, cramped and cold for it to lift, the soundlessness again impressed itself unpleasantly – it was intense, unnatural, acute.

And then it stirred.

The break in it was vague but positive; it might have been that, scarcely audible, the wind outside was rising, and yet not precisely that. I barely caught, and couldn't localise the sound.

Ella and King were dosing, they had had some snatches of uncomfortable sleep; I, I suppose, was preternaturally awake. I heard a key turn, and the swing back of a door, rapidly followed by a wave of voices breaking in. I put my hand out and touched King, and in a moment, both of them waked and started up.

I can't say how, but it at once occurred to us that quiet was our cue, that we were in for something singular.

The place was filling slowly with a chant, and then, emerging from the eastern end of the north aisle and travelling down just opposite, across the intervening dark, a line of light came into view, crossing the opening of the arches, cut by the massive piers, a moving, flickering line, advancing and advancing with the voices.

The outlines of the figures in the long procession weren't perceptible, the faces, palely lit and level with the tapers they were carrying, one rather felt than saw; but unmistakably the voices were men's voices, and the chant, the measured, reiterated cadences, prevailed over the wavering light.

Heavy and sombre as the stillness which it broke, vaguely akin to it, the chant swept in and gained upon the silence with a motion of the tide. It was a music neither of the senses, nor the spirit, but the mind, as set, as stately, almost as inanimate as the dark aisles through which it echoed; even, colourless and cold.

And then, quite suddenly, against its grave and passionless inflections something clashed, a piercing intermittent note, an awful discord, shrilling out and dying down and shrilling out again – a cry – a scream.

The chant went on; the light, from where we stood, was steadily retreating, and we ventured forward. Judging our whereabouts as best we could, we made towards the choir and stumbled up some steps, placing ourselves eventually behind one of the pillars of the apse. And from this point, the whole proceeding was apparent.

At the west end the line of light was turning; fifty or sixty monks (about – and at a venture) habited in brown and carrying tapers, walking two and two, were moving up the central aisle towards us, headed by three, one with the cross between two others bearing heavy silver candlesticks with tapers, larger than those carried by the rest.

Reaching the chancel steps, they paused; the three bearing the cross and candlesticks stood facing the altar, while those following diverged to right and left and lined the aisle. The first to take up this position were quite young, some almost boys; they were succeeded gradually by older men, those at the tail of the procession being obviously aged and infirm.

And then a figure, white and slight, erect – a woman's figure – struck a startling note at the far end of the brown line, a note as startling as the shrieks which jarred recurrently, were jarring still against the chant.

A pace or two behind her walked two priests in surplices, and after them another, vested in a cope. And on the whole impassive company her presence, her disturbance, made no mark. For them, in fact, she wasn't there.

Neither was she aware of them. I doubt if to her consciousness, or mine, as she approached, grew definite, there was a creature in the place besides herself.

She moved and uttered her successive cries as if both sound and motion were entirely mechanical – more like a person in some trance of terror or of anguish than a voluntary rebel; her cries bespoke a physical revulsion into which her spirit didn't enter; they were not her own – they were outside herself; there was no discomposure in her carriage, nor, when we presently saw it, in her face. Both were distinguished by a certain exquisite hauteur, and this detachment of her personality from her distress impressed one curiously. She wasn't altogether real, she didn't altogether live, and yet her presence there was the supreme reality of the unreal scene, and lent to it, at least as I was viewing it, its only element of life.

She had, one understood, her part to play; she wasn't, for the moment, quite prepared; she played it later with superb effect.

As she came up with the three priests, the monks closed in and formed a semi-circle round them, while the priests advanced and placed themselves behind the monks who bore the cross and candlesticks, immediately below the chancel steps, facing the altar. They left her standing some few paces back, in the half-ring of sickly light shed by the tapers.

Now one saw her face. It was of striking beauty, but its age? One couldn't say. It had the tints, the purity of youth – it might have been extremely young, matured merely by the moment; but for a veil of fine repression which only years, it seemed, could possibly have woven. And it was itself – this face – a mask, one of the loveliest that spirit ever wore. It kept the spirit's counsel. Though what stirred it then, in that unique emergency, one saw – to what had stirred it, or might stir it gave no clue. It threw one back on vain conjecture.

Put the match of passion to it – would it burn? Touch it with grief and would it cloud, contract? With joy – and could it find, or had it ever found, a smile? Again, one couldn't say.

Only, as she stood there, erect and motionless, it showed the faintest flicker of distaste, disgust, as if she shrank from some repellent contact. She was clad, I think I said, from head to foot in a white linen garment; head and ears were covered too, the oval of the face alone was visible, and this was slightly flushed. Her screams were changing into little cries or moans, like those of a spent animal, from whom the momentary pressure of attack has been removed. They broke from her at intervals, unnoticed, unsuppressed, and now on silence, for the monks had ceased their chanting.

As they did so one realised the presence of these men, who, up to now, had scarcely taken shape as actualities, been more than an accompaniment – a drone. They shifted from a mass of voices to a row of pallid faces, each one lit by its own taper, hung upon the dark, or thrown abruptly, as it were, upon a screen; all different; all, at first distinct, but linked together by a subtle likeness, stamped with that dye which blurs the print of individuality – the signet of the cloister.

Taking them singly, though one did it roughly, rapidly enough, it wasn't difficult at starting to detect varieties of natural and spiritual equipment. There they were, spread out for sorting, nonentities and saints and devils, side by side, and what was queerer, animated by one purpose, governed by one law.

Some of the faces touched upon divinity; some fell below humanity; some were, of course, merely a blotch of book and bell, and all were set impassively toward the woman standing there.

And then one lost the sense of their diversity in their resemblance; the similarity persisted and persisted till the row of faces seemed to merge into one face – the face of nothing human – of a system, of a rule. It framed the woman's and one felt the force of it: she wasn't in the hands of men.

There was a pause filled only by her cries, a space of silence which they hardly broke; and then one of the monks stepped forward, slid into the chancel and began to light up the high altar. The little yellow tongues of flame struggled and started up, till first one line and then another starred the gloom.

Her glance had followed him; her eyes were fixed upon that point of darkness growing to a blaze. There was for her, in that illumination, some intense significance, and as she gazed intently on the patch of brilliance, her cries were suddenly arrested – quelled. The light had lifted something, given back to her an unimpaired identity. She was at last in full possession of herself. The flicker of distaste had passed and left her face to its inflexible, inscrutable repose.

She drew herself to her full height and turned towards the men behind her with an air of proud surrender, of magnificent disdain. I think she made some sign.

Another monk stepped out, extinguished and laid down his taper, and approached her.

I was prepared for something singular, for something passably bizarre, but not for what immediately occurred. He touched her eyes and closed them; then her mouth, and made a feint of closing that, while one of the two priests threw over his short surplice a black stole and started audibly with a Sub venite. The monks responded. Here and there I caught the words or sense of a response. The prayers for the most part were unintelligible: it was no doubt the usual office for the dead, and if it was, no finer satire for the work in hand could well have been devised. Loudly and unexpectedly above his unctuous monotone a bell clanged out three times. An Ave followed, after which two bells together, this time muffled, sounded out again three times. The priest proceeded with a Miserere, during which they rang the bells alternately, and there was something curiously suggestive and determinate about this part of the performance. The real action had, one felt, begun.

At the first stroke of the first bell her eyelids fluttered, but she kept them down; it wasn't until later at one point in the response, "Non intres in judicium cum ancilla tua Domine," she yielded to an impulse of her lips, permitted them the shadow of a smile. But for this slip she looked the thing of death they reckoned to have made of her – detached herself, with an inspired touch, from all the living actors in the solemn farce, from all apparent apprehension of the scene. I, too, was quite incredibly outside it all.

I hadn't even asked myself precisely what was going to take place. Possibly I had caught the trick of her quiescence, acquiescence, and I went no further than she went; I waited – waited with her, as it were, to see it through. And I experienced a vague, almost resentful sense of interruption, incongruity, when King broke in to ask me what was up. He brought me back to Ella's presence, to the consciousness that this, so far as the spectators were concerned, was not a woman's comedy.

I made it briefly plain to them, as I knew something of the place and people, that any movement on our side would probably prove more than rash, and turned again to what was going forward.

They were clumsily transforming the white figure. Two monks had robed her in a habit of their colour of her order, I suppose, and were now putting on the scapular and girdle. Finally they flung over her the long white-hooded cloak and awkwardly arranged the veil, leaving her face uncovered; then they joined her hands and placed between them a small cross.

This change of setting emphasised my first impression of her face; the mask was lovelier now and more complete.

Two voices started sonorously, "Libera me, Domine," the monks took up the chant, the whole assembly now began to move, the muffled bells to ring again at intervals, while the procession formed and filed into the choir. The monks proceeded to their stalls, the younger taking places in the rear. The two who had assisted at the robing led the passive figure to the centre of the chancel, where the three who bore the cross and candlesticks turned round and stood a short way off confronting her. Two others, carrying the censer and bénitier, stationed themselves immediately behind her with the priests and the officiant, who now, in a loud voice, began his recitations.

They seemed, with variations, to be going through it all again. I caught the "Non intres in judicium" and the "Sub venite" recurring with the force of a refrain. It was a long elaborate affair. The grave deliberation of its detail heightened its effect. Not to be tedious, I give it to you in brief. It lasted altogether possibly two hours.

The priest assisting the officiant, lifting the border of his cope, attended him when he proceeded first to sprinkle, then to incense the presumably dead figure, with the crucifix confronting it, held almost like a challenge to its sightless face. They made the usual inclinations to the image as they passed it, and repeated the performance of the incensing and sprinkling with extreme formality at intervals, in all, I think, three times.

There was no break in the continuous drone proceeding from the choir; they kept it going; none of them looked up – or none at least of whom I had a view – when four young monks slid out, and, kneeling down in the clear space between her and the crucifix, dislodged a stone which must have previously been loosened in the paving of the chancel, and disclosed a cavity, the depth of which I wasn't near enough to see.

For this I wasn't quite prepared, and yet I wasn't discomposed. I can't attempt to make it clear under what pressure I accepted this impossible dénouement, but I did accept it. More than that, I was exclusively absorbed in her reception of it. Though she couldn't, wouldn't, see, she must have been aware of what was happening. But on the other hand, she was prepared, dispassionately ready, for the end.

All through the dragging length of the long offices, although she hadn't stirred or given any sign (except that one faint shadow of a smile) of consciousness, I felt the force of her intense vitality, the tension of its absolute impression. The life of those enclosing presences seemed to have passed into her presence, to be concentrated there. For to my view it was these men who held her in death's grip who didn't live, and she alone who was absorbently alive.

The candles, burning steadily on either side the crucifix, the soft illumination of innumerable altar lights confronting her, intensified the darkness which above her and behind her – everywhere beyond the narrow confines of the feeble light in which she stood – prevailed.

This setting lent to her the aspect of an unsubstantial, almost supernatural figure, suddenly arrested in its passage through the dark.

She stood compliantly and absolutely still. If she had swayed, or given any hint of wavering, of an appeal to God or man, I must have answered it magnetically. It was she who had the key to what I might have done but didn't do. Make what you will of it – we were inexplicably en rapport.

But failing failure I was backing her; it hadn't once occurred to me, without her sanction, to step in, to intervene; that I had anything to do with it beyond my recognition of her – of her part, her claim to play it as she pleased. And now it was – a thousand years too late!

They managed the illusion for themselves and me magnificently. She had come to be a thing of spirit only, not in any sort of clay. She was already in the world of shades; some power as sovereign and determinate as Death itself had lodged her there, past rescue or the profanation of recall.

King was in the act of springing forward; he had got out his revolver; meant, if possible, to shoot her before closing with the rest. It was the right and only workable idea. I held him back, using the first deterrent that occurred to me, reminding him of Ella, and the notion of her danger may have hovered on the outskirts of my mind. But it was not for her at all that I was consciously concerned. I was impelled to stand aside, to force him, too, to stand aside and see it through.

What followed, followed as such things occur in dreams; the senses seize, the mind, or what remains of it, accepts mechanically the natural or unnatural sequence of events.

I saw the grave surrounded by the priests and blessed; and then the woman and the grave repeatedly, alternately, incensed and sprinkled with deliberate solemnity; and heard, as if from a great distance, the recitations of the prayers, and chanting of interminable psalms.

At the last moment, with their hands upon her, standing for a second still erect, before she was committed to the darkness, she unclosed her eyes, sent one swift glance towards the light, a glance which caught it, flashed it back, recaptured it and kept it for the lighting of her tomb. And then her face was covered with her veil.

The final act was the supreme illusion of the whole. I watched the lowering of the passive figure as if I had been witnessing the actual entombment of the dead.

The grave was sprinkled and incensed again, the stone replaced and fastened down. A long sequence of prayers said over it succeeded, at the end of which, the monks put out their tapers, only one or two remaining lit with those beside the Crucifix.

The priests and the officiant at length approached the altar, kneeling and prostrating there some minutes and repeating "Pater Nosters", followed by the choir.

Finally, in rising, the officiant pronounced alone and loudly "Requiescat in pace." The monks responded sonorously, "Amen".

The altar lights were one by one extinguished; at a sign, preceded by the cross, the vague, almost invisible procession formed and travelled down the aisle, reciting quietly the "De Profundis" and guided now, by only, here and there, a solitary light. The quiet recitation, growing fainter, was a new and unfamiliar impression; I felt that I was missing something – what? I missed, in fact, the chanting; then quite suddenly and certainly I missed – the scream. In place of it there was this "De Profundis" and her silence. Out of her deep I realised it, dreamily, of course she would not call.

The door swung to; the church was dark and still again – immensely dark and still.

There was a pause, in which we didn't move or speak; in which I doubted for a second the reality of the incredibly remote, yet almost present scene, trying to reconstruct it in imagination, pit the dream against the fact, the fact against the dream.

"Good God!" said King at length, "what are we going to do?"

His voice awoke me forcibly to something nearer daylight, to the human and inhuman elements in the remarkable affair, which hitherto had missed my mind; they struck against it now with a tremendous shock, and mentally I rubbed my eyes. I saw what King had all along been looking at, the sheer, unpicturesque barbarity. What were we going to do?

She breathed perhaps, perhaps she heard us – something of us – we were standing not more than a yard or so away; and if she did, she waited, that was the most poignant possibility, for our decision, our attack.

Ella was naturally unstrung: we left her crouching by the pillar; later I think she partially lost consciousness. It was as well – it left us free.

Striking, as nearly as we could, the centre of the altar, working from it, we made a guess at the position of the stone, and on our hands and knees felt blindly for some indication of its loosened edge. But everywhere the paving, to our touch, presented an unevenness of surface, and we picked at random, chiefly for the sake of doing something. In that intolerable darkness there was really nothing to be done but wait for dawn or listen for some guidance from below. For that we listened breathless and alert enough, but nothing stirred. The stillness had become again intense, acute, and now a grim significance attached to it.

The minutes, hours, dragged; time wasn't as it had been, stationary, but desperately, murderously slow.

Each moment of inaction counted – counted horribly, as we stood straining ears and eyes for any hint of sound, of light.

At length the darkness lifted, almost imperceptibly at first; the big rose window to the west became a scarcely visible grey blot; the massive piers detached themselves from the dense mass of shadow and stood out, immense and vague; the windows of the lantern just above us showed a ring of slowly lightening panes; and with the dawn, we found the spot and set to work.

The implements we improvised we soon discovered to be practically useless. We loosened, but we couldn't move the stone.

At intervals we stopped and put our ears to the thin crevices. King thought, and still believes, he heard some sound or movement; but I didn't. I was somehow sure, for that, it was too late.

For everything it was too late, and we returned reluctantly to a consideration of our own predicament; we had, if possible, to get away unseen. And this time luck was on our side. The sacristan, who came in early by the cloister door which we had entered by, without perceiving us, proceeded to the sacristy.

We made a rapid and effectual escape.

We sketched out and elaborated, on our way back to the town, the little scheme of explanation to be offered to our host, which was to cover an announcement of abrupt departure. He received it with polite credulity, profound regret. He ventured to believe that the Señora was unfortunately missing a unique experience – cities, like men, had elements of beauty, or of greatness which escape the crowd; but the Señora was not of the crowd, and he had hoped she would be able to remain.

Nothing, however, would induce her to remain for more than a few hours. We must push on without delay and put the night's occurrences before the nearest British Consul. She made no comments and admitted no fatigue, but on this point she was persistent to perversity. She carried it.

The Consul proved hospitable and amiable. He heard the story and was suitably impressed. It was a truly horrible experience – remarkably dramatic – yes. He added it – we saw him doing it – to his collection of strange tales.

The country was, he said, extremely rich in tragic anecdote; and men in his position earned their reputation for romance. But as to doing anything in this case, as in others even more remarkable, why, there was absolutely nothing to be done!

The laws of Spain were theoretically admirable, but practically, well – the best that could be said of them was that they had their comic side.

And this was not a civil matter, where the wheels might often, certainly, be oiled. The wheel ecclesiastic was more intractable.

He asked if we were leaving Spain immediately. We said, "Perhaps in a few days." "Take my advice," said he, "and make it a few hours."

We did.

Ella would tell you that the horror of those hours hasn't ever altogether ceased to haunt her, that it visits her in dreams and poisons sleep.

She hasn't ever understood, or quite forgiven me my attitude of temporary detachment. She refuses to admit that, after all, what one is pleased to call reality is merely the intensity of one's illusion. My illusion was intense.

"Oh, for you," she says, and with a touch of bitterness, "it was a spectacle. The woman didn't really count."

For me it was a spectacle, but more than that: it was an acquiescence in a rather splendid crime.

On looking back I see that, at the moment in my mind, the woman didn't really count. She saw herself she didn't. That's precisely what she made me see.

What counted chiefly with her, I suspect, was something infinitely greater to her vision than the terror of men's dreams.

She lies, one must remember, in the very centre of the sanctuary – has a place uniquely sacred to her order, the traditions of her kind. It was this honour, satisfying, as it did, some pride of spirit or of race, which bore her honourably through.

She had, one way or other, clogged the wheels of an inflexible machine. But for the speck of dust she knew herself to be, she was – oh horribly, I grant you! – yet not lightly, not dishonourably, swept away.

The City of Blood
by Anna Kingsford

I dreamed that I was wandering along a narrow street of vast length, upon either hand of which was an unbroken line of high straight houses, their walls and doors resembling those of a prison. The atmosphere was dense and obscure, and the time seemed that of twilight; in the narrow line of sky visible far overhead between the two rows of house-roofs, I could not discern sun, moon, or stars, or colour of any kind. All was grey, impenetrable, and dim. Under foot, between the paving-stones of the street, grass was springing. Nowhere was the least sign of life: the place seemed utterly deserted.

I stood alone in the midst of profound silence and desolation. Silence? No! As I listened, there came to my ears from all sides, dully at first and almost imperceptibly, a low creeping sound like subdued moaning; a sound that never ceased, and that was so native to the place, I had at first been unaware of it. But now I clearly gathered in the sound and recognised it as expressive of the intensest physical suffering. Looking steadfastly towards one of the houses from which the most distinct of these sounds issued, I perceived a stream of blood slowly oozing out from beneath the door and trickling down into the street, staining the tufts of grass red here and there, as it wound its way towards me. I glanced up and saw that the glass in the closed and barred windows of the house was flecked and splashed with the same horrible dye.

"Some one has been murdered in this place!" I cried, and flew towards the door. Then, for the first time, I perceived that the door had neither lock nor handle on the outside, but could be opened only from within. It had, indeed, the form and appearance of a door, but in every other respect it was solid and impassable as the walls themselves. In vain I searched for bell or knocker, or for some means of making entry into the house. I found only a scroll fastened with nails upon a cross-beam over the door, and upon it I read the words:– "This is the Laboratory of a Vivisector." As I read, the wailing sound redoubled in intensity, and a noise as of struggling made itself audible within, as though some new victim had been added to the first. I beat madly against the door with my hands and shrieked for help; but in vain. My dress was reddened with the blood upon the doorstep. In horror I looked down upon it, then turned and fled. As I passed along the street, the sounds around me grew and gathered volume, formulating themselves into distinct cries and bursts of frenzied sobbing. Upon the door of every house some scroll was attached, similar to that I had already seen. Upon one was inscribed:– "Here is a husband murdering his wife": upon another:– "Here is a mother beating her child to death": upon a third:– "This is a slaughterhouse".

Every door was impassable; every window was barred. The idea of interference from without was futile. Vainly I lifted my voice and cried for aid. The street was desolate as a graveyard; the only thing that moved about me was the stealthy blood that came creeping out from beneath the doors of these awful dwellings. Wild with horror I fled along the street, seeking some outlet, the cries and moans pursuing me as I ran. At length the street abruptly ended in a high dead wall, the top of which was not discernible; it seemed, indeed, to be limitless in height. Upon this wall was written in great black letters — *"There is no way out."*

Overwhelmed with despair and anguish, I fell upon the stones of the street, repeating aloud — *"There is no way out."*

Dream Life and Real Life:
A Little African Story
by Olive Schreiner

Little Jannita sat alone beside a milk-bush. Before her and behind her stretched the plain, covered with red sand and thorny "Karroo" bushes; and here and there a milk-bush, looking like a bundle of pale green rods tied together. Not a tree was to be seen anywhere, except on the banks of the river, and that was far away, and the sun beat on her head. Round her fed the Angora goats she was herding; pretty things, especially the little ones, with white silky curls that touched the ground. But Jannita sat crying. If an angel should gather up in his cup all the tears that have been shed, I think the bitterest would be those of children.

By and by she was so tired, and the sun was so hot, she laid her head against the milk-bush, and dropped asleep.

She dreamed a beautiful dream. She thought that when she went back to the farmhouse in the evening, the walls were covered with vines and roses, and the "kraals" (*sheepfolds*) were not made of red stone, but of lilac trees full of blossom. And the fat old Boer smiled at her, and the stick he held across the door for the goats to jump over, was a lily rod with seven blossoms at the end. When she went to the house her mistress gave her a whole roaster-cake for her supper, and the mistress's daughter had stuck a rose in the cake; and her mistress's son-in-law said "Thank you!" when she pulled off his boots, and did not kick her.

It was a beautiful dream.

While she lay thus dreaming, one of the little kids came and licked her on her cheek, because of the salt from her dried-up tears. And in her dream she was not a poor indentured child any more, living with Boers. It was her father who kissed her. He said he had only been asleep — that day when he lay down under the thorn-bush; he had not really died. He felt her hair, and said it was grown long and silky, and he said they would go back to Denmark now. He asked her why her feet were bare, and what the marks on her back were. Then he put her head on his shoulder, and picked her up, and carried her away, away! She laughed — she could feel her face against his brown beard. His arms were so strong.

As she lay there dreaming with the ants running over her naked feet, and with her brown curls lying in the sand, a Hottentot came up to her. He was dressed in ragged yellow trousers, and a dirty shirt, and torn jacket. He had a red handkerchief round his head, and a felt hat above that. His nose was flat, his eyes like slits, and the wool on his head was gathered into little round balls. He came to the milk-bush, and looked at the little girl lying in the hot sun. Then he walked off, and caught one of the fattest little Angora goats, and held its mouth fast, as he stuck it under his arm. He looked back to see that she was still sleeping, and jumped down into one of the "sluits." (*The deep fissures, generally dry, in which the superfluous torrents of water are carried from the "Karroo" plains after thunderstorms.*) He walked down the bed of the "sluit" a little way and came to an overhanging bank, under which, sitting on the red sand, were two men. One was a tiny, ragged, old bushman, four feet high; the other was an English navvy, in a dark blue blouse. They cut the kid's throat with the navvy's long knife, and covered up the blood with sand, and buried the entrails and skin. Then they talked, and quarrelled a little; and then they talked quietly again.

The Hottentot man put a leg of the kid under his coat and left the rest of the meat for the two in the "sluit," and walked away.

When little Jannita awoke it was almost sunset. She sat up very frightened, but her goats were all about her. She began to drive them home. "I do not think there are any lost," she said.

Dirk, the Hottentot, had brought his flock home already, and stood at the "kraal" door with his ragged yellow trousers. The fat old Boer put his stick across the door, and let Jannita's goats jump over, one by one. He counted them. When the last jumped over: "Have you been to sleep to-day?" he said; "there is one missing."

Then little Jannita knew what was coming, and she said, in a low voice, "No." And then she felt in her heart that deadly sickness that you feel when you tell a lie; and again she said, "Yes."

"Do you think you will have any supper this evening?" said the Boer.

"No," said Jannita.

"What do you think you will have?"

"I don't know," said Jannita.

"Give me your whip," said the Boer to Dick, the Hottentot.

The moon was all but full that night. Oh, but its light was beautiful!

The little girl crept to the door of the outhouse where she slept, and looked at it. When you are hungry, and very, very sore, you do not cry. She leaned her chin on one hand, and looked, with her great dove's eyes — the other hand was cut open, so she wrapped it in her pinafore. She looked across the plain at the sand and the low karroo-bushes, with the moonlight on them.

Presently, there came slowly, from far away, a wild spring-buck. It came close to the house, and stood looking at it in wonder, while the moonlight glinted on its horns, and in its great eyes. It stood wondering at the red brick walls, and the girl watched it. Then, suddenly, as if it scorned it all, it curved its beautiful back and turned; and away it fled over the bushes and sand, like a sheeny streak of white lightning. She stood up to watch it. So free, so free! Away, away! She watched, till she could see it no more on the wide plain.

Her heart swelled, larger, larger, larger: she uttered a low cry; and without waiting, pausing, thinking, she followed on its track. Away, away, away! "I – I also!" she said, "I – I also!"

When at last her legs began to tremble under her, and she stopped to breathe, the house was a speck behind her. She dropped on the earth, and held her panting sides.

She began to think now.

If she stayed on the plain they would trace her footsteps in the morning and catch her; but if she waded in the water in the bed of the river they would not be able to find her footmarks; and she would hide, there where the rocks and the "kopjes" were.

(*"Kopjes," in the karroo, are hillocks of stones, that rise up singly or in clusters, here and there; presenting sometimes the fantastic appearance of old ruined castles or giant graves, the work of human hands.*)

So she stood up and walked towards the river. The water in the river was low; just a line of silver in the broad bed of sand, here and there broadening into a pool. She stepped into it, and bathed her feet in the delicious cold water. Up and up the stream she walked, where it rattled over the pebbles, and past where the farmhouse lay; and where the rocks were large, she leaped from one to the other. The night wind in her face made her strong — she laughed. She had never felt such night wind before. So the night smells to the wild bucks, because they are free! A free thing feels as a chained thing never can.

At last she came to a place where the willows grew on each side of the river, and trailed their long branches on the sandy bed. She could not tell why, she could not tell the reason, but a feeling of fear came over her.

On the left bank rose a chain of "kopjes" and a precipice of rocks. Between the precipice and the river bank there was a narrow path covered by the fragments of fallen rock. And upon the summit of the precipice a kippersol tree grew, whose palm-like leaves were clearly cut out against the night sky. The rocks cast a deep shadow, and the willow trees, on either side of the river. She paused, looked up and about her, and then ran on, fearful.

"What was I afraid of? How foolish I have been!" she said, when she came to a place where the trees were not so close together. And she stood still and looked back and shivered.

At last her steps grew wearier and wearier. She was very sleepy now, she could scarcely lift her feet. She stepped out of the river-bed. She only saw that the rocks about her were wild, as though many little "kopjes" had been broken up and strewn upon the ground, lay down at the foot of an aloe, and fell asleep.

———————————

But, in the morning, she saw what a glorious place it was. The rocks were piled on one another, and tossed this way and that. Prickly pears grew among them, and there were no less than six kippersol trees scattered here and there among the broken "kopjes." In the rocks, there were hundreds of homes for the coneys, and from the crevices wild asparagus hung down. She ran to the river, bathed in the clear cold water, and tossed it over her head. She sang aloud. All the songs she knew were sad, so she could not sing them now, she was glad, she was so free; but she sang the notes without the words, as the cock-o-veets do. Singing and jumping all the way, she went back, and took a sharp stone, and cut at the root of a kippersol, and got out a large piece, as long as her arm, and sat to chew it. Two coneys came out on the rock above her head and peeped at her. She held them out a piece, but they did not want it, and ran away.

It was very delicious to her. Kippersol is like raw quince, when it is very green; but she liked it. When good food is thrown at you by other people, strange to say, it is very bitter; but whatever you find yourself is sweet!

When she had finished she dug out another piece, and went to look for a pantry to put it in. At the top of a heap of rocks up which she clambered she found that some large stones stood apart but met at the top, making a room.

"Oh, this is my little home!" she said.

At the top and all round it was closed, only in the front it was open. There was a beautiful shelf in the wall for the kippersol, and she scrambled down again. She brought a great branch of prickly pear, and stuck it in a crevice before the door, and hung wild asparagus over it, till it looked as though it grew there. No one could see that there was a room there, for she left only a tiny opening, and hung a branch of feathery asparagus over it. Then she crept in to see how it looked. There was a glorious soft green light. Then she went out and picked some of those purple little ground flowers – you know them – those that keep their faces close to the ground, but when you turn them up and look at them they are deep blue eyes looking into yours! She took them with a little earth, and put them in the crevices between the rocks; and so the room was quite furnished. Afterwards she went down to the river and brought her arms full of willow, and made a lovely bed; and, because the weather was very hot, she lay down to rest upon it.

She went to sleep soon, and slept long, for she was very weak. Late in the afternoon she was awakened by a few cold drops falling on her face. She sat up. A great and fierce thunderstorm had been raging, and a few of the cool drops had fallen through the crevice in the rocks. She pushed the asparagus branch aside, and looked out, with her little hands folded about her knees. She heard the thunder rolling, and saw the red torrents rush among the stones on their way to the river. She heard the roar of the river as it now rolled, angry and red, bearing away stumps and trees on its muddy water. She listened and smiled, and pressed closer to the rock that took care of her. She pressed the palm of her hand against it.

When you have no one to love you, you love the dumb things very much. When the sun set, it cleared up. Then the little girl ate some kippersol, and lay down again to sleep. She thought there was nothing so nice as to sleep. When one has had no food but kippersol juice for two days, one doesn't feel strong.

"It is so nice here," she thought, as she went to sleep, "I will stay here always."

Afterwards the moon rose. The sky was very clear now, there was not a cloud anywhere; and the moon shone in through the bushes in the door, and made a lattice-work of light on her face. She was dreaming a beautiful dream. The loveliest dreams of all are dreamed when you are hungry. She thought she was walking in a beautiful place, holding her father's hand, and they both had crowns on their head, crowns of wild asparagus. The people whom they passed smiled and kissed her; some gave her flowers, and some gave her food, and the sunlight was everywhere. She dreamed the same dream over and over, and it grew more and more beautiful; till, suddenly, it seemed as though she were standing quite alone. She looked up: on one side of her was the high precipice, on the other was the river, with the willow trees, drooping their branches into the water; and the moonlight was over all. Up, against the night sky the pointed leaves of the kippersol trees were clearly marked, and the rocks and the willow trees cast dark shadows.

In her sleep she shivered, and half awoke.

"Ah, I am not there, I am here," she said; and she crept closer to the rock, and kissed it, and went to sleep again.

It must have been about three o'clock, for the moon had begun to sink towards the western sky, when she woke, with a violent start. She sat up, and pressed her hand against her heart.

"What can it be? A coney must surely have run across my feet and frightened me!" she said, and she turned to lie down again; but soon she sat up. Outside, there was the distinct sound of thorns crackling in a fire.

She crept to the door and made an opening in the branches with her fingers.

A large fire was blazing in the shadow, at the foot of the rocks. A little Bushman sat over some burning coals that had been raked from it, cooking meat. Stretched on the ground was an Englishman, dressed in a blouse, and with a heavy, sullen face. On the stone beside him was Dirk, the Hottentot, sharpening a bowie knife.

She held her breath. Not a coney in all the rocks was so still.

"They can never find me here," she said; and she knelt, and listened to every word they said. She could hear it all.

"You may have all the money," said the Bushman; "but I want the cask of brandy. I will set the roof alight in six places, for a Dutchman burnt my mother once alive in a hut, with three children."

"You are sure there is no one else on the farm?" said the navvy.

"No, I have told you till I am tired," said Dirk; "the two Kaffirs have gone with the son to town; and the maids have gone to a dance; there is only the old man and the two women left."

"But suppose," said the navvy, "he should have the gun at his bedside, and loaded!"

"He never has," said Dirk; "it hangs in the passage, and the cartridges too. He never thought when he bought it what work it was for! I only wish the little white girl was there still," said Dirk; "but she is drowned. We traced her footmarks to the great pool that has no bottom."

She listened to every word, and they talked on.

Afterwards, the little Bushman, who crouched over the fire, sat up suddenly, listening.

"Ha! what is that?" he said.

A Bushman is like a dog: his ear is so fine he knows a jackal's tread from a wild dog's.

"I heard nothing," said the navvy.

"I heard," said the Hottentot; "but it was only a coney on the rocks."

"No coney, no coney," said the Bushman; "see, what is that there moving in the shade round the point?"

"Nothing! you idiot," said the navvy. "Finish your meat; we must start now."

There were two roads to the homestead. One went along the open plain, and was by far the shortest; but you might be seen half a mile off. The other ran along the river bank, where there were rocks, and holes, and willow-trees to hide among. And all down the river bank ran a little figure.

The river was swollen by the storm full to its banks, and the willow-trees dipped their half-drowned branches into its water. Wherever there was a gap between them, you could see it flow, red and muddy, with the stumps upon it. But the little figure ran on and on; never looking, never thinking; panting, panting! There, where the rocks were the thickest; there, where on the open space the moonlight shone; there, where the prickly pears were tangled, and the rocks cast shadows, on it ran; the little hands clenched, the little heart beating, the eyes fixed always ahead.

It was not far to run now. Only the narrow path between the high rocks and the river.

At last she came to the end of it, and stood for an instant. Before her lay the plain, and the red farm-house, so near, that if persons had been walking there you might have seen them in the moonlight. She clasped her hands. "Yes, I will tell them, I will tell them!" she said; "I am almost there!" She ran forward again, then hesitated. She shaded her eyes from the moonlight, and looked. Between her and the farm-house there were three figures moving over the low bushes.

In the sheeny moonlight you could see how they moved on, slowly and furtively; the short one, and the one in light clothes, and the one in dark.

"I cannot help them now!" she cried, and sank down on the ground, with her little hands clasped before her.

———————————

"Awake, awake!" said the farmer's wife; "I hear a strange noise; something calling, calling, calling!"

The man rose, and went to the window.

"I hear it also," he said; "surely some jackal's at the sheep. I will load my gun and go and see."

"It sounds to me like the cry of no jackal," said the woman; and when he was gone she woke her daughter.

"Come, let us go and make a fire, I can sleep no more," she said; "I have heard a strange thing to-night. Your father said it was a jackal's cry, but no jackal cries so. It was a child's voice, and it cried, 'Master, master, wake!'"

The women looked at each other; then they went to the kitchen, and made a great fire; and they sang psalms all the while.

At last the man came back; and they asked him, "What have you seen?" "Nothing," he said, "but the sheep asleep in their kraals, and the moonlight on the walls. And yet, it did seem to me," he added, "that far away near the 'krantz' [precipice] by the river, I saw three figures moving. And afterwards – it might have been fancy – I thought I heard the cry again; but since that, all has been still there."

———————————

Next day a navvy had returned to the railway works.

"Where have you been so long?" his comrades asked.

"He keeps looking over his shoulder," said one, "as though he thought he should see something there."

"When he drank his grog to-day," said another, "he let it fall, and looked round."

Next day, a small old Bushman, and a Hottentot, in ragged yellow trousers, were at a wayside canteen. When the Bushman had had brandy, he began to tell how something (he did not say whether it was man, woman, or child) had lifted up its hands and cried for mercy; had kissed a white man's hands, and cried to him to help it. Then the Hottentot took the Bushman by the throat, and dragged him out.

Next night, the moon rose up, and mounted the quiet sky. She was full now, and looked in at the little home; at the purple flowers stuck about the room, and the kippersol on the shelf. Her light fell on the willow trees, and on the high rocks, and on a little new-made heap of earth and round stones. Three men knew what was under it; and no one else ever will.

Lily Kloof,
South Africa.

An Engagement
by Ella D'Arcy

When Owen suddenly made up his mind again to tempt Fortune, and to invest the remnants of his capital in the purchase of Carrel's house and practice at Jacques-le-Port, he brought with him to the Island a letter of introduction to Mrs. Le Messurier, of Mon Désir.

But with the business of settling down upon his hands – and another distraction also – nearly six weeks went by before he remembered to call. Then, having inquired his way, he walked up to the house one mild, blue afternoon.

He found a spruce semi-detached villa, standing back from the road, with a finely sanded path running from the gate, right and left, up to the hall door. In the centre of the large oval flower-bed which the path thus enclosed, rose a tall and flourishing monkey-tree, with the comically ugly appearance to which Owen's eyes had grown familiarised since his coming to the Island. In front of nearly every villa is planted an araucania-tree.

Mon Désir was of two storeys, painted white, and had green wooden shutters turned back against the walls. Dazzlingly clean and very stiff lace curtains hung before the windows. Owen was favourably impressed, and, actuated by an unusual sentiment of diffidence, wondered who were the persons he should find within, and what sort of a reception awaited him.

The outer door of the house stood open, and the plate-glass panel of an inner door permitted him to see along a cool dark hall, tiled in black and white, into a sunny garden beyond. While he waited there, looking into the garden, a girl and boy passed across his range of vision, from one side to the other.

The girl was tall and slight, swung a gardening basket in one hand, and had the other arm laid round the shoulders of the boy, who was a whole head shorter than she. Although dowdily dressed in a frock of some dark material, although wearing a hideous brown mushroom hat, although she and her companion had scarcely come into sight before they had passed out of it again, nevertheless, Owen received in that fleeting moment the impression that she was pretty. And it left him absolutely indifferent.

Then a maid appeared from behind the staircase, received his card and letter, and showed him into a small sitting-room on the left of the hall, a room so full of furniture, and at the same time so dark, that for a moment or two he was unable to find a seat. The light was not only materially obscured by the lace curtains he had noticed from the outside, but there were voluminous stuff curtains as well, and a green venetian blind had been let more than half-way down. Probably, earlier in the day the February sunshine had fallen upon the window, and consideration for the best parlour furniture is almost a religious cult among certain classes in the Island; stray sunbeams are fought against with the same assiduity as stray moths. In all the neat villas which border the roads leading out from Jacques-le-Port, the best parlour is invariably a room of gloom, never used but on ceremonious occasions, or for the incarceration of such a chance and uninvited guest as was Owen to-day.

As his eyes accustomed themselves to the darkness he began to distinguish a multiplicity of Berlin wool cushions and bead-worked footstools, of rosewood *étagères* loaded with knick-knacks, and rosewood tables covered with photograph albums and gilt-bound books. He took up one or two of these and read the titles: "Law's Serious Call," "The Day and the Hour, or Notes on Prophecy," "Lectures on the Doctrine of the Holy Spirit." Such titles said nothing to him, and he put the volumes down again unopened. He began to study on the opposite wall a large coloured photograph of the Riviera; the improbably blue sea, the incurving coastline, the verdure-clothed shore, dotted with innumerable white villas. But it interested him little more than the books had done, his acquaintance with foreign parts extending no farther than Paris.

He waited a few moments longer, and then two persons entered the room – a very old lady and the young girl he had caught a glimpse of in the garden. Seen now, without her hat, she was decidedly pretty, but Owen glanced past her to devote all his attention to Mrs. Le Messurier.

Giving him her hand, the old lady had said "How do you do?" waiting until he had satisfied her as to the state of his health. Then she invited him to be seated, and introduced the young girl as "Agnes Allez, my granddaughter," only she pronounced the name "Orlay," which is the custom of the Island.

Miss Allez had said "How do you do?" too, with a little air of prim gentility, which was the exact youthful counterpart of her grandmother's. After which she sat silent, with her hands lightly folded in her lap, and listened to the conversation.

Mrs. Le Messurier began with a few inquiries after the mutual acquaintance in England who had sent him to call upon her, and Owen replied suitably, while taking stock of her personality. She was dressed entirely in black, with a black silk apron over a black stuff gown, a black knitted shawl, a monumental cap of black lace and flowers and trembling bugles. The dress was fastened at the throat by a large gold brooch, framing a medallion of hair ingeniously tormented into the representation of a tombstone and a weeping willow-tree. An old-fashioned watch-chain of pale gold hung in two long festoons below her waist, and on her poor hand – a hand with time-stained, corrugated nails, with swollen, purple veins, with enlarged finger joints – a worn wedding-ring turned loosely.

Owen noted the signs of her age, of her infirmity, with half-conscious satisfaction; they promised him a patient before very long. And in the pleasant evidences of means all about him, he foresaw how satisfactorily he might adjust his sliding scale of charges.

She was speaking to him of his prospects in the Island, saying, with a melancholy motion of the head: "Ah, there, but for sure, you will have some trouble to work up Carrel's practice again. He have let it go all to pieces. An' such a good practice as it was in old Doctor Bragé's time. But you know the reason?"

Owen knew the reason well. His predecessor had been steadily drinking himself to death for the last ten years, and his practice was as dilapidated as were his house, his dog-cart, his reputation. It was just on account of their dilapidations that Owen had bought these articles cheap; while Carrel's reputation was of as little account to him as it was to Carrel himself, although it seemed likely, in spite of everything, to hang together longer than its owner would have any use for it.

"Well, I must try to work up Bragé's business again," said Owen self-confidently. With nervous tobacco-stained fingers he twisted and pointed one end of his black moustache, and became aware that the young girl was watching him covertly.

"There don't seem to be too many of us doctors here," he went on, "and from all I hear Le Lièvre is very much behind the times. There ought to be a good opening, I should think, for a little new life, eh? A little new blood?"

His voice touched an anxious note. The necessity of beginning to earn something pressed upon him. But Mrs. Le Messurier's reply was not reassuring.

"Ah, my good! Doctor Le Lièvre is, maybe, old-fashioned – I don't know nothing about that – but he is very much thought of. He is very safe, and he has attended us all. My poor boy John, who died of consumption in '67; and my daughter, Agnes's mother, whom we lost when Freddy was born; and my dear husband" – her knotted fingers went up to fondle mechanically the glazed tomb and willow-tree – "and poor Thomas Allez, my son-in-law, who went in '85."

Her dates came with all the readiness of constant reference. She entered into details of the various complaints, the various remedies, the reasons they had failed.

Owen's face wore that smooth mask of sympathetic attention with which the profession equips every medical man, but he was embittered by the praises of Le Lièvre, and drawing the two ends of his moustache into his mouth he chewed them vexedly.

His discontented glance fell upon the young girl. A sudden pink overflowed her cheeks. He pointed his moustache again, smiled a little, and let his dark eyes fix hers with an amused complacency. He saw he had made an impression. She blushed a warmer rose, and looked away.

He wondered whether she talked the same broken English her grandmother did. He hoped not; but the four words she had as yet uttered left him in doubt.

Mrs. Le Messurier could not pronounce the "th." She had said just now, speaking of Le Lièvre, "I don't know nodding' 'bout dat, but he is very much tought of." And she laid stress on the unimportant words; she accented the wrong syllables. Owen felt it would be a pity if so kissable a mouth as Agnes Allez's were to maltreat the words it let slip in the same fashion.

He undertook to make her speak. The old lady had reached the catalogue of "Freddy's" infantile disorders, and as she coupled his name with no prefatory adjective of affection or commiseration, Owen concluded that he, at least, was still among the living, was probably the boy he had seen.

He turned to the young girl: "Then that was your brother you were with just now in the garden, I suppose?"

She told him "Yes," and in reply to a further question, "Yes, he is only fifteen, and I shall be eighteen in May."

She spoke always with that little primness he had noticed in her reception of him, but her pronunciation was correct, was charming.

It occurred to him that the sunny February garden, and the companionship of the girl, would be an agreeable exchange for the starched and darkened atmosphere of the parlour and Mrs. Le Messurier's lugubrious reminiscences. He drew the conversation once and once again garden-wards, but without success.

To be guilty of anything so informal as to invite a stranger to step into the garden on his first visit was not to be thought of. The unconventional, the unexpected, are errors which the Islanders carefully eschew. Mrs. Le Messurier merely said: "Yes, you must come up and drink tea with us one day next week, will you not, and the children will be very pleased to show you the garden then. What day shall it be?"

The evening meal was at that moment ready laid out in the next room, and Owen, who had a long walk before him, would have been only too glad of an invitation to share it; but it is not customary in the Islands to ask even a friend to take a cup of tea, unless the day and the hour have been settled at least a week in advance.

When Owen got back to his house in the Contrée Mansel, he found Carrel sitting over the fire in the dining-room, in a more than usually shaky condition. Carrel was always cold, and pleaded for the boon of a fire upon the warmest days. He paid Owen a pound a week for the privilege of boarding in the house where he had once been master, and spent the remainder of a small annuity on spirits. Owen made no effort to check him, not considering it worth his while. He saw that before long his room would be preferable to his company. However, for the present, he had his uses, he knew the Islands well, and when Owen chose to ask information from him, he could always give it.

He mentioned therefore where he had been, and inquired carelessly whether the old woman was worth money. Carrel, although very fuddled, was still instructive. Oh yes, she had money sure enough; was a regular old Island woman, with her head screwed on the right way about. But Carrel doubted whether Owen would ever see the colour of it. "Le Lièvre's got the key of the situation there, my boy, and if he don't go off the hooks before she does, he'll hold it till her death. Unless, indeed, you can get round the soft side of the granddaughter, little Agnes, hey? Little Agnes Allez. Good Lord, what a smashing fine girl her mother was five-and-twenty years ago, before she married that fool Tom Allez. He was her cousin, too, and they were both the children of first cousins. No wonder the boy's a natural. Did ye see him, also?"

Owen meditated; then, referring to the grandmother, asked what she was worth. Carrel thought she would cut up for ten thousand pounds.

"Which, laid out in good sound *rentes*, would bring in £500 a year, and you would have the house, and a nice little wife into the bargain. And a family doctor is bound to marry, my boy, hey? Which reminds me to tell you," concluded Carrel, with a spirituous laugh, "that your scarlet devil of a Margot was here while you were out, inquiring after you. I wonder what she'll do when she hears you are making eyes at the little Allez girl, hey?"

"She may do as she damn pleases," said Owen, equably; "do you imagine I'm in any way bound to a trull like that?"

But all the same he was sorry to hear that the red-haired witch had been round and that he had missed her. He had not seen her now for over a week.

An Island tea is a square, sit-down meal eaten in the living-room with much solemnity. It is taken at half-past five, and is the last meal of the day; you are offered nothing after it but a glass of home-made wine and a biscuit. It consists entirely of sweets; jams, cakes, and various *gôches* – *gôches à pommes, gôches à groseilles, gôches à beurre*. Sugar and milk are put liberally into every cup; and such hyper-inquisitiveness as a desire to know whether you take one or neither never occurs to the well-regulated Island mind. When you have eaten all you are able, you are urgently pressed to take a little more. It is considered good manners to do so.

When on the appointed day Owen found himself again at Mon Désir, he looked at Agnes Allez for the first time with a genuine interest. The ten thousand pounds mentioned by Carrel had stuck fast in the younger man's mind.

The girl sat at the tea-tray, and her grandmother faced her. The guest was at one side of the table, and the boy Frederick Allez on the other. Owen observed in him the same soft eyes, the same regular, well-proportioned features as his sister's. But his mouth would not stay shut, his fingers were never at rest, he laughed foolishly when he encountered Owen's gaze.

"I love dogs, they are so faithful," he told the visitor suddenly, *à propos* of nothing.

Owen assented.

His grandmother and sister did not pay him much attention, but a maid waited on him as though he were a child of six, passed him his tea, and placed wedges of cake and *gôche* upon his plate.

Mrs. Le Messurier ate little, folded her decrepit hands on the edge of the table, and looked on.

"I sometimes can't remember," she said, "that a whole generation has been taken away from me. When I look at Agnes and Freddy I could think it was the other Agnes and my boy John, who used to sit just so with me forty years ago. But we lived down in town then. Ah, but it is a pitée, a pitée, that they should have been taken, and a poor useless old woman like me left behind!"

Owen was infinitely bored by her regrets. He had no natural sympathy or patience with the old. He gave an audible sigh of relief when, tea over, it was proposed that Agnes should show him the garden. Small and well-kept, its paths were soon explored; but at the end was a little observatory reached by a dozen wooden steps. A red-cushioned bench ran round the interior, and the front of the construction, of glass and three-sided, gave an admirable view over immense skies and an island-strewn sea.

"It's beautiful, is it not?" said Agnes, with a gentle pride in its beauty. "To me it seems quite as beautiful as the Riviera. Not that I've ever been there, of course, but gran'ma took poor Uncle John there the last year of his life, and we have a picture of it hanging in the drawing-room."

She named to Owen the different islands. "That one is St. Maclou, and further on is the Ile des Marchants. Over there to the left is the Petite Ste. Marguerite. We can't often see the Grande Ste. Marguerite without the glasses, but Freddy will go and get them."

The boy who had given them his company the whole time, punctuating their phrases with his foolish laugh, blundered off on this errand with an expression of consequential glee. Owen and the girl were left alone.

The vast expanse of sea below them still glittered in the light of the afterglow, but the cloud-curtain of evening was drawing over the eastern sky – a dreamy, delicious cloud-curtain of a soft lilac colour, opaque and yet transparent, permitting scintillating hints of the blue day behind to pierce through. And across its surface floated filmy wreaths of a fading rose-colour, while high above the observatory trembled the first faintly-shining star.

But Owen looked only at the young girl, and she grew embarrassed beneath his gaze. He knew it was on his account she wore that elaborate, but hopelessly provincial, Sunday frock; on his account, that before coming out she had gone upstairs to fetch her Sunday hat, instead of putting on the every-day one which hung in the hall. He knew it was for him that she was blushing so warmly; that it was to give herself a countenance she fingered her sleeve so nervously, unhooking it at the wrist, trying to hook it again, not succeeding, and persisting in the attempt, while every instant tinged her cheeks with a livelier rose.

He watched her a few seconds, smiling behind his moustache, before he leaned over, took hold of her hand, and fastened the sleeve for her. He was pleasantly stimulated by the tremor he felt running through her when his fingers touched her skin.

Then the boy burst open the door, handed his sister the glasses, and flung himself down, with his wearying laugh, on the cushion by her side.

"I love dogs," he said to Owen, just as he had done at tea, "don't you? They are so faithful." It appeared to be a stock phrase of his, beyond which he could not get.

During the next six weeks Owen was often at Mon Désir, and his visits to Agnes and his assignations with Margot afforded him agreeable alternative recreation from his work.

He had known for long, however, that Agnes was in love with him – he had for long made up his mind that she and her ten thousand pounds were desirable possessions – before he said any word to the girl herself. And then, as generally happens, the crisis came fortuitously, unpremeditatedly. They were out on the cliffs together. She had been showing him Berceau Bay, which lies below Mon Désir. They had stepped from a door in the garden into a green lane, and had followed it down, down through veils and mazes of April greenness, until it suddenly stopped with them on a grassy plateau overlooking the winged bay. At their feet the shadow of the hill behind them lay upon the water, but out beyond the shadow, the sea sparkled with jewel-like colour and brilliancy. When they had climbed the steep cliff path on the other side, they had stopped a moment to notice the gulls and cormorants perched on the rock-ledges beneath them, and all at once the decisive words had passed his lips, and the girl was looking up at him with soft brown eyes that overflowed with love, with tears, before he quite knew how it had come about. But after all, he was glad to have it settled, and to have the engagement sealed and confirmed that same night by Mrs. Le Messurier's tremulous, hesitating, not over-cordial sanction.

No, she was not over-cordial, the old skin-flint, he told himself as he went away, not so grateful as she should have been, but all the same, this disconcerting element in her attitude did not prevent him from boasting complacently of his good fortune to Carrel, the moment he got home.

Carrel happened to be comparatively sober, and his mood then was invariably a fleering one. For his heart fed on a furious hatred and envy of Owen. He envied him his twenty-eight years, he envied his sobriety, his strength of character. He hated his ill-breeding, his cock-sureness, his low ambitions. And though he had been glad enough when Owen had purchased the house and practice, he chose now to consider him an interloper who had ousted him from his proper place. He therefore at once planted a knife in Owen's vanity, and gave him some information he had previously held back.

"So you are going to marry little Agnes Allez? Well, you might do worse. The old lady is bound to leave her a nice little nest egg, but I expect she'll tie it up pretty tight too. She and the old man didn't spend forty years of their lives in the drapery business, saving ha'pence, for the first vagrant Englishman who comes along to have the squandering of."

"What's that?" said Owen sharply, unable to conceal his disgust.

Carrel turned the knife round with dexterous fingers. "You didn't suppose she was one of the Le Mesuriers of Rozaine, did you? Pooh! She kept the shop in the High Street which Roget has now, and that's where the money comes from."

Owen, the son of a third-rate London attorney, naturally recoiled from the prospect of an alliance with retail trade. But perhaps Allez, the father, had been a gentleman?

Carrel quenched this hope at once.

"Tom Allez was son of a man who kept a fruit-stall in the Arcade. He couldn't afford to stock himself, but sold for the growers on commission. However, towards the end of his life, he began to grow tomatoes himself out Cottu way, and was doing very well when he died, and Tom, who was always an ass, brought everything to rack and ruin. But he was already married to Agnes Le Messurier, so the old people took the pair of 'em home, to live with them. And Tom never did anything for the rest of his life but develop Bright's disease, which carried him off when he was forty-one. The boy is an imbecile, as you see. And, by the bye, in counting your eggs he must be reckoned with. Half the money will go to him, you may be sure. I doubt whether little Agnes will get more than two hundred a year after all."

For twenty-four hours Owen meditated on this news, weighing in the balance his social ambitions against a possible five thousand pounds.

Then he came to Carrel again. "Look here," he said, "you understand these damned little Islands better than I do. Would it really make any difference in my career to contract such a marriage?"

"It would only keep you out of the society of the precious Sixties you're so anxious to cultivate, for the rest of your life," chuckled Carrel; "it would only be remembered against you to the sixth generation. At present, as an outsider, a stranger, you are in neither camp, but once you marry a Le Messurier with two s's, you place yourself among the Forties for ever."

From this date onwards, Owen's speculations were given to the problem of how he could easiest get loose from his engagement.

Agnes Allez stood in her bedroom, tortured by apprehension and suspense. She asked herself what could be going on in the best parlour below where Owen was closeted with her grandmother, and she forbidden to join them. Her grandmother had written to Owen, asking him to call upon her, and had said to the girl, before he came, "Now, perhaps I shall send for you, but until I do, remain in your room."

Already, half an hour, three quarters of an hour, had gone by, and the longed-for summons did not reach her; her keen ears still detected the murmurous rumble of voices downstairs. Then, of a sudden, they ceased: she heard the glass door of the hall shut to, and, from outside, firm steps grind down the gravel. She ran to the open window, and through the slots of the shutters saw Owen's tall figure pass down the path and out of the gate. He never once turned his head, but, taking the road to Jacques-le-Port, was lost to view behind its trees. Then came her grandmother calling to her from the hall, and she went down.

Mrs. Le Messurier told her, with kindness indeed, but with the melancholy satisfaction also, which the very old find in evil tidings, that her engagement with Dr. Owen must be considered at an end. She had never completely approved of him, but lately she had heard stories, which, if true, could only merit the severest condemnation. She had given him the opportunity of demonstrating their falsehood. He had failed to do so to her satisfaction, and thereupon she had told him, as she now told Agnes, that the engagement between them was at an end.

The girl's first feeling was one of burning indignation against the persons who had dared to slander the man she loved. She knew little of what had been said, she understood less, but she was sure, she was convinced, before hearing anything, that it was all untrue.

"Pedvinn talks of bringing an action against Thoumes and his wife," Mrs. Le Messurier told her, "for misappropriating poor Louis Renouf's property."

"But not against Jack, I suppose, because he could not keep the poor old man alive!" Agnes cried, with flaming cheeks. Renouf was a patient of Owen's who had died about three weeks before.

"The girl Margot has been seen going in and out of the surgery ever since your engagement, child."

"And suppose she has," cried Agnes, astonished, "what harm is there in that?"

But when her first anger had cooled down she awoke to a sense of her own misery, to a sense of the cruelty of her fate. She had not been engaged three months, and already the beautiful dream which had come into her life was shattered at a touch. Until the unforgettable moment when Owen had first called at Mon Désir, she had led such dull, such monotonous days; not unhappy ones, simply because she had known no happier ones to gauge them by. She had often smiled since to remember that she had been used to find excitement in a summer picnic with the de Gruchy girls at Rocquaine, in a winter lecture with magic-lantern illustrations at the Town Library.

In those days she had known of love in much the same vague unrealising way that she had known of the Desert of Sahara; although she had touched the fringe of courtship when young Mallienne, the builder's son, had offered her peppermints during evening chapel one Sunday last December. When she met him after that she used to smile and blush.

She, of course, had always supposed that she should some day marry. Everybody did. Last summer her friend Caroline de Gruchy had married Mr. Geraud, *pharmacien* at St. Héliers; but he was bald, forty years of age, and not at all handsome, and although Agnes had been one of the bridesmaids, the affair had left her cold and unmoved.

But with Owen's first visit she had awoke suddenly to the knowledge of love, and this wonderful fact, this stupendous miracle rather, had changed for her the whole world. It was as though she were endowed with a new sense; she saw meaning and beauty everywhere; her perceptions acquired clearness at the same time that her eyes grew deeper, more intense, that her cheek took on a lovelier colour, her mouth a sweeter, a more engaging smile.

Every hour, every moment, that she had spent in Owen's company was indelibly engraved on her memory. She could call up each particular occasion at will. She had learned his portrait off by heart at that first visit, she had done nothing but add graces to it ever since. She thought him the most handsome, the most distinguished-looked man she had ever seen. She admired his black hair, his dark eyes, his sallow skin. She admired the way he held himself, the way he dressed, although she had observed on the same occasion that the stiff edges of his cuffs were frayed, although she had seen, as she watched him away from the door, that his boot-heels were trodden down on the outside. But in spite of his shabby clothes, he looked a thousand times the superior of young Mallienne, of any of the young men she knew, in their best Sunday broadcloth.

And this was before she had formulated, even to herself, her feelings for him; long before that ecstatic, that magical moment when he had taken her into his arms, had kissed her, had kissed her mouth, had said, "Well, little one, do you know I am very fond of you, and I fancy you don't altogether dislike me, eh?"

That had happened on a Sunday afternoon, April 28th; a date she could never forget. They were out upon the *côte*; Freddy was nominally with them, but in point of fact had wandered away to gather the wild hyacinths which just then carpeted the ground with blue. He kept bringing her bunches of these to take care of; she could feel again the thick, pale-green, shiny stems grasped in her hand. She and Owen climbed the steep path which winds up from the bay to the brow of the cliff; her dress brushed against the encroaching gorse and bracken, and her eyes followed a couple of white butterflies gyrating on ahead; when she looked down from the height on which she stood, she saw the smooth sea below her, paving, as with a green translucent marble, every inlet, every crevice of the bay.

Then the path had bent outwards to skirt a great boulder of granite, and there, right under the shelter of the rock, was a circular clearing, a resting-place, spread with the sweet, short cliff-grass, where a broad ledge of the stone offered a natural seat.

It was here that he had kissed her, and the flowers had fallen in blue confusion at her feet, and, "Oh, I love you so," she had whispered, and he had laughed, and said, "Yes, child, I could see that from the very first."

Then they had sat down, he with his arm round her waist. "Well, I must call you Agnes now, I suppose," he had said; and she had timidly asked him his name, and he had told her, John Ashford Owen, but that his friends commonly called him Jack. "Then I may call you Jack, too, because I am going to be your best friend of all," she had answered, and on this Freddy had come up and broken into loud lamentation over the scattered flowers. To appease him they had both knelt down in the grass and helped him gather them up.

Jack had kissed her many times since, but never perhaps in quite the same way. At least, she had never experienced since quite the same sweet tremulous emotion. And yet she loved him more devotedly every day. Every day her affection sent out fresh delicate tendrils which rooted themselves inextricably in him.

And now these were to be rudely torn up; at a word all her joy, all her heaven was to come to an end. It was too cruel. And for what reason? Because wicked, envious people invented calumnies concerning him. It was too monstrous.

She passed a miserable night, but with the morning plucked up faint heart again. For it was impossible her engagement should really for ever be at an end. With a little time, a little patience, things must come right. Her sufferings were now all for Jack. How wounded, how outraged he must have felt, never even to have looked back when on Saturday he had left the house.

Oh, she must write to him, must tell him to have courage, not to give her up, and all would yet be well.

In the warm, silent solitude of her shuttered bedroom she wrote her first love-letter, an adorable, naïve, rambling letter; and waited in fluttering expectation during three interminable days for his reply. When it came, she had to read it twice over before she understood it. Correctly expressed, formal, in his rather illegible hand sprawling over two sides of the paper, Owen wrote that he had too much self-respect to wish to force himself on a family where he was not appreciated, and too high a sense of honour to accept her well-meant proposal for a clandestine engagement.

When understanding came, she broke into floods of weeping; then dried her tears, and sought excuses for his seeming coldness. She found them in his pride; it was naturally up in arms, after the rebuff it had received. If he had addressed her merely as "My dear Agnes," that was because he thought it probable Mrs. Le Messurier would see the letter; but he had signed himself "Yours, nevertheless." This was intended to show her he loved her still. Before evening, the very cause of her morning's anguish was converted into another proof of the nobility of her lover's mind.

By the end of twenty-four hours she had persuaded herself she ought to write to him again, to reproach him gently, tenderly, for his attitude towards her, to assure him of her unalterable constancy, to implore him, too, to be true. This letter was written on a Sunday, and she carried it to evening chapel with her, inside the bosom of her frock, both to sanctify it as it were, and to have the pleasure of feeling it against her heart as long as possible. Happy letter! by to-morrow morning it was to have the joy, the glory, of lying in *his* hand. Her grandmother never went to chapel a second time, and Freddy made no objection to passing round by the letter-box on the way home.

There was a day of long suspense, but when Agnes came down to breakfast on Tuesday morning, purposely earlier than the others, she found Owen's answer lying on her plate.

With her heart beating violently, she took it up, studied every line, every dot of the superscription, noticed that the stamp had been put on crookedly, that the flap of the envelope went down into a long point. She turned it over and over in her hand, filled with a sort of sweet terror as she speculated on its contents. But the fear that in a few moments she would no longer be alone came to determine her. She pulled it hastily open, tearing the envelope into great jags, and unfolded a sheet of note-paper which contained five lines. They began, "Dear Miss Allez," expressed polite regret that Mrs. Le Messurier's decided action in the matter made it impossible the writer should permit himself any longer the pleasure of corresponding with her, and were signed "Very truly yours, J. Ashford Owen."

The girl turned red, then white. Her hands trembled, her blood ran cold. She heard her grandmother and Freddy in the hall. To hide her emotion, she got up and walked over to the window. The August flowers in the garden seemed to look at her with crooked jeering eyes.

Jack had written her a horrible letter; she repeated this to herself over and over again during the day. He had no heart. She thought of all that had passed between them; she called up, line by line, every word of her letter to him. Her cheeks burned with shame. She hated him, hated him. She would renounce him entirely, never think of him again. But even while she said it, she burst into tears, flung herself upon her bed, and kissed and passionately kissed the letter which had pierced her heart.

Therewith she began again the eternal rehabilitative process, in which every woman shows herself such an adept in relation to the man she loves.

Jack had not meant to be cruel, but he was quick-tempered; he resented the treatment he had received. Still smarting from a sense of injury, he would naturally be unjust towards every one, angry even with her. But, of course, he loved her all the same. He had loved her only a few weeks ago. One could not change so absolutely in so short a time. One could not love and not love as one puts on and off a coat. It was she who was wicked to doubt him, who was unreasonable not to make allowances, who was stupid not to read his real feelings beneath the disguising words.

But no sooner was her idol again set upon his altar, than doubt, suspicion, assailed her anew. And so the struggle continued between her longing to believe her lover perfect and the revolt of her reason, her dignity, against his conduct towards her. Yet with every victory love flowed stronger, resentment ebbed insensibly away.

The last traces of resentment vanished when one Saturday in town she met him suddenly face to face. She was passing the Town Library, and exactly as she passed, Owen came out, standing still, as he saw her, on the step.

Her pulses beat tumultuously, the colour ran to her cheeks.

"Oh, Jack," she cried, taking his hand, "how could you write to me so coldly, so cruelly? If you knew what I have suffered! And it was not my fault ..."

From the first moment of seeing her, Owen had stood transfixed, silent. Now he pushed back the swing door, and held it wide.

"At least come in here," he said slowly; "don't let us have a scene in the street."

They stood together in a corner of the great granite-flagged hall, which offered such cool, quiet contrast with the sunshine and turmoil outside.

"You don't care for me any more?" she asked, keen for the denial, which came indeed, but which to her supersensitiveness seemed to lack emphasis.

But his excuses were emphatic enough.

"It's no more my fault than it's yours," he told her; "it's your grand-mother who won't have anything to say to me, the Lord knows why?"

He spoke interrogatively, and she flamed a deprecating crimson.

"I can't very well force my way into the house against her wishes, can I?" he went on.

"No; but, dearest Jack, you needn't be angry with me, and we can wait a little, and I know everything will come right. If only you will go on loving me. You do love me still?" she asked him, "I shall die if you don't!"

He smiled down upon her, twisting his moustache-end. A softer look came into his eyes.

"So, the poor little girlie can't live without me?" he said, and gently squeezed her arm. Her heart welled up with adoration and gratitude.

A stranger coming down the polished wooden staircase cast a sympathetic glance at this little Island love idyll.

But Owen looked at his watch.

"Oh, confound it! Half-past twelve already, and I ought to be up at Rohais by now. I've an appointment there. I don't like to leave you, but —"

"Is it *very* important?" she asked wistfully.

"It's a new patient."

"Oh, then in that case, of course you must go," she admitted, with ready abnegation of her pleasure where it clashed with his interests. "But when shall I see you again? Ah, do let me see you."

"Oh, … well, … all right! I'll stroll up to-morrow in the course of the afternoon, to Berceau Bay … but if I'm prevented, you'll be coming to market, next Saturday, I suppose, eh?"

And he was gone.

Agnes sat down for a few moments to recover her composure. Her eyes rested on the red gold-fish swimming futilely round and round the glass bowl in the centre of the hall; but at her ear was the joy-killing whisper that the appointment had been a fictitious one.

Nevertheless, she persuaded herself he would come next day. She spent three hours, hidden in the bracken, at a point whence she could overlook the whole bay. When he did not come, she deferred her hopes to the following Saturday, to be again disappointed. He was not to be seen. Neither in the Market Place, nor at the Library, nor yet in the Contrée Mansel; for she could not refrain from the poor pleasure of passing along the street in which he lived, of glancing shame-facedly at his house, of envying wildly the servant she saw for an instant at an upper window. She would have thought it a privilege to be allowed to clean his boots.

But when she found herself at home that evening she was seized by an access of silent despair. There seemed nothing on earth to do: nothing to live for.

Yet the buoyancy of youth is hard to extinguish. Repeated blows are needed to beat it down, just as the tears shed at eighteen may be bitter indeed, but do not furrow the cheeks.

As the year brought round another spring, Agnes found that her spirits grew brighter with the days. She loved Jack more than ever. It was impossible to be absolutely unhappy with such a love in her heart; with the knowledge that she lived in the same Island with him; that once a week at least she could walk through the streets he daily trod; that any day she ran the chance of meeting him again, of speaking with some one who had just spoken with him.

Against dates on which she heard his name thus mentioned, she put a cross of red ink in the little calendar she carried in her purse. When she was having her new summer frock fitted, the dress-maker's three-year-old child ran into the room. Agnes, who was fond of children, said a kind word to him; but the mother, kneeling on the floor with upstretched arms and a mouthful of pins, shook her head menacingly.

"Ah, Johnnie's a bad boy. He won't take his medicine. I'll have to tell Dr Owen 'bout him."

"Does Dr. Owen attend him?" Agnes asked, flutteringly; and the woman explained Owen was the doctor of the club to which her husband belonged.

"He's a very clever doctor," ventured Agnes, all covered with blushes. "Don't you think so?"

"Ah, my good!" said the other, as who should say, doctors are necessary evils, and there's not much to choose between them. "But he give Johnnie a fine new double piece last time he come, didn't he, Johnnie? 'Tisn't the value I ever looks at," she explained to Agnes, "but the kind thought."

Agnes felt a glow of pride at the generosity, the good-heartedness of her lover, and on going away she pressed a whole British shilling into Johnnie's treacly little paw. Against this day she placed two crosses in her calendar, and the episode filled her thoughts for a week, to be succeeded by a still more precious one.

The annual picnic came round, provided by the Chapel for its Sunday-school. Agnes, as one of the teachers, went with the rest. They drove in waggonnettes to Rocquaine, and the only point of the day to which she looked forward with pleasure, was the passing Owen's house on the way back late at night. They went by a longer way, but they always came down the Contrée Mansel on the way home. She distinguished from quite a distance *his* illuminated parlour window; but the white blind was drawn down; she was just going to be bitterly disappointed, when a shadow, *his* shadow, passed across it. She thrilled with excitement, with gratitude for her great good luck, and answered young Mallienne, who sat beside her, with strange irrelevancy.

For in spite of everything she could not realise to herself that Owen did not love her; her heart refused to envisage it. Although he made no effort to see her, although he gave no sign, she clung to the belief that all would yet be well. She leaned on Fate; something would be sure to happen … some day, when she was her own mistress … She thought of him constantly, loved him as tenderly as before.

The summer was extraordinarily fine. The heat which had begun in March lasted right through to September; in the middle of the day from July onwards, it was almost unbearable. Agnes, one Saturday, having been into town as usual, was obliged to walk home laden with purchases, for the omnibus filled up with waiting passengers almost the moment it reached the Market Place. But when, very warm and a little weary, she reached Mon Désir, she found Frederic in one of those states of nervous excitement from which he periodically suffered. Mrs. Le Messurier had given him a soothing draught, the last in the house. It was essential to have more in case another were required during the night or the next day.

Agnes, pleased at the chance of a second journey into town, since it gave her a second chance of meeting Owen, volunteered to go back for it. Mrs. Le Messurier told her she looked done up with the heat already, but that she might go when she had had her dinner, and that she must take the omnibus both ways.

It was half-past two when she reached town, crossed over to Mauger's and waited there while the prescription was made up. She had then ten minutes on her hands before the three o'clock omnibus left for St. Gilles.

An old family friend, Mr. de Gruchy, stood in his shirt-sleeves on the threshold of his shop. Agnes stopped to speak to him, and to inquire after the girls. They were all away from home, and doing well. Their mother received cheerful letters every week. Agnes charged him with kind messages for them, and turned to go. He shook her hand heartily. "Well, good-bye, my dear," he said, in his comfortable, resonant voice, "my love to your grand'ma, and ask her when she's going to spend another day with us, eh?"

Coming down the street were a lady and two gentlemen. The men were in tennis flannels, and carried racquets and balls. The girl wore a lilac and white frock, fashioned with a simplicity and *chic* that spoke of St. Héliers at least, if not of Paris.

Agnes recognised the youngest Miss d'Aldernois, her brother the Captain, just back from India, and between the two, Jack Owen. Jack was looking straight towards her.

The delighted blood sprang to her cheek, her eyes sparkled, her mouth smiled. She took a step forward, she half extended her hand … and he looked her full in the face without a sign of recognition and passed on.

Miss d'Aldernois' silk-lined skirt brushed with a light frou-frou against hers, as, with her pretty head held high, she chattered volubly with her pretty lisp. The Captain walked in the roadway.

Agnes stood and watched the three figures with their short, slanting shadows retire further and further down the sunny street.

"Come in and take something, my dear," she heard de Gruchy saying at her elbow; "a little drop of raspberry vinegar now, it will do you good. Or go up and have a chat with mother, eh? You will find her in the drawing-room. She would like to read you Lucy's last letter, I know. It's downright clever."

Agnes shook her head, stammered excuses in a voice that sounded strange in her own ears, and left him.

He had cut her dead; Jack, the man she worshipped. The only man who had ever taken her in his arms and kissed her; the only man by whom she ever wished to be kissed and held. In broad daylight, openly, before witnesses, he had cut her.

Mr. de Gruchy had seen what had happened; he had understood; he had pitied her.

An illumination came. Jack was ashamed of her. Because she had shaken hands with the old man, he was ashamed to recognise her before his new friends. She was connected with trade; a child of trade; and he was now received among the Sixties.

A profound humiliation overpowered her, sapped the rest of her strength. The glare of the sun became suddenly intolerable ... she longed to be at home, to be in darkness.

She discovered that in her preoccupation she had taken the wrong turning. She hurried back, but the market clock showed seven minutes past three. The omnibus must be already half-way up Constitution Hill.

There was nothing to do but to walk, as she had walked in the morning. She set out with automatic movements, with a suffering endurance.

When you step away from the last bit of shadow of the town, and, steeply climbing, reach the level hill-top, you have before you a long unsheltered stretch of road until you come to the trees of St. Gilles. It is a white and dusty road with sun-parched fields on either side; and in July there is a blazing sky above you, to your left a blazing sea.

It seemed to Agnes that the sun was darting his rays straight down into her brain, that the ground was scorching the soles of her feet. But it did not occur to her to open her umbrella.

The passing scarlet jacket of a soldier made her close her eyes with pain. The whistle of a boy behind her set all her nerves ajar.

Should she ever get home? ... She dragged on with leaden feet and prayed persistently for darkness.

But when at last she lay upon her bed in such darkness as closed shutters and drawn curtains can give, all she could say was, "Oh, the sun, the sun!" all she could do was to lift her hand indeterminately towards her head. And when, a few hours before the end, she lost the power of speech, still her hand wandered up every now and again automatically towards her head.

Mrs. Le Messurier sits alone with her grandson in the living-room of Mon Désir. He cuts out pictures from the illustrated papers, and she gazes tirelessly through dim and tearless eyes into the past. Bright crowds of long-dead men and women pass before her, and among them the two Agneses are never absent long. Then, all at once, as the boy, with his mirthless laugh, looks up to claim her attention, the vision is scattered into thin wreaths of smoke.

The Hour of Her Life
by Mabel E. Wotton

It was at the beginning of last season that a flower-shop was started in the heart of Clubland, which, had it continued open, would have been town-famed long ere this. Instead of holding the orthodox stiff-backed chairs and counter, the interior was as prettily arranged a little nook as could be found in all London. Bits of old brocades and trailing plants covered the walls, and the stock-in-trade, which consisted exclusively of men's buttonholes, was dispensed by so beautiful a woman that she was able to make it a rule from the very first, that whatever might be the price of the flowers when sold by her two assistants, they doubled in value when touched by her own fair hands. Annette was the name over the window, and it very soon became 'the thing' with a certain section of society to lounge into the flower-shop on spring afternoons, and to waste a fair amount of time and money over the excellent tea (which was given gratis), and the purchase of flowers, whose perfection and cost put a certain *cachet* upon the customers. A favoured few were occasionally admitted into an inner sanctum, and this, though it was merely divided from the outer room by a curtain, it became the fashion to desire to enter. The place was fitted in Liberty's best style, the lounges were luxurious, and the object was flirtation.

The piquancy of it, such as it was, lay in Annette herself. A small, impudent-toned, rosy-faced girl would have vulgarised the affair at once; it was so exactly what would have been expected. But Annette was a graceful, loose-limbed woman, whose complete indifference stood her in lieu of dignity, and whose absolutely colourless face, crowned by a mass of dyed auburn hair, to which only one man was so fastidious as to object, brought into greater prominence a pair of big changeful eyes, which were long-lashed, and of a perfect forget-me-not blue. Her manner was usually grave to sombreness, and, as Freddy Calvin averred, it was not altogether unlike making love to an iceberg. It being pointed out to him that this could scarcely be deemed a satisfactory occupation, he shifted both his ground and his simile, and vowed it more resembled wooing an angel, and made him feel kind of churchy and good. And, besides, he never knew when she would snub him, and when fall in with radiant delight with his own plans; and this perhaps held the case in a nutshell.

One morning early in May, Mr. Freddy Calvin – heart-whole, strictly inoffensive, and heir to Lord Sydthorpe, he was registered in the matchmaker's books that season – came strolling along Piccadilly in the glossiest of new hats, and the broadest of smiles. He was a young gentleman who was invariably on excellent terms both with himself and the world at large, and he thought the universe at that moment held no greater bliss than the knowledge he was going to Annette, and felt tolerably assured of his welcome.

"I shall marry that woman if she will have me," he had said to Luke Felstead the night before, and it had left him totally unruffled that his friend had rudely replied: "Then, my dear Freddy, the more fool you."

Felstead was the one man who objected to Annette's dyed hair, and was also the mentor who occasionally took Freddy to task. Farthermore, though this is a detail, he was the one man for whom Annette cared a rush.

Freddy reached his destination, and finding the shop empty but for the two little blue-gowned white-capped maids, begged one of them to find out if mademoiselle would admit him to the inner room. To brush past the curtain uninvited was more than the most courageous of the men would have dared.

"Mam'selle says 'Please come in,'" was the message brought back, and Freddy, with sufficient delicacy to feel he should sink the trade in the courtship, left on the table the rose he had just purchased, and went in with alacrity.

Annette was doing some needlework, some lacey sort of stuff, but put it down at once to stretch a greeting hand towards him.

"I am so glad to see you!" and there was enough music in her soft tones to make the words sound not commonplace.

"It is downright good of you to let me come in," responded Freddy heartily; he was barely of age, and his diction was still boyish. "Is that a thing that wants holding, Annette? My cousin Mary is always doing work that wants another fellow holding, and I'll do it for you at once. Uncle Sydthorpe is in town again."

"Is he?" asked his hostess. Freddy's chatter bored her, because she knew there was so much of it she should have to sit through before he could be helped on to the one subject which interested her keenly, and of which only he could tell her.

To-day, however, her patience was less severely taxed than usual, for when he had continued discussing his relations for some minutes, he broke off abruptly to remark he had seen Felstead last night, and to quote his opinions anent his cousin Mary.

Annette's indifference vanished.

"What did you say he said of Miss Calvin?" she asked breathlessly.

"Oh, he admires her."

"She is pretty?"

"Pretty?" Freddy whistled. "No, she is plain, but Felstead cares nothing for looks. He likes a Vere de Vere individual, who would rather die than send you in to dinner with the wrong girl."

Annette's laugh sounded forced.

"And I was studying up the Peerage last night to understand the carriage panels," she said. "Ah, well! it takes all sorts to make a world, doesn't it?"

"As if you weren't a whole century better than she in every way," Freddy cried out indignantly. "I only wish you cared half as much for yourself as I care for you, and then you'd die of self-love."

"A pleasing ending," replied Annette.

She spoke listlessly, for what was the use of it all, when everything she could learn of Luke Felstead tended to show the sharp line of demarcation he drew between women of his own class, and others? What was the use of enduring the society of this talkative lad, if it never brought her nearer his friend?

Freddy was going on in a more ardent strain now, not quite venturing on the intended proposal, but making as hot love as his honest heart and limited vocabulary would allow. Annette thought her own thoughts the while, and when they grew too bitter, dismissed him almost curtly.

Five minutes after his departure she caught the tones of another voice enquiring for her, a pleasant, full-toned voice this one, and as courteous in its manner of addressing the white-capped maids as if they had been royal. Annette passed swiftly through the curtain, and confronted a grave-looking middle-aged man, with a pale pink flush rising slowly in her cheeks.

"Yes, Mr Felstead?" she said.

The newcomer raised his hat. "I am an early visitor, but I thought I should find Freddy here," he explained, and his listener chose to construe his sentence into; "Otherwise I should not have come."

So she answered defiantly that he had been, and had stayed a long time, and all the while had a miserable knowledge that she would regret the words as soon as Felstead had left her.

"I saw you last night," she continued.

"And I you," he responded, "though I did not go in myself. I hope you liked the play?"

"No. I was with Roger Bryant, and he always palls on me after a bit. You will ask me why I go with him then?"

"Certainly not," said Felstead suavely. "I should not be so impertinent as to question your movements."

Adding a good day, he went off, and Annette retreated into the inner room. Had she done anything wrong? she asked herself, in a white heat of rage. No, she knew she had not, for ladies — real ladies — went out in the evening with men who were not their husbands: the society papers said so; so how dared he say in that distant polished voice: "Certainly not."

The days went on. May came to an end, and June dawned amid all the sunny-houred fashion and fuss which inaugurates so much enjoyment, and disguises so much of tragedy. Annette had disposed of the amorous Bryant by snubbing him so effectually that that hero went flowerless for a week; and then, in the natural reaction from misery to annoyance, took to buying his buttonholes at another shop.

"We were talking away in quite a friendly fashion," he informed his brother some months later, "when she told me suddenly I had gone too far, and must stop. I declare to you I was trying to be as agreeable as possible. As I didn't at once well, what do you imagine this extraordinary woman did? She just rang the bell, and told one of her maids to stay in the room with us; and then she turned to me with the most beaming of smiles. 'You were saying —' she said sweetly."

Bryant deposed, left Freddy Calvin an undisputed first, and a rare round of delight he had, in which the river and many theatres played prominent parts, and which were as innocent, and undoubtedly as enjoyable, as if they had been shared by the most lynx-eyed of chaperons.

At length came the day when Luke Felstead saw that if ever he intended to win Freddy from a not over-desirable influence, now was the time to do it. Why he interested himself in the young man, with whom he had but little in common, is not to be related here. It took its rise from a memory associated with his mother, and was an unwritten chapter of Felstead's lonely life. Enough that Freddy, left to himself, would inevitably drift downwards, and accordingly must be taken in hand at once.

So his mentor, with a vast amount of self-pity, for he hated interfering with other people's affairs, betook himself to Charing Cross in order to meet the train which brought up the two from a half day at Richmond, and there asked Annette, as simply as if it were not thoroughly alien to his ordinary line of conduct, if she would accord him an interview the following morning. It hardly required the demure "Yes, I shall be very pleased," for her eyes shone for the moment, and the quick breath parted her lips.

"It is a sad waste of expression," thought Felstead, half-contemptuously, as he watched her companion put her into a cab. "What a flirt she is!"

Next morning Annette was up betimes. She wanted both herself and her room to look their prettiest, and he had not said at what hour he would call. But as the time dragged leadenly by, she was seized with a great nervousness, and was fit for nothing more than to sit trembling, with her ears strained to catch the first sound of his approach. He was coming to her of his own free will! The thought rang like a jubilant note of victory. She knew she was beautiful; she had but little vanity, but she could not help knowing that; had he grown to think so too?

Was he coming to her because her tactics of patient waiting had been crowned with success at last? Was her double endeavour never to force their possible friendship, but to learn of his desires through Freddy, and then be swayed by them, while at the same time she trusted he might be piqued by her apparent preference for another man, — was it to yield her happiness to-day? She pushed up the hair which was growing damp with anxiety upon her forehead, and rubbed her hands to bring some warmth into them. Then —

"Can I see your mistress? She is expecting me."

"Yes, sir, if you will go in to her, please," and Luke Felstead entered the room. The hour of her life had come.

"Will you — will you sit down?" she said, when the maid had pulled to an inner door behind the curtain, for he had not relinquished her fingers, but was looking at her gravely. "What is it?" she added involuntarily.

"I think it is good of you to see me," he told her, seating himself at some little distance, and scanning her as she stood before him, a straight motionless figure in her dark blue gown. "You do not know me at all well, and I have no right to ask it."

She murmured something inaudible, and he continued —

"Will you promise not to turn me out of the room, for I am going to be impertinent, and shall deserve it?"

Even had Annette been a novice in the hearing of love vows, which she certainly was not, she would have taken heart from the direct personal tone of his words; but she controlled herself, and answered him very quietly.

"You have always been scrupulously careful, Mr. Felstead. Even if you were, as you say, 'impertinent,' I would forgive you, now."

She had dropped on to a couch with loosely-clasped hands and half-averted head. It made no impression on him, but having her here to himself, Felstead began dimly to comprehend somewhat of the fascination she might possess for younger men.

"You are too young and too beautiful to be here by yourself," he said abruptly. "Haven't you people of your own to live with?"

She shook her head.

"My father was an officer — Lion Browning of the Guards; perhaps you have heard of him — Mad Lion, they called him. He cut the service when he married my mother, and I was born in France. She sold oranges in Drury Lane; and I have been told he was tipsy at the time. But I won't think that. He was my father, and I like to think he was a gentleman, and be proud of him."

Watching her kindling eyes, and the eloquent little gesture with which she flung back her head, Felstead thought so too.

"I see," he said kindly. "And being your father's child, you did not care much about your other relations."

"That was just it," she answered. "I went to my grandfather — his father, you know — once, and he turned me from the house. A low-looking man, I think he said he was a coster, found me out another time, and insisted he was my uncle, so I did the same friendly office by him. I am a sort of Mahomet's coffin, Mr. Felstead, and hang between the two worlds without belonging to either."

Felstead was silent. This explained much which had hitherto puzzled him.

"I came to ask you a big kindness," he said at last. "I came to you yourself, direct, because if I can read faces at all, yours proves you are good-hearted. Are you fond of Freddy Calvin, Miss Browning?"

Annette hesitated.

"Why?" she asked.

"Because I want you to give up the boy, and let him go."

The woman's heart beat almost to suffocation. Was this tantamount to saying, "that I may take his place?"

"Why?" she said again, and stopped short.

Then he told her. What he said was as delicately veiled as was compatible with absolute clearness; not by one expression or inflexion of his voice would he wantonly wound her; but the naked truth was unmistakable. A woman in her position, who had been fêted by a vast number of the fastest men in town; whose beauty had enabled her to sell flowers at fancy prices, and whose life generally since the opening of the shop had proved she was answerable to no one for her actions, was assuredly not the sort of woman to become the future Lady Sydthorpe. He did not fancy her affection could really have been caught by the errant fancy of a boy some year or two her junior. Would she not show herself capable of a great goodness, and break the chains which held him?

Annette heard him steadily to the end. A dull brickdust red had suffused her pale cheeks, and her eyes had darkened.

"I may not know the ways of your world, Mr. Felstead," she said when he had finished, "but I am not a bad woman."

The man flushed in his turn.

"You and I may not much like each other," he told her, "but if any man in my presence dared to say that you were, I would knock him down for a liar."

Annette had set her teeth so hard, that it was with physical effort she unclenched them to answer him.

"Then why can't I marry him?" she demanded. "Understand that I do not say I would, I do not say I care two straws about him. I only say, why shouldn't I?"

Her companion murmured something about an impressionable lad like Calvin wanting a wife who would hold him up, and not pull him down in the social scale; but Annette had risen to her feet, and broke in upon his words with a sudden passion and energy that made them fail upon his lips.

"Why should you try to spare your friend?" she cried. "What have I done? My father's birth was as good as his own; you yourself admit that whatever I may do, it is in the open daylight; I am well favoured enough to have won his love, and I have wit enough to keep it. I have got my own living, it is true, but is that a shame to me? When the men I know overstep the bounds of friendship, I send them away. I don't keep my discarded lovers dangling about me. Is that so much lower than the fine ladies of your own set? When the —"

What Luke Felstead might have answered had her impetuous ringing speech continued to its end, remained unspoken, for as the words came pouring forth as she stood fronting the man who, perfectly unmoved, perfectly courteous, listened to her, a chance remark of his which Freddy had repeated flashed through her brain. Felstead could only care for a woman who would 'rather die,' as the boy had phrased it, than commit the slightest social solecism, and this sudden remembrance tolled the death-knell to her hopes. She stood silent, and looked at him piteously.

"Could a woman of my class never make a man of yours happy?"

"Never," said Felstead, firmly. "There would be the same difficulty, Miss Browning, if you were a princess. To be happy the boy should marry in his own swim."

"Couldn't my love for my husband do anything?" Her voice was dangerously sweet, her blue eyes were liquid with tears she was too proud to shed. "It should teach me to sink my old life utterly; I would have no will nor aim but his."

The face she was watching did not soften, and Annette drew back a step, as though the quiet figure had struck her.

"I see. I am a fool." she said, and the pleading had died from her voice. Then: "You want me to send him away, Mr. Felstead? If I do, it will be to please you." She turned from him abruptly, and walking over to the mantel-shelf rested her elbow on its ledge, her chin on her hand. "I wonder if I shall do it."

"To please me?"

Felstead rose from his seat, startled, bewildered. What did she mean?

"Yes," said Annette, slowly, "you. I – I am whimsical, Mr. Felstead, and just because, as you say, we two don't much like each other, I've a fancy – to be well thought of – by you." She spoke unsteadily, almost jerkily. "Come back to-morrow morning, will you, and bring Freddy with you? I," her fingers stole over her quivering mouth, and hid it from him, "I will do what you want? Will you shake hands with me – now?"

That day the flower-shop was closed, and a neat placard affixed to its shutters, which the friends read next morning with a conviction on at least the elder man's part that the announcement meant for always. 'Gone away' was what it said.

'The World's Slow Stain'
by Ella Hepworth Dixon

I

"I'm going to marry a man who jilted me ten years ago."

She stood up, facing him, instinctively taking the attitude in which she had been told, often enough, that she looked best. A woman of thirty — perhaps over — who was vaguely supposed to be twenty-six. Adela Buller was getting a little hard-looking now, but she wore her clothes with an air. She had on a simple, well-made dress, but the effect was spoiled by the quantity of rings which covered her fingers; rings with little hearts depending from them, rings with mysterious inscriptions, and rings of strange design.

Gilbert Vincent gazed at the two little plump hands resting on the empty chair facing him, and smiled a dubious smile. He had a fat, white face, which expressed nothing in repose. When he smiled, people had a brief vision of unclean things.

"It's a subtle form of revenge," he said, after a constrained pause. "Though I didn't know you wanted to marry."

"Well, I do."

"Why? I thought you had come to the conclusion that it was much more agreeable not to be tied; to let us all adore you. For you know we are *all* devoted ..." said Vincent, in the soft, half-amused voice in which, in his capacity of successful dramatist, he was permitted to make the most outrageous statements. "I am sure," he went on, with a curiously un-English movement of his small white hands, "if I were a woman, nowadays, I should think so."

"Yes, you're all devoted enough," admitted Adela, with candour. She never took the trouble to be anything but candid with Gilbert Vincent. She had known him too long. "But, all the same, one doesn't care to *afficher* oneself too much"

"Oh, as for that, who cares much about anything? You don't mean to tell me you're going to turn prudish?"

"I was a nice girl once. It's a hundred years ago; but I was really!"

"Were you ever 'nice'?" said Vincent. "A nice girl like one reads of in books? I can't believe you ever belonged to that variety of the British bore."

Adela laughed a rather unpleasant laugh.

"No, I don't think I was ever a bore," she said, crossing to the mantelpiece and taking up a Japanese ivory, which she twisted about and examined on all sides as she spoke. "But I was a good girl, with deep feelings, and ideals, and all that sort of thing ... I — I imagined that men were ... decent, you know, and that the women who were treated unfairly were the exceptions, and that it was their own fault, generally, if they were. I did not know that women were stuffed with idiotic theories from their very childhood, and that all my life I should suffer, suffer, suffer, for what I had been taught then. We are not told" she went on with rising excitement, "what life is, what it all means, or how to play the game. We are like children to whom a pack of cards is thrown, and who are set down to play a strange game with men who are confirmed gamblers. The rules are never told us, so that we blunder helplessly along, and unless we cheat outrageously, or mark the cards, there's small chance of our winning. And what's so funny is, that most 'good' men like us to be like that, ignorant, silly, helpless — even cheats. They think it pretty."

"I believe you're right," said Vincent, with languid surprise, This was a new phase of Adela Buller, of whom he always had vague visions, in which he saw her forming one of quartette suppers at the Carlton, of hearing of her 'running over to Paris' (she had been especially fond, of late years of that particular form of dissipation so dear to the Londoner), of seeing her, in an exaggerated 1840 gown which slipped off her white shoulders, reciting suggestive little poems in French to a small audience of young men.

He got up, and, leaning one elbow on the mantelpiece, watched her with a new curiosity. Her eyes were strangely bright — had she been putting belladonna into them again, he wondered? He could see the pulse in her wrist beating furiously against the dark blue vein ... Vincent hoped devoutly she was not going to have a *crise de nerfs*. What excellent 'copy' she would make; what a capital *type* she would be on the stage; the young lady who is forever hovering on the brink, but who has 'kept straight' all the same. Really, he must make an exhaustive study of Adela.

"Poor little girl!" he said softly, watching her as she tried to balance the fat Japanese divinity on his head. "And so you're going to take your revenge by marrying him. Well, it's not a bad way, either. Who was the fool the other night at the club who was saying that your modern woman wasn't complex at all — only hysterical? By Jove, and who's the lucky beggar?"

"Anthony Mellingham. He wrote from Mexico. I haven't seen him, you know, for seven or eight years. He's made some money, I believe, and apparently he's got remorse! It seems curious now, how I loved that man — ten years ago."

"Then all's for the best in the best of all possible worlds," said Vincent, with his dubious smile. "When are you going to see him? To-night?"

"Oh no, to-morrow morning. I look so worn at night ... But in a cotton frock, in the morning, with my hair done rather neatly ... That's how they like to come back and find a woman, don't they?" said Adela, with the drawl which had become habitual to her. There was a world of weariness, of disillusionment in her tone.

"Well, he's a lucky man," repeated Gilbert, taking her dimpled hand and giving it a lengthened pressure.

"Don't do that — it bores me."

"What am I to give you for a wedding present? Another ring?"

"Oh, anything. No, not a ring. I — I — hate them. I'm never going to wear rings any more."

"Except the fatal one," said Vincent, retreating. "By the bye," he asked, exhibiting his curious smile on the first step of the staircase, turning back as he did so to take in every detail of the pretty woman he was leaving, "what's he like?"

"Fairish; rather good-looking, rather stupid."

"Oh, then it's the fellow you did in that novel you wrote?"

"What, that idiotic thing? Oh, I don't know! I've forgotten all about it," said Adela peevishly. "I only wrote the thing because I was — miserable. And nobody would have bought it, only it was a one-and-sixpenny book printed the wrong way up."

"It had a success," said the dramatist, in the strictly indifferent tone of one artist to another.

"Have *I* ever had a success?" said Adela wearily.

"Curious girl, but only one of a new species," said Vincent to himself as he made his way down the Kensington street. "She's all right, I daresay, but she wouldn't like us to think so ... She calls it 'dull' of a woman not to have had emotional experiences, and wouldn't thank you if you altered your conversation to spare her blushes ... Yet she can be very sweet, very attractive; and she is curiously feminine — for a modern type. She knows enough to be always *très femme* when she wants to be really charming. And, by Jove, she *can* be charming! It's extraordinary how fond one can be of her — at times, and in certain moods ... I wonder," he asked himself, as he stopped to light a cigar, "if it is possible I shall feel it if Adela really were to marry?"

II

Adela Buller sat waiting for her lover. Every now and then she got up, fidgeting about, now to throw into a drawer some audacious French novel which challenged the eye with its yellow cover, now to put into the background the signed photograph of a famous comedian, again to slightly lower the blind which let in the glaring July sunshine, and then to give one final look into the glass.

Adela had an artistic sense of the eternal fitness of things. She looked her part to perfection. Her face had undergone careful massage at the hands of her maid, so that, for the moment, the cheeks had regained something of the roundness, the freshness of youth, and she had insisted on Sarah brushing out the artificial waves of her hair. The lilac cotton gown showed, without insisting on, the plump lines of her figure; her pretty hands were absolutely bare.

"Mr. Mellingham," said the servant, and Anthony entered, revealing himself, after these ten years, as a not ill-looking man of thirty-six, burnt almost to bronze colour, so that he made a somewhat incongruous appearance in his brand-new London clothes. For the rest, his blue eyes were placed slightly too close together, and there was a curious mixture of sensuality and caution in his face. The latter quality had become accentuated in the course of eight years' knocking about in Mexico. Both tendencies had always existed deep down in his nature, and had accounted for the everyday tragedy of his having loved Adela, and yet having ridden away.

He stepped forward, glancing tentatively round the room.

"Adela!" he said, putting his arms round her, and turning her face upwards so that their lips could meet.

Heavens! How horrible it was, she thought ... He had so completely passed out of her life during the last eight years, that this embrace seemed well-nigh as outrageous as that of a stranger. As he kissed her, she remembered the caresses, the passionate words of other men ... How many — how many had there been since they had seen each other? It could never be the same again; she was not the same woman; Time had besmirched her, year by year, with his horrible, corroding finger. Ah, if she could only have died then — when Tony went away ...

"Why, you're looking as young and pretty as when I left," he declared, his spirits rising. "Hanged if I don't think you're better-looking. And you have cared about me a little bit all this time, Adela?" he went on anxiously. "You haven't let any of those other fellows snap you up?"

"Marry me, do you mean?"

"Why, of course."

"N — no. I must have been a young person of exemplary fidelity," she said, smiling. "For no one, as far as I remember, has even wanted to marry me."

"Oh, that's all rot — a pretty girl like you, too. But you were always so horribly proud. How jolly it is in London, with the Park, and the theatres, and all that sort of thing. I say, we'll have some fun together, won't we? And then, at the end of the month, we'll get turned off in proper style, and then we can go to Scotland. Hang it, Adela, I've waited long enough."

They looked at each other, and the ludicrousness of his phrase made them both laugh. Anthony Mellingham felt more comfortable. Adela had been looking so serious — although uncommonly pretty — ever since he had arrived. He had marvelled how little she had changed. Well, girls weren't like men; they hadn't got to rough it, they didn't lead the lives that men did ... Nowadays, girls, when they were hipped or disappointed, took up bridge or started a hat-shop. He wondered if Adela had started a hat-shop?

Well, bygones must be bygones; he had come back now, having made enough out there to live comfortably at home. What he wanted, he told himself, was a nice little place in Dorsetshire or Sussex, where he could get a bit of hunting in the winter, and of which Adela, who was always a handy girl, with lots of notions about things, could do the honours to the few friends he still possessed in England. If he had behaved badly all those years ago, he was sorry for it, especially as his eye dwelt agreeably on the rounded lines of Adela's figure, on her soft blonde hair, and her little bare plump hands. By Jove! she was just the nice-looking, amiable, simple-minded little woman he wanted. There had been a girl on the steamer, coming home, who had reminded him immensely of Adela. She might have been ten years younger, but there was no essential difference. He and she, he remembered with a smile, had had an uncommonly good time together.

Before Anthony left, which was not till after luncheon, they had made half a hundred projects; but what struck Adela as the strangest, most unlikely project of all, was that the wedding was to take place at the end of the month.

III

All the rooms in the little house in Kensington were filled to overflowing. It had been an early wedding, and the young couple were to catch the two o'clock train to Edinburgh. The rooms were stifling, and through the open door of the microscopic dining-room came a potent mingling of odours, comprising, among others, those of hothouse flowers, of champagne, of anchovy sandwiches, and of heated humanity, together with a brief vision of black coats struggling round a buffet, the rest of the room being filled with the pale, clear tones of women's summer dresses. Viewed from above, the headgear of the ladies resembled a flowerbed in full bloom. The drawing-room was chiefly filled with aunts and cousins of the bride (for Anthony Mellingham had no relations, and he had so far lost sight of his old friends that Gilbert Vincent had been, somewhat unwillingly, forced to officiate as best man) — aunts and cousins who surged tearfully round that self-possessed young lady, pressing damp kisses on a cheek which had been touched ever so slightly with powder. The bridegroom was downstairs drinking champagne with all and sundry, in radiant spirits, and wearing already the checked suit in which he was to travel. Adela's little boudoir was too high up to be made use of in the scurry of a wedding, and so the copper lamps, the silver-plated bacon-dishes, and the etchings after Leader, which always loom so largely in marriage offerings, were set out in the little room at the end of the hall passage.

Gilbert Vincent, his face pale with a pallor which was uncanny-looking, paced the little room upstairs in which he had spent so many hours of his life. He had often enough waited there for Adela, for she was of the order of unpunctual women, and he was waiting for her now.

Though he had professed himself amused, even delighted, with Miss Buller's prospective husband during the many theatre and river parties which had been got up during the last month, he felt curiously injured to-day, when she was at last separated from him for good ... Indeed, Vincent hardly realised it now. How could Adela Buller do anything so trite as to turn British matron? The thing was preposterous — it was worse, it was inartistic. He had been accustomed to drop in when he liked and read her scenes from his new plays (he was a man who was curiously dependent on feminine sympathy), even to make love to her when he felt so inclined, and here was Adela the legal property of a blundering, idiotic British Philistine, who stared when he propounded one of his elaborate aphorisms. Well, anyhow, she had promised to see him for a few moments alone, on her way upstairs to put on her travelling-dress. Deuce take her, why didn't she come? In a minute, he must jump into a hansom and drive to Euston, where he was to see to the tickets and procure for the bridal pair a carriage to themselves.

There was the rustling of a silk train, and Adela was in the room.

"It *is* good of you, I — I wanted to see you, before you went, Adela," he murmured, detaining her with both hands.

"Well, what is it?"

"I daresay it's ridiculous, but I feel quite sentimental."

"*You* sentimental! O Heavens!" She brushed past him to the looking-glass, where she began to fumble with the diamond pin which fastened her bridal veil.

"It *is* ridiculous!" admitted Vincent, with a wave of his white hands, "but these things occur. You're — you're not going to throw me over altogether?" he went on, surprised, himself, at the agitation in his voice. "You won't give me up?"

"Give you up?" — with a shrug. "How do you mean? We have been friends — nothing more."

"Friends!" said the man. She resented his sneer.

"Listen, once for all, Gilbert. You and I say good-bye to-day for good. I'm not going to see you, I'm not going to see any of the set I've been in for the last few years. I hate, I loathe the whole worldly lot ... For Heaven's sake, give me a chance ... I — I — oh, don't speak to me any more as long as I live."

He had a vision of her disappearing up the narrow little staircase, a foam of white tulle and shimmering satin. Then he looked round the room. Presently he smiled his singularly unpleasant smile. What had he agitated himself about this particular woman for? ... All that she had said to him just now meant nothing — except exasperated nerves ... She was essentially a comedian, and she evidently thought it part of her *rôle* as bride to talk in such a fashion on her wedding day ... Sooner or later, she would come back to him; he would sit in her boudoir, read her a scene from his new play, make love to her when he felt inclined ... But the husband? Well, he had better know at once that he hadn't married a Philistine, that he would never be able to turn Adela, after all these years, into the conventional British wife. Why, she was not only clever, she was something of an artist. There was that bitter little story of hers which he had helped her to write, in which she had hit off Mellingham to the life; now that he knew Anthony, he saw how merciless the character-drawing was. And of course, like all amateurs, and most women-novelists, she had drawn on her own experience ... Vincent smiled as he remembered how well some of those love scenes, the 'riding away' of the lover, and the subsequent career of the heroine had been done ... His eye fell on a row of narrow booklets. *A Man of Pleasure,* by Andrew Burn; there it was. It struck him suddenly, what a dramatic effect you could get by making a young husband read his bride's version of his life ... If Vincent could only be there to see! Well, the sooner Mr. Anthony Mellingham knew, the better. He slipped the thin little calico-covered novelette into his pocket, and, running downstairs, made his way to Euston.

The Scotch express flew northwards, bearing the married pair in a carriage by themselves. The blue cushions were littered with yellow leather bags, with newspapers, with tea-baskets, while, carefully wrapped in a Scotch plaid, Adela lay dozing with her back to Anthony. He took out his watch. Not ten o'clock yet; it would be a whole hour before they arrived in Edinburgh. No wonder Adela was tired out, he thought; there was that idiotic fussation of the morning — all the excitement, and all those people staring at her. And Adela, as he remembered, had always been rather a shy, modest little woman ... Knowing she didn't mind smoke, he lit a cigarette, and, leaning back on the cushions, congratulated himself on his having 'done the right thing' by her, after all ... Perhaps she had taken him a bit too seriously, all those years ago; at any rate, it was hardly his fault that he had been obliged to leave England. Adela hadn't a penny of her own, and he possessed, at the time of their love affair, exactly three hundred a year ... Well, it had all come right now. He thought of his banking account with complacence, and determined that there was literally nothing on earth to prevent their being as jolly a couple as he knew of.

There was a yawning yellow bag in front of him, containing silver flasks, evening newspapers, and novels. He dipped his hand in, and drew one out. A small, narrow volume, bound in calico, printed, according to the fashion of a few years ago, in a sort of column. *A Man of Pleasure,* by Andrew Burn. Who was the author? He had never heard of him. Oh, by Jove, this was the book that Vincent had slipped into his bag at the station, telling him it was A1. Well, Vincent was a dramatist, or a literary chap of sorts, and he ought to know.

Anthony Mellingham opened the book and began to read. The train rattled northwards, shaking the occupants of the carriage from side to side like inanimate objects. Adela did not move. The yellow lamplight fell straight on to Mellingham's curly yellow hair. Any one who had been watching him as he read on and on would have seen, first a perceptible creasing up of the line between his brows; then that his face had deepened into a copper colour through the bronze; finally, that his mouth seemed to have transformed itself into an ugly slit. He wore no moustache, so that the expression of the lips was plainly visible. The happy bridegroom seemed to have aged ten years in that hour.

The monotonous thud and whirl of the flying train made a strange accompaniment to his reading. No one, he saw at a glance, could have written the book but the sleeping woman opposite him. His very words had been repeated, and there was even a love scene — the one in which they had said farewell —which she had described with curious fidelity: yes, there was the boat-house at Wargrave, filled with cool, green twilight, the flopping of the river against the boats, the rain which fell in a white sheet outside. And he, Anthony Mellingham, the 'Man of Pleasure' of the book, had been carefully painted as an insufferable cad and egoist.

And she had married him.

The express stopped with a jerk on the outskirts of Edinburgh. Adela sat up, startled. Opposite her was her husband, with his changed face. The book fell from his hand. In an instant she had guessed the whole odious situation. Her face grew haggard, the deep circles which fatigue had scooped round her eyes were accentuated by the vertical rays from the carriage lamp. There was something faded yet hard, weary yet worldly, in the whole woman's personality.

Husband and wife gazed steadily at each other without a word. No word was needed, for in that look there passed, like a sword-thrust, the vision of an eternal rancour.

"I suppose we shall be able to get something decent to eat?" said the bride, pretending to yawn.

He turned his eyes away as he answered: "I believe Vincent telegraphed to the Palace about supper."

The Quicksand
by Edith Wharton

I

As Mrs. Quentin's victoria, driving homeward, turned from the Park into Fifth Avenue, she divined her son's tall figure walking ahead of her in the twilight. His long stride covered the ground more rapidly than usual, and she had a premonition that, if he were going home at that hour, it was because he wanted to see her.

Mrs. Quentin, though not a fanciful woman, was sometimes aware of a sixth sense enabling her to detect the faintest vibrations of her son's impulses. She was too shrewd to fancy herself the one mother in possession of this faculty, but she permitted herself to think that few could exercise it more discreetly. If she could not help overhearing Alan's thoughts, she had the courage to keep her discoveries to herself, the tact to take for granted nothing that lay below the surface of their spoken intercourse: she knew that most people would rather have their letters read than their thoughts. For this super-feminine discretion Alan repaid her by — being Alan. There could have been no completer reward. He was the key to the meaning of life, the justification of what must have seemed as incomprehensible as it was odious, had it not all-sufficingly ended in himself. He was a perfect son, and Mrs. Quentin had always hungered for perfection.

Her house, in a minor way, bore witness to the craving. One felt it to be the result of a series of eliminations: there was nothing fortuitous in its blending of line and colour. The almost morbid finish of every material detail of her life suggested the possibility that a diversity of energies had, by some pressure of circumstance, been forced into the channel of a narrow dilettantism. Mrs. Quentin's fastidiousness had, indeed, the flaw of being too one-sided. Her friends were not always worthy of the chairs they sat in, and she overlooked in her associates defects she would not have tolerated in her bric-à-brac. Her house was, in fact, never so distinguished as when it was empty; and it was at its best in the warm fire-lit silence that now received her.

Her son, who had overtaken her on the door-step, followed her into the drawing-room, and threw himself into an arm-chair near the fire, while she laid off her furs and busied herself about the tea-table. For a while neither spoke; but glancing at him across the kettle, his mother noticed that he sat staring at the embers with a look she had never seen on his face, though its arrogant young outline was as familiar to her as her own thoughts. The look extended itself to his negligent attitude, to the droop of his long fine hands, the dejected tilt of his head against the cushions. It was like the moral equivalent of physical fatigue: he looked, as he himself would have phrased it, dead-beat, played out. Such an air was so foreign to his usual bright indomitableness that Mrs. Quentin had the sense of an unfamiliar presence, in which she must observe herself, must raise hurried barriers against an alien approach. It was one of the drawbacks of their excessive intimacy that any break in it seemed a chasm.

She was accustomed to let his thoughts circle about her before they settled into speech, and she now sat in motionless expectancy, as though a sound might frighten them away.

At length, without turning his eyes from the fire, he said: "I'm so glad you're a nice old-fashioned intuitive woman. It's painful to see them think."

Her apprehension had already preceded him. "Hope Fenno —?" she faltered.

He nodded. "She's been thinking — hard. It was very painful — to me at least; and I don't believe she enjoyed it: she said she didn't." He stretched his feet to the fire. "The result of her cogitations is that she won't have me. She arrived at this by pure ratiocination — it's not a question of feeling, you understand. I'm the only man she's ever loved — but she won't have me. What novels did you read when you were young, dear? I'm convinced it all turns on that. If she'd been brought up on Trollope and Whyte-Melville, instead of Tolstoi and Mrs. Ward, we should have now been vulgarly sitting on a sofa, trying on the engagement-ring."

Mrs. Quentin at first was kept silent by the mother's instinctive anger that the girl she has not wanted for her son should have dared to refuse him. Then she said: "Tell me, dear."

"My good woman, she has scruples."

"Scruples?"

"Against the paper. She objects to me in my official capacity as owner of the *Radiator*."

His mother did not echo his laugh.

"She had found a solution, of course — she overflows with expedients. I was to chuck the paper, and we were to live happily ever afterward on canned food and virtue. She even had an alternative ready — women are so full of resources! I was to turn the *Radiator* into an independent organ, and run it at a loss to show the public what a model newspaper ought to be. On the whole, I think she fancied this plan more than the other — it commended itself to her as being more uncomfortable and aggressive. It's not the fashion nowadays to be good by stealth."

Mrs. Quention said to herself: "I didn't know how much he cared!" Aloud she murmured: "You must give her time."

"Time?"

"To move out the old prejudices and make room for new ones."

"My dear mother, those she has are brand-new; that's the trouble with them. She's tremendously up-to-date. She takes in all the moral fashion-papers, and wears the newest thing in ethics."

Her resentment lost its way in the intricacies of his metaphor. "Is she so very religious?"

"You dear archaic woman! She's hopelessly irreligious; that's the difficulty. You can make a religious woman believe almost anything: there's the habit of credulity to work on. But when a girl's faith in the Deluge has been shaken, it's very hard to inspire her with confidence. She makes you feel that, before believing in you, it's her duty as a conscientious agnostic to find out whether you're not obsolete, or whether the text isn't corrupt, or somebody hasn't proved conclusively that you never existed, anyhow."

Mrs. Quentin was again silent. The two moved in that atmosphere of implications and assumptions where the lightest word may shake down the dust of countless stored impressions; and speech was sometimes more difficult between them than had their union been less close.

Presently she ventured, "It's impossible?"

"Impossible?"

She seemed to use her words cautiously, like weapons that might slip and inflict a cut. "What she suggests."

Her son, raising himself, turned to look at her for the first time. Their glance met in a shock of comprehension. He was with her against the girl, then! Her satisfaction overflowed in a murmur of tenderness.

"Of course not, dear. One can't change — change one's life ..."

"One's self," he emended. "That's what I tell her. What's the use of my giving up the paper if I keep my point of view?"

The psychological distinction attracted her. "Which is it she minds most?"

"Oh, the paper — for the present. She undertakes to modify the point of view afterward. All she asks is that I shall renounce my heresy: the gift of grace will come later."

Mrs. Quentin sat gazing into her untouched cup. Her son's first words had produced in her the hallucinated sense of struggling in the thick of a crowd that he could not see. It was horrible to feel herself hemmed in by influences imperceptible to him; yet if anything could have increased her misery it would have been the discovery that her ghosts had become visible.

As though to divert his attention, she precipitately asked: "And you —?"

His answer carried the shock of an evocation. "I merely asked her what she thought of *you*."

"Of me?"

"She admires you immensely, you know."

For a moment Mrs. Quentin's cheek showed the lingering light of girlhood: praise transmitted by her son acquired something of the transmitter's merit. "Well —?" she smiled.

"Well — you didn't make my father give up the *Radiator*, did you?"

His mother, stiffening, made a circuitous return: "She never comes here. How can she know me?"

"She's so poor! She goes out so little." He rose and leaned against the mantelpiece, dislodging with impatient fingers a slender bronze wrestler poised on a porphyry base, between two warm-toned Spanish ivories. "And then her mother —" he added, as if involuntarily.

"Her mother has never visited me," Mrs. Quentin finished for him.

He shrugged his shoulders. "Mrs. Fenno has the scope of a wax doll. Her rule of conduct is taken from her grandmother's sampler."

"But the daughter is so modern — and yet —"

"The result is the same? Not exactly. *She* admires you — oh, immensely!" He replaced the bronze and turned to his mother with a smile. "Aren't you on some hospital committee together? What especially strikes her is your way of doing good. She says philanthropy is not a line of conduct but a state of mind — and it appears that you are one of the elect."

As, in the vague diffusion of physical pain, relief seems to come with the acuter pang of a single nerve, Mrs. Quentin felt herself suddenly eased by a rush of anger against the girl. "If she loved you —" she began.

His gesture checked her. "I'm not asking you to get her to do that."

The two were again silent, facing each other in the disarray of a common catastrophe — as though their thoughts, at the summons of danger, had rushed naked into action. Mrs. Quentin, at this revealing moment, saw for the first time how many elements of her son's character had seemed comprehensible simply because they were familiar: as, in reading a foreign language, we take the meaning of certain words for granted till the context corrects us. Often as, in a given case, her maternal musings had figured his conduct, she now found herself at a loss to forecast it; and with this failure of intuition came a sense of the subserviency which had hitherto made her counsels but the anticipation of his wish. Her despair escaped in the moan, "What *is* it you ask me?"

"To talk to her."

"Talk to her?"

"Show her — tell her — make her understand that the paper has always been a thing outside your life — that hasn't touched you — that needn't touch *her*. Only, let her hear you — watch you — be with you — she'll see ... she can't help seeing ..."

His mother faltered. "But if she's given you her reasons —?"

"Let her give them to you! If she can — when she sees you ..." His impatient hand again displaced the wrestler. "I care abominably," he confessed.

II

On the Fenno threshold a sudden sense of the futility of the attempt had almost driven Mrs. Quentin back to her carriage; but the door was already opening, and a parlour-maid, who believed that Miss Fenno was in, led the way to the depressing drawing-room. It was the kind of room in which no member of the family is likely to be found except after dinner or after death. The chairs and tables looked like poor relations who had repaid their keep by a long career of grudging usefulness: they seemed banded together against intruders in a sullen conspiracy of discomfort. Mrs. Quentin, keenly susceptible to such influences, read failure in every angle of the upholstery. She was incapable of the vulgar error of thinking that Hope Fenno might be induced to marry Alan for his money; but between this assumption and the inference that the girl's imagination might be touched by the finer possibilities of wealth, good taste admitted a distinction. The Fenno furniture, however, presented to such reasoning the obtuseness of its black-walnut chamferings; and something in its attitude suggested that its owners would be as uncompromising. The room showed none of the modern attempts at palliation, no apologetic draping of facts; and Mrs. Quentin, provisionally perched on a green-reps Gothic sofa with which it was clearly impossible to establish any closer relation, concluded that, had Mrs. Fenno needed another seat of the same size, she would have set out placidly to match the one on which her visitor now languished.

To Mrs. Quentin's fancy, Hope Fenno's opinions, presently imparted in a clear young voice from the opposite angle of the Gothic sofa, partook of the character of their surroundings. The girl's mind was like a large light empty place, scantily furnished with a few massive prejudices, not designed to add to any one's comfort but too ponderous to be easily moved. Mrs. Quentin's own intelligence, in which its owner, in an artistically shaded half-light, had so long moved amid a delicate complexity of sensations, seemed in comparison suddenly close and crowded; and in taking refuge there from the glare of the young girl's candour, the older woman found herself stumbling in an unwonted obscurity. Her uneasiness resolved itself into a sense of irritation against her listener. Mrs. Quentin knew that the momentary value of any argument lies in the capacity of the mind to which it is addressed; and as her shafts of persuasion spent themselves against Miss Fenno's obduracy, she said to herself that, since conduct is governed by emotions rather than ideas, the really strong people are those who mistake their sensations for opinions. Viewed in this light, Miss Fenno was certainly very strong: there was an unmistakable ring of finality in the tone with which she declared:

"It's impossible."

Mrs. Quentin's answer veiled the least shade of feminine resentment. "I told Alan that where he had failed there was no chance of my making an impression."

Hope Fenno laid on her visitor's an almost reverential hand. "Dear Mrs. Quentin, it's the impression you make that confirms the impossibility."

Mrs. Quentin waited a moment: she was perfectly aware that, where her feelings were concerned her sense of humour was not to be relied on. "Do I make such an odious impression?" she asked at length, with a smile that seemed to give the girl her choice of two meanings.

"You make such a beautiful one! It's too beautiful — it obscures my judgment."

Mrs. Quentin looked at her thoughtfully. "Would it be permissible, I wonder, for an older woman to suggest that, at your age, it isn't always a misfortune to have what one calls one's judgment temporarily obscured?"

Miss Fenno flushed. "I try not to judge others —"

"You judge Alan."

"Ah, *he* is not others," she murmured with an accent that touched the older woman.

"You judge his mother."

"I don't; I don't."

Mrs. Quentin pressed her point. "You judge yourself, then, as you would be in my position — and your verdict condemns me."

"How can you think it? It's because I appreciate the difference in our point of view that I find it so difficult to defend myself —"

"Against what?"

"The temptation to imagine that I might be as *you* are — feeling as I do."

Mrs. Quentin rose with a sigh. "My child, in my day love was less subtle." She added, after a moment: "Alan is a perfect son."

"Ah, that again — that makes it worse!"

"Worse?"

"Just as your goodness does, your sweetness, your immense indulgence in letting me discuss things with you in a way that must seem almost an impertinence."

Mrs. Quentin's smile was not without irony. "You must remember that I do it for Alan."

"That's what I love you for!" the girl instantly returned; and again her tone touched her listener.

"And yet you're sacrificing him — and to an idea!"

"Isn't it to ideas that all the sacrifices that were worth while have been made?"

"One may sacrifice one's self."

Miss Fenno's colour rose. "That's what I'm doing." she said gently.

Mrs. Quentin took her hand. "I believe you are," she answered. "And it isn't true that I speak only for Alan. Perhaps I did when I began; but now I want to plead for you too — against yourself." She paused, and then went on with a deeper note: "I have let you, as you say, speak your mind to me in terms that some women might have resented, because I wanted to show you how little, as the years go on, theories, ideas, abstract conceptions of life, weigh against the actual, against the particular way in which life presents itself to us — to women especially. To decide beforehand exactly how one ought to behave in given circumstances is like deciding that one will follow a certain direction in crossing an unexplored country. Afterward we find that we must turn out for the obstacles — cross the rivers where they're shallowest — take the tracks that others have beaten — make all sorts of unexpected concessions. Life is made up of compromises: that is what youth refuses to understand. I've lived long enough to doubt whether any real good ever came of sacrificing beautiful facts to even more beautiful theories. Do I seem casuistical? I don't know — there may be losses either way … but the love of the man one loves … of the child one loves … that makes up for everything …"

She had spoken with a thrill which seemed to communicate itself to the hand her listener had left in hers. Her eyes filled suddenly, but through their dimness she saw the girl's lips shape a last desperate denial: "Don't you see it's because I feel all this that I mustn't — that I can't?"

III

Mrs. Quentin, in the late spring afternoon, had turned in at the doors of the Metropolitan Museum. She had been walking in the Park, in a solitude oppressed by the ever-present sense of her son's trouble, and had suddenly remembered that some one had added a Beltraffio to the collection. It was an old habit of Mrs. Quentin's to seek in the enjoyment of the beautiful the distraction that most of her acquaintances appeared to find in each other's company. She had few friends, and their society was welcome to her only in her more superficial moods; but she could drug anxiety with a picture as some women can soothe it with a bonnet.

During the six months which had elapsed since her visit to Miss Fenno she had been conscious of a pain of which she had supposed herself no longer capable: as a man will continue to feel the ache of an amputated arm. She had fancied that all her centres of feeling had been transferred to Alan; but she now found herself subject to a kind of dual suffering, in which her individual pang was the keener in that it divided her from her son's. Alan had surprised her: she had not foreseen that he would take a sentimental rebuff so hard. His disappointment took the uncommunicative form of a sterner application to work. He threw himself into the concerns of the *Radiator* with an aggressiveness which almost betrayed itself in the paper. Mrs. Quentin never read the *Radiator*, but from the glimpses of it reflected in the other journals she gathered that it was at least not being subjected to the moral reconstruction which had been one of Miss Fenno's alternatives.

Mrs. Quentin never spoke to her son of what had happened. She was superior to the cheap satisfaction of avenging his injury by depreciating its cause. She knew that in sentimental sorrows such consolations are as salt in the wound. The avoidance of a subject so vividly present to both could not but affect the closeness of their relation. An invisible presence hampered their liberty of speech and thought. The girl was always between them; and to hide the sense of her intrusion they began to be less frequently together. It was then that Mrs. Quentin measured the extent of her isolation. Had she ever dared to forecast such a situation, she would have proceeded on the conventional theory that her son's suffering must draw her nearer to him; and this was precisely the relief that was denied her. Alan's uncommunicativeness extended below the level of speech, and his mother, reduced to the helplessness of dead-reckoning, had not even the solace of adapting her sympathy to his needs. She did not know what he felt: his course was incalculable to her. She sometimes wondered if she had become as incomprehensible to him; and it was to find a moment's refuge from the dogging misery of such conjectures that she had now turned in at the Museum.

The long line of mellow canvases seemed to receive her into the rich calm of an autumn twilight. She might have been walking in an enchanted wood where the footfall of care never sounded. So deep was the sense of seclusion that, as she turned from her prolonged communion with the new Beltraffio, it was a surprise to find that she was not alone.

A young lady who had risen from the central ottoman stood in suspended flight as Mrs. Quentin faced her. The older woman was the first to regain her self-possession.

"Miss Fenno!" she said.

The girl advanced with a blush. As it faded, Mrs. Quentin noticed a change in her. There had always been something bright and banner-like in her aspect, but now her look drooped, and she hung at half-mast, as it were. Mrs. Quentin, in the embarrassment of surprising a secret that its possessor was doubtless unconscious of betraying, reverted hurriedly to the Beltraffio.

"I came to see this," she said. "It's very beautiful."

Miss Fenno's eye travelled incuriously over the mystic blue reaches of the landscape. "I suppose so," she assented; adding, after another tentative pause: "You come here often, don't you?"

"Very often," Mrs. Quentin answered. "I find pictures a great help."

"A help?!

"A rest, I mean ... if one is tired or out of sorts."

"Ah," Miss Fenno murmured, looking down.

"This Beltraffio is new, you know," Mrs. Quentin continued. "What a wonderful background, isn't it? Is he a painter who interests you?"

The girl glanced again at the dusky canvas, as though in a final endeavour to extract from it a clue to the consolations of art. "I don't know," she said at length; "I'm afraid I don't understand pictures," She moved nearer to Mrs. Quentin and held out her hand.

"You're going?"

"Yes."

Mrs. Quentin looked at her. "Let me drive you home," she said impulsively. She was feeling, with a shock of surprise, that it gave her, after all, no pleasure to see how much the girl had suffered.

Miss Fenno stiffened perceptibly. "Thank you; I shall like the walk."

Mrs. Quentin dropped her hand with a corresponding movement of withdrawal, and a momentary wave of antagonism seemed to sweep the two women apart. Then, as Mrs. Quentin, bowing slightly, again addressed herself to the picture, she felt a sudden touch on her arm.

"Mrs. Quentin," the girl faltered, "I really came here because I saw your carriage." Her eyes sank, and then fluttered back to her hearer's face. "I've been horribly unhappy!" she exclaimed.

Mrs. Quentin was silent. If Hope Fenno had expected an immediate response to her appeal, she was disappointed. The older woman's face was like a veil dropped before her thoughts.

"I've thought so often," the girl went on precipitately, "of what you said that day you came to see me last autumn. I think I understand now what you meant — what you tried to make me see ... Oh, Mrs. Quentin," she broke out, "I didn't mean to tell you this — I never dreamed of it till this moment — but you *do* remember what you said, don't you? You must remember it! And now that I've met you in this way, I can't help telling you that I believe — I begin to believe — that you were quite right, after all."

Mrs. Quentin had listened without moving; but now she raised her eyes with a slight smile. "Do you wish me to say this to Alan?" she asked.

The girl flushed, but her glance braved the smile. "Would he still care to hear it?" she said fearlessly.

Mrs. Quentin took momentary refuge in a renewed inspection of the Beltraffio; then, turning, she said, with a kind of reluctance: "He would still care."

"Ah!" broke from the girl.

During this exchange of words the two speakers had drifted unconsciously toward one of the benches. Mrs. Quentin glanced about her: a custodian who had been hovering in the doorway sauntered into the adjoining gallery, and they remained alone among the silvery Vandykes and flushed bituminous Halses. Mrs. Quentin sank down on the bench and reached a hand to the girl.

"Sit by me," she said.

Miss Fenno dropped beside her. In both women the stress of emotions was too strong for speech. The girl was still trembling, and Mrs. Quentin was the first to regain her composure.

"You say you've suffered," she began at last. "Do you suppose *I* haven't?"

"I knew you had. That made it so much worse for me — that I should have been the cause of your suffering for Alan!"

Mrs. Quentin drew a deep breath. "Not for Alan only," she said. Miss Fenno turned on her a wondering glance. "Not for Alan only. *That* pain every woman expects — and knows how to bear. We all know our children must have such disappointments, and to suffer with them is not the deepest pain. It's the suffering apart — in ways they don't understand." She breathed deeply. "I want you to know what I mean. You were right — that day — and I was wrong."

"Oh," the girl faltered.

Mrs. Quentin went on in a voice of passionate lucidity. "I knew it then — I knew it even while I was trying to argue with you — I've always known it! I didn't want my son to marry you till I heard your reasons for refusing him; and then — then I longed to see you his wife!"

"Oh, Mrs. Quentin!"

"I longed for it; but I knew it mustn't be."

"Mustn't be?"

Mrs. Quentin shook her head sadly, and the girl, gaining courage from this mute negation, cried with an uncontrollable escape of feeling:

"It's because you thought me hard, obstinate, narrow-minded? Oh, I understand that so well! My self-righteousness must have seemed so petty! A girl who could sacrifice a man's future to her own moral vanity — for it *was* a form of vanity; you showed me that plainly enough — how you must have despised me! But I am not that girl now — indeed I'm not. I'm not impulsive — I think things out. I've thought this out. I know Alan loves me — I know *how* he loves me — and I believe I can help him — oh, not in the ways I had fancied before — but just merely by loving him." She paused, but Mrs. Quentin made no sign. "I see it all so differently now. I see what an influence love itself may be — how my believing in him, loving him, accepting him just as he is, might help him more than any theories, any arguments. I might have seen this long ago in looking at *you* — as he often told me — in seeing how you'd kept yourself apart from — from — Mr. Quentin's work and his — been always the beautiful side of life to them — kept their faith alive in spite of themselves — not by interfering, preaching, reforming, but by — just loving them and being there —" She looked at Mrs. Quentin with a simple nobleness. "It isn't as if I cared for the money, you know; if I cared for that, I should be afraid—"

"You will care for it in time." Mrs. Quentin said suddenly.

Miss Fenno drew back, releasing her hand. "In time?"

"Yes; when there's nothing else left." She stared a moment at the pictures. "My poor child," she broke out, "I've heard all you say so often before!"

"You've heard it?"

"Yes — from myself. I felt as you do. I argued as you do, I acted as I mean to prevent your doing, when I married Alan's father."

The long empty gallery seemed to reverberate with the girl's startled exclamation — "Oh, Mrs. Quentin—"

"Hush; let me speak. Do you suppose I'd do this if you were the kind of pink-and-white idiot he ought to have married? It's because I see you're alive, as I was, tingling with beliefs, ambitions, energies, as I was — that I can't see you walled up alive, as I was, without stretching out a hand to save you!" She sat gazing rigidly forward, her eyes on the pictures, speaking in the low precipitate tone of one who tries to press the meaning of a lifetime into a few breathless sentences.

"When I met Alan's father," she went on, "I knew nothing of his — his work. We met abroad, where I had been living with my mother. That was twenty-six years ago, when the *Radiator* was less — less notorious than it is now. I knew my husband owned a newspaper — a great newspaper — and nothing more. I had never seen a copy of the *Radiator*; I had no notion what it stood for, in politics — or in other ways. We were married in Europe, and a few months afterward we came to live here. People were already beginning to talk about the *Radiator*. My husband, on leaving college, had bought it with some money an old uncle had left him, and the public at first was merely curious to see what an ambitious, stirring young man without any experience of journalism was going to make out of his experiment. They found first of all that he was going to make a great deal of money out of it. I found that out too. I was so happy in other ways that it didn't make much difference at first; though it was pleasant to be able to help my mother, to be generous and charitable, to live in a nice house, and wear the handsome gowns he liked to see me in. But still it didn't really count — it counted so little that when, one day, I learned what the *Radiator* was, I would have gone out into the streets barefooted rather than live another hour on the money it brought in ..." Her voice sank, and she paused to steady it. The girl at her side did not speak or move. "I shall never forget that day," she began again. "The paper had stripped bare some family scandal — some miserable bleeding secret that a dozen unhappy people had been struggling to keep out of print — that *would* have been kept out if my husband had not — Oh, you must guess the rest! I can't go on!"

She felt a hand on hers. "You mustn't go on," the girl whispered.

"Yes, I must — I must! You must be made to understand." She drew a deep breath. "My husband was not like Alan. When he found out how I felt about it he was surprised at first — but gradually he began to see — or at least he fancied he saw — the hatefulness of it. At any rate he saw how I suffered, and he offered to give up the whole thing — to sell the paper. It couldn't be done all of a sudden, of course — he made me see that — for he had put all his money in it, and he had no special aptitude for any other kind of work. He was a born journalist — like Alan. It was a great sacrifice for him to give up the paper, but he promised to do it — in time — when a good opportunity offered. Meanwhile, of course, he wanted to build it up, to increase the circulation — and to do that he had to keep on in the same way — he made that clear to me. I saw that we were in a vicious circle. The paper, to sell well, had to be made more and more detestable and disgraceful. At first I rebelled — but somehow — I can't tell you how it was — after that first concession the ground seemed to give under me: with every struggle I sank deeper. And then — then Alan was born. He was such a delicate baby that there was very little hope of saving him. But money did it — the money from the paper. I took him abroad to see the best physicians — I took him to a warm climate every winter. In hot weather, the doctors recommended sea air, and we had a yacht and cruised every summer. I owed his life to the *Radiator*. And when he began to grow stronger the habit was formed — the habit of luxury. He could not get on without the things he had always been used to. He pined in bad air; he drooped under monotony and discomfort; he throve on variety, amusement, travel, every kind of novelty and excitement. And all I wanted for him his inexhaustible foster-mother was there to give!

"My husband said nothing, but he must have seen how things were going. There was no more talk of giving up the *Radiator*. He never reproached me with my inconsistency, but I thought he must despise me, and the thought made me reckless. I determined to ignore the paper altogether — to take what it gave as though I didn't know where it came from. And to excuse this I invented the theory that one may, so to speak, purify money by putting it to good uses. I gave away a great deal in charity — I indulged myself very little at first. All the money that was not spent on Alan I tried to do good with. But gradually, as my boy grew up, the problem became more complicated. How was I to protect Alan from the contamination I had let him live in? I couldn't preach by example — couldn't hold up his father as a warning, or denounce the money we were living on. All I could do was to disguise the inner ugliness of life by making it beautiful outside — to build a wall of beauty between him and the facts of life, turn his tastes and interests another way, hide the *Radiator* from him as a smiling woman at a ball may hide a cancer in her breast! Just as Alan was entering college his father died. Then I saw my way clear. I had loved my husband — and yet I drew my first free breath in years. For the *Radiator* had been left to Alan outright — there was nothing on earth to prevent his selling it when he came of age. And there was no excuse for his not selling it. I had brought him up to depend on money, but the paper had given us enough money to gratify all his tastes. At last we could turn on the monster that had nourished us. I felt a savage joy in the thought — I could hardly bear to wait till Alan came of age. But I had never spoken to him of the paper, and I didn't dare speak of it now. Some false shame kept me back, some vague belief in his ignorance. I would wait till he was twenty-one, and then we should be free.

"I waited — the day came, and I spoke. You can guess his answer, I suppose. He had no idea of selling the *Radiator*. It wasn't the money he cared for — it was the career that tempted him. He was a born journalist, and his ambition, ever since he could remember, had been to carry on his father's work, to develop, to surpass it. There was nothing in the world as interesting as modern journalism. He couldn't imagine any other kind of life that wouldn't bore him to death. A newspaper like the *Radiator* might be made one of the biggest powers on earth, and he loved power, and meant to have all he could get. I listened to him in a kind of trance. I couldn't find a word to say. His father had had scruples — he had none. I seemed to realize at once that argument would be useless. I don't know that I even tried to plead with him — he was so bright and hard and inaccessible! Then I saw that he was, after all, what I had made him — the creature of my concessions, my connivances, my evasions. That was the price I had paid for him — I had kept him at that cost!

"Well — I *had* kept him, at any rate. That was the feeling that survived. He was my boy, my son, my very own — till some other woman took him. Meanwhile the old life must go on as it could. I gave up the struggle. If at that point he was inaccessible, at others he was close to me. He has always been a perfect son. Our tastes grew together — we enjoyed the same books, the same pictures, the same people. All I had to do was to look at him in profile to see the side of him that was really mine. At first I kept thinking of the dreadful other side — but gradually the impression faded, and I kept my mind turned from it, as one does from a deformity in a face one loves. I thought I had made my last compromise with life — had hit on a *modus vivendi* that would last my time.

"And then he met you. I had always been prepared for his marrying, but not a girl like you. I thought he would choose a sweet thing that would never pry into his closets — he hated women with ideas! But as soon as I saw you I knew the struggle would have to begin again. He is so much stronger than his father — he is full of the most monstrous convictions. And he has the courage of them, too — you saw last year that his love for you never made him waver. He believes in his work; he adores it — it is a kind of hideous idol to which he would make human sacrifices! He loves you still — I've been honest with you — but his love wouldn't change him. It is you who would have to change — to die gradually, as I have died, till there is only one live point left in me. Ah, if one died completely — that's simple enough! But something persists — remember that — a single point, an aching nerve of truth. Now and then you may drug it — but a touch wakes it again, as your face has waked it in me. There's always enough of one's old self left to suffer with ..."

She stood up and faced the girl abruptly. "What shall I tell Alan?" she said.

Miss Fenno sat motionless, her eyes on the ground. Twilight was falling on the gallery — a twilight which seemed to emanate not so much from the glass dome overhead as from the crepuscular depths into which the faces of the pictures were receding. The custodian's step sounded warningly down the corridor. When the girl looked up she was alone.

The Man in the Scented Coat
by Sarah Grand

Josepha, well known for her talents, much loved for her charming personality, a little alarming to her friends on account of her occasional eccentricities, but always interesting, was having tea late one winter's afternoon with a lady who lived in one of those great sarcophagus houses in Portland Place, a gloomy region, suggestive of merry microbes seeking whom they may devour. Several times Josepha had risen to go, but her friend was loath to lose her, and darkness had descended upon them, the lamps had been lighted and the curtains drawn long before they finally shook hands.

"How do you mean to get back?" her friend asked.

"By train," Josepha rejoined; "the quickest and warmest way. It is only a step to the station."

They parted at the head of the stairs, her hostess returned to the drawing-room, and Josepha ran down into the hall.

"There is a dense fog, madam," the footman said, standing with his hand on the latch of the door, but hesitating to open it. "Shall I call a cab?"

"Let me see the fog? " she answered.

He opened the door, and the light in the hall fell upon what looked like a thundercloud filling up the aperture. She could see nothing through it, not the twinkle of the nearest lamps, nor could she hear a sound. For a moment the mist seemed solid as a wall, but the heat of the house meeting it melted its density, frayed it at the edges, and released it, so that it came streaming into the hall, fast filling it with vapour, which rapidly spread itself over everything, gauzily, like a veil, bedimming the brilliant lamps, shrouding the luxurious furnishings, and adding to all that touch of mystery which dignifies commonplace ordinary elegance with interest.

"I never saw anything like it!" she exclaimed, stepping out into the portico.

"You'll surely not attempt to walk madam," the man remonstrated. "You'll lose yourself the first few yards."

"Oh, impossible!" she said. "I know the way so well. And I never was out in anything like this before!"

With the words on her lips, she ran down the steps, and it was as if she had plunged into space, she was so instantly engulfed. In reality she was only a few yards from the door, clinging to an area railing, gasping and giddy, trying to collect herself. The first few breaths of the sulphur-laden fog were like pure smoke; she thought for a moment she should suffocate. She was inclined to return to the house, but hesitated, and walked on a little way, guiding herself by the railing. Then she decided that she would go back, and turned about to do so. It was a fatal move, for she had no sooner let go of the railing than she lost it; and at the same time, she discovered that it was impossible to see any houses at all, let alone find a particular one. Whether she had gone round twice in her bewilderment, or come to a turn in the street, she could not tell; but the railing ought to have been on her left, and, with outstretched hand, she moved cautiously sideways, expecting to come in contact with it. The next thing she did, however, was to stumble off the curb into the roadway. The house she had left in Portland Place was close to a turn, and she now supposed that she had somehow rounded the comer, and was going down another street. If so, it would lead her into Portland Road, and, once there, she thought she should easily find the station, or someone to direct her. So far she had not encountered a soul or heard a sound of traffic, and this silence in a neighbourhood usually teeming with life and movement, had a strange effect upon her — an effect, not exactly exhilarating, but certainly exciting. She found herself being rapidly wound up into the mood for adventures. Her quick imagination began to present possibilities to her. She might easily have to wander on all night, Heaven knew whither; and she might encounter people, desirable or undesirable, but interesting, at all events. She might be run over too — and just as she realized the danger a great thing like a mountain moving loomed up over her, coming down upon her, but at a foot pace, fortunately. It was probably an omnibus which had strayed on to the pavement.

"You'd better pull up, John," a voice shouted hoarsely. "We're all out on it."

Josepha was about to address the voice when another vehicle came into her consciousness. This is the only way to express it, for she could neither hear nor see it properly; she just perceived it. Two bright lamps from it made two illuminated circles in the yellow mist, which did not, however, render anything the more distinct.

"Sheer off," said someone up in the air. "Sheer off if there's any pusson or thing there, fur I'm dashed if I can either 'old my 'orse still or drive 'im on."

"Where are we? " Josepha shrieked up to him.

"Blowed if I know, my dear," he answered. "If it isn't Peckham it's Piccadilly, or may be Portland Place."

"That's a p — posterous statement," said the driver of the other vehicle.

"'Old on, mate," said the first speaker.

"You'll knock me off my box if you do that again!"

Then they both laughed loudly, the horses began to prance on the pavement, making a hideous clattering with their iron hoofs, and Josepha, moving with outstretched hands, got hastily out of the way.

The next thing she realized was greater darkness, if possible, and a current of fresh air. She must have come into a more open space. The fog had affected the gas, and the lamps were either out all together or reduced to ineffectual sparks. Josepha had stumbled up against a lamp-post and now stood holding on to it. All about her was absolute silence. Nothing moved that she could perceive. It was as if she herself were the centre of a universe of frightful fog.

As she stood there, not knowing what to do next, she suddenly found herself thinking of growing flowers — flowers in a warm garden, with the summer sun on them. It was the perfume of flowers which made her think of them, a heavy perfume, of which she was distinctly conscious for some time before it struck her as strange that there should be an actual perfume in such an atmosphere. She looked round to discover from whence it came — looked, that is to say, if it could be called looking when there was nothing to be seen but a sort of shine through a thick cloud. The perfume had been quite strong when she first noticed it, but now she found that it was growing gradually fainter, and, without any formed intention, she began to walk on, following the direction from which it seemed to come, and guiding herself by the sense of smell instead of the sense of sight. She went on pretty rapidly, moving her arms in front of her, as if she were swimming, to save herself from coming into collision with things; and as she advanced, the perfume became more distinct, so that she knew that she was on the right track. Who was the perfumed person? she wondered, and what should she do when she came up with her — or him? Ask the way, she supposed; and even as she determined to do so, she found in front of her what seemed to be two shadows of unequal height moving in the mist — shadows of men, she concluded, but more by their voices than from what she could see of them as she overtook them. Whether they were the voices of gentlemen or not she had no time to decide, for just as she came abreast of them, a band of roughs, carrying links, rushed out upon them from somewhere, howling a discordant chorus. By the light of the links Josepha now saw, with relief, that they were well-dressed men, and presumably gentlemen, whom she had overtaken, and she would have claimed their protection could she have made herself heard; but this was impossible because of the din kept up by the roughs, who had surrounded all three, and were dancing about them, howling and jeering like fiends. The gentlemen seemed singularly alarmed for their own safety, and tried to break through the circle, now on this side and now on that, to the great delight of the louts, who separated as if to let them pass, but when they made for the gap, closed up again with shouts of derision.

Josepha, afraid that if they made their escape she would be left alone in the hands of the enemy, kept close behind them.

One of the gentlemen was tall and thin, the other short and stout. The latter had a white silk muffler wound round his throat, so as to conceal the lower part of his face; and it was from his coat that the strong perfume proceeded.

"My, ain't 'e a rosebud!" yelled one of the roughs. "You could smell 'im a mile off."

"I knaow 'im! I knaow 'oo the little fat 'un is," another shouted excitedly. "I see 'im in the percession, bowin' like this, wi' 'is 'at off."

"It is!" "It is!" "It's 'im!"

"'E's mufflin' up 'is 'ole face."

"'E's got a beard under 'is muffler."

"Let's give 'im three cheers."

"Let's duck 'im. We don't want to support no more blamed expensive royal aristocrats, we don't."

"'Ere's a princess, too!"

"'Ow much fur a kiss, yer 'ighness?"

The roughs pressed closer and closer. Both gentlemen were too anxious to make their own escape to think of Josepha; but the latter was watching her opportunity. It came of the recklessness of their tormentors, who hurried them on, heedless of where they might be going, till finally they ran into a heavy dray, drawn by two huge horses, which had been pulled up close to the curb, and compelled to stop there, fog-bound, waiting for the air to clear. When the lights of the links flared in their eyes, the horses became unmanageable, swerved, plunged, and finally bolted right through the roughs, scattering them. Josepha saw the man in the scented coat wrest a link from one of the lads, and hand it to his companion. Then both set off as hard as they could go, and Josepha followed them. The link was not enough to light them, but they must have known where they were pretty well, for they pursued their way without hesitation, and at such a rate that Josepha could not catch up with them. She called to them, but if they heard, they only hurried on the faster. There was not a soul to be seen but themselves, and not a cab or a carriage. The air was less stagnant now, happily. A breeze had arisen, and was swirling the fog about, and Josepha could both breathe and see better.

The gentlemen turned into what appeared to be a long, wide street, with shops on both sides of it, all of which were shut. Half way up, they dashed at a narrow black door, which seemed to be pinched for room between the shutters of two great shop windows. The man in the scented coat hurriedly thumped on the door in a peculiar manner. It was instantly opened, and he and his companion passed in. Josepha arrived in time to prevent the door being shut again, and entered also, without ceremony. The door must have been worked from above, for there was no one near it. It shut of itself when Josepha let it go. A dim lamp burning on a bracket showed that it opened directly on to a narrow, steep staircase between two walls. The gentlemen had disappeared by this time, and Josepha ran up after them intrepidly. At the top she found herself in a very ordinary sort of parlour, the furniture of which belonged to the green rep period. A round table, with a lamp upon it, stood in the middle of the room, and there were some cheap engravings on the walls. The fireplace was at the end on her left as she entered, and in the recess on the left-hand side of it there stood a tall mahogany bookcase full of books. The tall gentleman had extinguished the link, and now stood fumbling with the bookcase, which presently revolved as if on a pivot, disclosing an inner room beyond. The gentlemen were passing through the aperture when Josepha called, "Stop! Wait for me!" The man in the scented coat turned round in consternation. His face was still half hidden by the muffler, and he spoke through it, with a slight intonation as of a foreigner whose English is excellent, or an Englishman very much accustomed to speak foreign languages.

"May I ask whom I have the honour to address, madam?" he said stiffly.

"Alice in Wonderland," Josepha rejoined. "Oh I am out of breath! Why didn't you stop when I called to you?"

Both gentlemen stood looking at her much embarrassed. At last the tall one said to the other, "A spy, I suppose, sir. This is extremely unfortunate."

Josepha walked up to him and took off her hat and veil. She was one of the best known women of the day, her portraits were everywhere, and the man in the scented coat recognised her face the moment he saw it.

"Surely I have the honour to address —," he said, with a bow.

"That is my name," Josepha answered, curtsying to the pair.

Then there was an awkward pause. The bookcase had revolved end on to her, leaving an aperture on either side, in which the gentlemen remained standing, the tall one on the right, the short one on the left, looking, from Josepha's point of view, like the little figures that live in pasteboard castles on cottage mantelpieces, and pop in and out to tell the weather. To her own astonishment, she burst out laughing.

"May I ask, madam," said the man in the scented coat, very stiffly, "if there is anything we can do to oblige you."

"Thank you, yes," Josepha answered, still unable to control her countenance. It was one of her weaknesses that she dearly loved a joke, and never could resist the temptation to indulge in one whatever it might cost her. "I shall be greatly obliged if you will kindly give me food, rest, and shelter till the fog is over, and then see me safe home."

"*Madam!* —" the tall man began.

"No, really," Josepha interrupted him, raising her hand and speaking in a tone of remonstrance; "I could not think of imposing on your good nature to any greater extent. I lost myself in the fog, and don't in the least know where I am; but I place myself under your protection with confidence, and rely altogether upon your discretion."

The man in the scented coat bowed profoundly, then stepped out of his aperture as if to make way for her to pass. "I thank you, madam, for your confidence," he said, "and I promise you that it shall not be misplaced. And to prove that *I* also rely upon *your* discretion, I venture to ask you to come this way —"

"*Sir!*" the tall man remonstrated, popping out of his aperture.

The other waved him back impatiently, and Josepha passed into the inner room; the gentlemen followed her. Then the bookcase, answering to a touch, noiselessly revolved upon its pivot, closing the apertures. They were now in a good-sized apartment furnished in heavy, costly, hotel fashion, with saddlebag chairs, gilt consoles, and engravings; but no mirrors. In the centre of the room was a table covered with green baize, and on one of the consoles were piles of packs of cards. A large lamp stood in the middle of the table, so shaded that the light fell only on the cloth, the faces of those who might sit round being left in comparative obscurity. Josepha drew her own conclusions from these arrangements, but her countenance remained immovable. She threw herself into an easy chair, pillowed her head on the back of it, and looked up at the ceiling.

"Oh, I am so glad to sit down!" she exclaimed.

The perfectly unaffected simple, cheerful human nature of her began to delight the man in the scented coat. He took off his muffler, drew up a chair, and sat down to talk to her. Finding him so good-natured, she felt some compunction for imposing her presence upon him. "I do hope my intrusion is not causing you any serious inconvenience," she said.

"Not at all," he answered. "I have merely changed a pleasant arrangement for a still pleasanter one. My — eh — that gentleman —"

"Shall we call him Colonel Perturbation for convenience sake?" Josepha suggested.

" By all means; and do me the favour to call me —"

"The Man in the Scented Coat," Josepha ventured, seeing him hesitate.

"Capital!" he said. "Colonel Perturbation will put off the guests I expected in order to leave me full liberty to do my best to entertain the — eh — charming guest I did not expect."

Colonel Perturbation had been busying himself about the room, and now Josepha saw to her surprise that there was another person present, a sort of waiter-man, of furtive appearance, with a chronic curve in his back as if he were saving himself the trouble of bowing incessantly by holding himself always in the attitude of a bow. He was laying a table, and Josepha observed that everything was being sent up from below on a lift, the shaft of which was on the wall outside, the dishes being taken in through a window, which was obscured by thick opaque glass, and, when shut, fitted closely. This arrangement prevented any sound being conducted by the shaft. It was also evident that the lift was strong enough to be used on occasion for heavier weights than dishes. Colonel Perturbation busied himself in superintending the arrangements. He had a fair skin tanned to a sandy colour, his hair and moustache being of much the same shade, which gave him that curiously dried-up look fair men sometimes have in middle life. He wore rings up to the first joint of the third finger of either hand, with a variety of stones in them, the different colours of which produced a tawdry effect. The deference which he paid to his stout companion was somewhat intermittent, like that of an inferior who forgets himself every now and then, and presumes. While they waited, the Man in the Scented Coat kept up an animated conversation with Josepha; but, in spite of the utmost effort to be polite, he could not keep his eyes from wandering to the packs of cards piled upon the console. They were within reach, and at last, as if the temptation were too strong for him, he possessed himself of one of them, stripped off the outside wrapper, and began to stay his hunger to be handling them, by slowly shuffling them, until Josepha, not able to stand it any longer, took pity on him.

"Shall we have a game?" she said.

The change that came over him, the lightening and brightening of his whole being, was extraordinary; but it was pitiable also, and pathetic.

They sat down at the card-table, and began a childish game of betting on the card that should turn up. The luck fluctuated at first from one to the other, but finally set in steadily in favour of the Man in the Scented Coat, and by the time supper was ready he had won all Josepha's money, and every ornament she had on. The effect of his success was interesting. Beaming about him during the meal, he described, with much animation to Colonel Perturbation, the unexpected runs which had come upon various suits, the curious way in which certain cards had turned up again in pack after pack, proving how impossible it would be to use the same pack twice satisfactorily, as Josepha, to his horror, had suggested that they should. His recollection of the details was extraordinary. Only once was he at fault, and then he called for a fresh pack, and recovered the clue when he had cleared a space, and spread out the cards on the table before him. Josepha watched him as he sat there (they were still at the supper table) in a high-backed armchair, which he filled to overflowing, holding his bearded chin in his left hand, a part of the pack in his right, and gazing, with absorbed concentration in his large, full eyes, at the cards he had laid out before him on the white cloth; and she could not help thinking of the part such a man might play in life if only he devoted himself with the same conscientious intelligence to nobler pursuits.

Colonel Perturbation having offered Josepha a cigarette, which she accepted, they continued to sit there, smoking and chatting. One subject of interest led on to another, and the time went well enough to be forgotten; and the fog had cleared; and still they sat and talked, and might have continued to sit and talk much longer, too, but for another interruption.

Without warning, the window of the lift flew open, and the waiter-man appeared in a state of breathless agitation.

"Gentlemen —" he gasped.

The gentlemen jumped to their feet.

"Must we take to the lift?" the Man in the Scented Coat demanded.

The waiter-man signified that they must. Colonel Perturbation made for the lift incontinently, but the Man in the Scented Coat waited to secure his silk muffler, and to gather up his winnings from the card-table and pocket them.

Only one at a time could descend. The Man in the Scented Coat suggested politely that Josepha should go first; but Josepha objected. She did not know what might await her at the bottom — well-water, or a rope or dagger being among the possibilities which she rapidly foresaw.

"You'd better go first yourself, sir," Colonel Perturbation urged in an agitated manner. The Man in the Scented Coat stepped on to the lift, and descended into darkness. There was what seemed to be a long interval before the machine reappeared. When it stopped, Colonel Perturbation almost pushed Josepha on to it. The waiter-man showed her how to work the apparatus, and warned her that it was a goodish way down, but someone would "holler" when it was time to stop. She went on and on so long, however, and at such a rapid rate, that she thought she must be in the bottomless pit by the time she heard the shout. There was no light in the lift, and none where she stopped; but the Man in the Scented Coat announced that he was there, awaiting her.

"Hold out your hand to me," he said, "and don't be alarmed. I will see you safely home."

She gave him her left hand, and he hurried her on and on in the dark, all she knew of it being that they were walking on some soft substance, probably clay. She did not see Colonel Perturbation or the waiter-man again, nor did she ask any questions. When at last they stopped, her companion opened a door. It led into a quiet street, and when shut looked like an innocent garden gate in a high brick wall, over which branches of trees showed reassuringly. A close carriage was drawn up to the curb; the door was held open by a servant in black, and Josepha entered at the request of her companion, who followed her, having first asked where she wished to be put down, and repeated to the coachman the address she gave.

"You are a cool-headed lady," he remarked, as they drove off rapidly.

"Yes, I *am* cool headed," she answered. "I am fond of life, and devote myself to the study of it in all its phases; and this leads to occasional adventures; but I am prepared for anything. I have a little companion here which I always carry in case of accidents." As she spoke, she touched his hand for a moment with something hard and cold. "I know that that is a melodramatic touch," she said. "But the boundary between melodrama and true tragedy is ill-defined; the one passes on to the other often, unexpectedly."

Her companion sat still for some time, reflecting.

"What shall you say about this adventure?" he asked at last in an easy manner, which, however, did not conceal a very real anxiety from

Josepha's quick intuition. It was still pitch dark outside, but they could see each other distinctly enough by the light of the carriage lamps.

"How do you mean?" she asked blandly.

"Well," he began, with embarrassment, "will you think it necessary to tell — eh — shall you think our conversation sufficiently interesting to repeat?"

She gave him that smiling look-direct which makes the meaning of an answer somewhat uncertain. "In matters of this kind, I hope I shall always answer to expectation," she said. This diplomatic reply was as unsatisfactory as she could make it, to punish him for the doubt implied in his question.

He smiled, however, and bowed; then, after a little pause, which she felt to be tentative, he said, "I trust you utterly."

"Just in so far as you trust me you will find me loyal," she assured him.

"I hope you will remember this evening not unpleasantly," he said.

"It will be associated in my mind with many interesting impressions," she replied.

"May I venture to hope that we shall meet again?" he asked.

She answered slowly, "In that your wishes must be consulted."

Months passed, and not a single soul had received a hint of that night's adventure — not even a hint that there had been an adventure. Then one day Colonel Perturbation appeared before Josepha carrying a costly present.

"I have been sent," he said, "to offer this as a tribute of respect to a woman who can hold her tongue."

"Take back your tribute," Josepha answered with royal scorn. "It would not have been accepted at any time. But this offer of it to me now means that I have been on my trial all these months. I should have been trusted, not tried. That is my message to your master."

A Cowl in Cracow
by Ménie Muriel Dowie

It was while I was in Cracow, spending my days happily and quietly in wanderings whose vagueness I jealously guarded from the narrowing influences of the guide-book. My excursions had been governed by a principle which holds a vast amount of satisfaction — for me: each morning I had sallied forth and walked to the root of some impressive spire which had seemed to call me, and I could never tell the world of old houses and rich pink brick-work that I delighted in as I went.

One spire only puzzled me. Twice I had started for it, each time I had arrived, hot and interested, quite elsewhere. Needless to say, it gathered an imaginary importance, and I marked it down finally with a sporting eye, and started to walk it up scientifically, keeping it well to windward, and making use of all available cover. I skirted the somewhat French quarter of the town, and passed through the Jewish colony, and thence away by a road that seemed aiming for the open country, when at length I recognised my spire caught in a thicket of big trees from which grew the long sides of a raspberry-coloured building of many windows and a pervading silence. Silences slept in its courtyard and beneath the empty arches of its doorways, silence browsed with the brown cow in the centre of its grass-plot. In all the rooms and ways of it, nothing was stirring. And yet it did not seem dead; on the contrary, windows were open, and curtains not a fortnight starched fluttered at its sills. My intrusion — for I intruded quite promptly — excited no attention; unless perhaps the cow noticed me. I surveyed the two storeys on three sides of me, and the tower in the trees, and I could come to no conclusion; if it were a nunnery (which might account for the tower) why had it not the traditional high-wall all round it? Why was it open to the little by-way and gate, through which I had approached? Where was the surly porter who, through a grating, should have kept the world at bay?

Now, I do not need any one to tell me that my next act was inexcusable. I know this, but perhaps it was justified. However, you are to hear, and can judge. I walked in at one of those doorways, choosing, for preference, one through which a sunbeam was preceding me, and I set a resolute but reasoning foot upon the stairway. It was thus I reasoned: the worst that could happen to me would be to be turned out, which would not be injurious; and the best that could happen to me would be to discover my whereabouts, and perhaps have an amusing conversation with an inmate. At the best, I could apologise with such wit and grace as the moment vouchsafed me; at the worst, I could but appear a stupid and intrusive foreigner.

It was in this philosophic spirit that I ascended two flights of stairs and turned with a degree of deprecation along a flagged corridor; but it was not exactly in this spirit that I found myself opposite an open door, and regarding a young man shaving himself before a glass; a young man attired in a more surprising costume than I have ever happened to imagine. He did not see me, it was his profile that I was regarding, and my eye travelled from the cheek he was elaborately scraping, to the curious cream-woollen and cotton dress which clothed him. Then it struck me that he was some kind of a priest or monk. I was in a monastery! It will not hurt me to admit that a thrill, strange to me since, years before, I depleted a store-cupboard of some preserved American limes, flickered and prickled in the nape of my neck and down my spine. It was then that the young man put down his razor, and in turning sideways caught sight of my quite motionless figure. I expect monks are a pretty transcendental kind of people, and perhaps a little exalted in their minds; at any rate, that one treated me with the respectful stare one would lavish on a being from another world. Certainly he did not think I was real; and I do not blame him. To me, he appeared a creature in a front scene, I one of the audience, of whom nothing but attention was expected. He began speaking in a tremulous rapid undertone, in Polish, and I, feeling the situation so absurd and so unreal, laughed and begged him, in French, to forgive my invasion. I felt, in a silly sort of way, that my simple person stood for the outside world, and vanity, and folly, and perhaps wickedness — and it amused me, and made me wish I knew how to giggle, and could have giggled then. But he wiped the soap from his face with a long strip of the hardest huck-a-back towelling I have ever seen, which hung by a tag from the wall, and looked at me, still with a rather dazed face, but conciliatory.

"Madame, are you an apparition?" he said gently, and with a smile glimmering through his surprise.

I nodded pleasantly.

"And how is it that ... do you want anything of me?" He had altered his phrase, and this second one had in it a note of eagerness that did not chime in with my ideas of the conventual manner.

"Thank you, I do not know that I want anything now," I replied. "I did want to know what this place was, and I came up.—" Here the feebleness of my case overcame me, and I did not proceed with my explanations. The young man, however, did not seem to notice any flaws in my remarks; he was rather thinking within himself as he reached a white serge garment from a narrow bed, and slipped into it mechanically. "I am a stranger; I think I just wanted to be — interested," I supplemented.

"You are the only stranger that has set foot within this building," he said gravely, "since I came here, a stranger, fifteen months ago."

"But there is nothing to prevent anybody coming in, that I can see," said I, in defence of my presence. "It's all quite open."

"We are known, the views of our order and its laws, in Cracow; no one belonging to this place would pass that first gateway."

"Wouldn't they indeed?" said I, much interested.

"And why did you come here?" The minute I had said it, I felt this remark to be inquisitive, but I must have appeared so inquisitive altogether that a little more or less could not matter. And the young Brother in no way resented the inquiry.

"I came here by — a trick!" he replied, with some fierceness. And I leaned back upon the stonework and blinked at him. The oddness of my position struck me far more forcibly than before, and though he was speaking, even asking me questions, it all went by me as though I watched it in a dream, until at last I woke, and he seemed to be telling me about himself.

"I was intended for the Austrian Diplomatic Service," he was saying, "and was passing through a course at the University in Paris. I had never had great sympathy with my family, and I disliked the Austrian ideas and influence. I am a Pole, and I love my *own* country. In Paris I met others of the same mind . I became one of them. ... We had our dreams, and we hoped. I see now that I abused my father's confidence, but my punishment has been bitter. For ten months I laboured secretly, put aside my title, and travelled to Switzerland, to London, lectured and spoke for our cause, and told my family no word of what I was doing. It does not matter, it would not matter if I told you the whole of it now, for I am as dead to the world as if I were in a silver tomb in the vaults of Wawel; but it broke up my life. A lady at whose house I visited in Paris learned something of my pursuits, and wrote to my family. I do not say that she meant ill. I was recalled to Vienna to join my father, who has a high position there, and is much favoured by the Emperor. He spoke to me of the ruin of our house, of my mother and sisters; in spite of his name, he is a modern, he swims — with the tide. I was at once offered a post at a court, and compelled to mix with men of my father's opinions. And I could not bear it. I promised my father to follow any profession, to enter on any way of life that did not entail my bending my pride so low, my living in a nest of lies, eating them, breathing them, lying down at night with them. "Any life?" said my father.

"*Any* life," I answered. "A Czernowietzki never breaks his word," said he. "Nor binds himself to false oaths," said I. That was the end. I left my father at his Government office, and on my return to the hotel of my brother a note awaited me. It announced that this" — the young man waved his arm in the direction of his narrow bed and single prie-dieu— "was my father's choice for me. For fifteen months I have seen no one belonging to the world — the world I love. No one till you came, Mademoiselle! Your chance visit — I think you have dropped from the skies — excites all my old longing for the life I have left."

"Why not leave this life and go back to Paris? Cut yourself off from your family — you are cut off from them now — and make your own life what you please."

The Brother smiled and shook his head, looking dreamily into the elm-branches that smothered the root of my spire.

"Do you know Paris?" he said wistfully.

"Well. I have just left there."

"And you return ...?" he said, with sudden eagerness.

"Oh, in about three months, perhaps."

"Mademoiselle, you have it in your power to do me the greatest possible service ... you comprehend ... *the greatest possible service*. Will you do it? It will not trouble you much, you who have fallen from the clouds to give me comfort! Will you do it?"

He was extraordinarily excited; his face, which was pale, flushed a very dark colour, and he panted as he spoke. I stood away from the cold stone balustrade on which I had been leaning during this remarkable interview, and put a foot over the threshold of his cell.

"But certainly I will do it, I will do anything in my power that will really serve you," I said. "Only tell me ..." A bell — such a nasty, tinny, ascetic, inhuman sort of bell — rang out from the spire. The young man looked nervously towards his window, but began speaking rapidly to me, as though time were precious.

"I left Paris hastily, as you have heard; there was not time to see or explain to all my friends; one of them, ... Mademoiselle, I am trusting you, and speaking with my soul, and yet even a dead man hesitates to talk of that which is his heart's lining, so to say; ... but I have thought so much and there is no way; my mother, my sisters would not help me, even if I could get word to them, but letters are inspected, and I, sacred God, I am supposed to have given up such thoughts!"

"You cannot mean that you are going to spend all your life here, doing nothing? Oh, do not be so mad. Come away! Come away now, no one saw me enter, none will see you go out. Come, and let me help you back to Paris — I have money if you need it — let me help you back to ... to the lady you have not forgotten." It was a venture, but I never was surer of anything than of that lady's existence when I spoke. He stooped with a strange graceful suddenness, and kissed my hand.

"Dear lady," he said, "there is my oath," and the words choked him as he said them. "But time is short, let me think ... a Brother might pass at any moment; I must write a letter, and you, ah, I am afraid it is too hard for you to find her and to deliver it! She may not be in the same place, she may be — no, God is not cruel ... she is not married." The simple faith of that man's voice, as he said these last words, is what I have never heard, nor ever expect to hear the like of. I knew very soon I should be crying.

"Well, won't you write?" I said. "I will find her. Tell me only your name," I added with a sudden inspiration, "and be quick and write the letter." He had already found his paper and pen; it was a stiff, curious piece of paper, and he was flinging words upon it.

"I am Stanislaw Czernowietzki, Count, of the province of ..."

"You are Brother Stanislaw, of the Order of the White Brothers of Jesus and John," said a voice in the corridor.

I have never been so startled in my life, as when, with chill, frozen slowness, I turned, and saw that white man standing behind me.

It was not for myself I was frightened, for nothing could happen to me — but the poor Count! And his half-written letter! For ten seconds — fifteen perhaps — no one spoke. I admit I had quite lost my head, but it only struck me that all Poles do not know German, and I assumed that the Superior did not and that the Count did.

"For heaven's sake, the address, only the address!" I exclaimed, with the stray South German accent of my school-days which recurs to me in moments of excitement; but the Count's hands had fallen to his sides, and the new-comer was addressing him over my head in Polish and with great severity. I knew it was about me, but my wits had not come back to me quite or I would have behaved with more dignity. I put out my hand for the letter.

"The name, just the bare name!" I said, wildly.

"Ah, no! Go, Madame, pray go ... I beg of you."

It was the Count speaking with strange bitter self-possession, and that should have brought me to myself. I turned to the Superior ... I do not know exactly what I said, but I smiled, in my nervousness, actually smiled on the horrid creature who had appeared so inopportunely.

"Madame, of your goodness — go — and thank you!" said the soft voice of the Count behind me.

And without a word more I went. Down the stairs and out into the court unmolested, and the slamming of one heavy door — that of the Count's cell, I felt sure — was the sound that followed me into the sunshine.

The Yellow Wall-paper
by Charlotte Perkins Gilman

It is very seldom that mere ordinary people like John and myself secure ancestral halls for the summer.

A colonial mansion, a hereditary estate, I would say a haunted house, and reach the height of romantic felicity – but that would be asking too much of fate!

Still I will proudly declare that there is something queer about it.

Else, why should it be let so cheaply? And why have stood so long untenanted?

John laughs at me, of course, but one expects that in marriage.

John is practical in the extreme. He has no patience with faith, an intense horror of superstition, and he scoffs openly at any talk of things not to be felt and seen and put down in figures.

John is a physician, and *perhaps* – (I would not say it to a living soul, of course, but this is dead paper and a great relief to my mind) – *perhaps* that is one reason I do not get well faster.

You see he does not believe I am sick!

And what can one do?

If a physician of high standing, and one's own husband, assures friends and relatives that there is really nothing the matter with one but temporary nervous depression – a slight hysterical tendency – what is one to do?

My brother is also a physician, and also of high standing, and he says the same thing.

So I take phosphates or phosphites – whichever it is, and tonics, and journeys, and air, and exercise, and am absolutely forbidden to "work" until I am well again.

Personally, I disagree with their ideas.

Personally, I believe that congenial work, with excitement and change, would do me good.

But what is one to do?

I did write for a while in spite of them; but it *does* exhaust me a good deal – having to be so sly about it, or else meet with heavy opposition.

I sometimes fancy that in my condition if I had less opposition and more society and stimulus – but John says the very worst thing I can do is to think about my condition, and I confess it always makes me feel bad.

So I will let it alone and talk about the house.

The most beautiful place! It is quite alone, standing well back from the road, quite three miles from the village. It makes me think of English places that you read about, for there are hedges and walls and gates that lock, and lots of separate little houses for the gardeners and people.

There is a *delicious* garden! I never saw such a garden – large and shady, full of box-bordered paths, and lined with long grape-covered arbors with seats under them.

There were greenhouses, too, but they are all broken now.

There was some legal trouble, I believe, something about the heirs and co-heirs; anyhow, the place has been empty for years.

That spoils my ghostliness, I am afraid, but I don't care – there is something strange about the house – I can feel it.

I even said so to John one moonlight evening, but he said what I felt was a *draught,* and shut the window.

I get unreasonably angry with John sometimes. I'm sure I never used to be so sensitive. I think it is due to this nervous condition.

But John says if l feel so, I shall neglect proper self-control; so I take pains to control myself – before him, at least, and that makes me very tired.

I don't like our room a bit. I wanted one downstairs that opened on the piazza and had roses all over the window, and such pretty old-fashioned chintz hangings! but John would not hear of it.

He said there was only one window and not room for two beds, and no near room for him if he took another.

He is very careful and loving, and hardly lets me stir without special direction.

I have a schedule prescription for each hour in the day; he takes all care from me, and so I feel basely ungrateful not to value it more.

He said we came here solely on my account, that I was to have perfect rest and all the air I could get. "Your exercise depends on your strength, my dear," said he, "and your food somewhat on your appetite; but air you can absorb all the time." So we took the nursery at the top of the house.

It is a big, airy room, the whole floor nearly, with windows that look all ways, and air and sunshine galore. It was nursery first and then playroom and gymnasium, I should judge; for the windows are barred for little children, and there are rings and things in the walls.

The paint and paper look as if a boys' school had used it. It is stripped off – the paper – in great patches all around the head of my bed, about as far as I can reach, and in a great place on the other side of the room low down. I never saw a worse paper in my life.

One of those sprawling flamboyant patterns committing every artistic sin.

It is dull enough to confuse the eye in following, pronounced enough to constantly irritate and provoke study, and when you follow the lame uncertain curves for a little distance they suddenly commit suicide – plunge off at outrageous angles, destroy themselves in unheard of contradictions.

The color is repellant, almost revolting; a smouldering unclean yellow, strangely faded by the slow-turning sunlight.

It is a dull yet lurid orange in some places, a sickly sulphur tint in others.

No wonder the children hated it! I should hate it myself if I had to live in this room long.

There comes John, and I must put this away, – he hates to have me write a word.

We have been here two weeks, and I haven't felt like writing before, since that first day.

I am sitting by the window now, up in this atrocious nursery, and there is nothing to hinder my writing as much as I please, save lack of strength.

John is away all day, and even some nights when his cases are serious.

I am glad my case is not serious!

But these nervous troubles are dreadfully depressing.

John does not know how much I really suffer. He knows there is no *reason* to suffer, and that satisfies him.

Of course it is only nervousness. It does weigh on me so not to do my duty in any way!

I meant to be such a help to John, such a real rest and comfort, and here I am a comparative burden already!

Nobody would believe what an effort it is to do what little I am able, – to dress and entertain, and order things.

It is fortunate Mary is so good with the baby. Such a dear baby!

And yet I *cannot* be with him, it makes me so nervous.

I suppose John never was nervous in his life. He laughs at me so about this wall-paper!

At first he meant to repaper the room, but afterwards he said that I was letting it get the better of me, and that nothing was worse for a nervous patient than to give way to such fancies.

He said that after the wall-paper was changed it would be the heavy bedstead, and then the barred windows, and then that gate at the head of the stairs, and so on.

"You know the place is doing you good," he said, "and really, dear, I don't care to renovate the house just for a three months' rental."

"Then do let us go downstairs," I said, "there are such pretty rooms there."

Then he took me in his arms and called me a blessed little goose, and said he would go down cellar, if I wished, and have it whitewashed into the bargain.

But he is right enough about the beds and windows and things.

It is an airy and comfortable room as any-one need wish, and, of course, I would not be so silly as to make him uncomfortable just for a whim.

I'm really getting quite fond of the big room, all but that horrid paper.

Out of one window I can see the garden, those mysterious deep-shaded arbors, the riotous old-fashioned flowers, and bushes, and gnarly trees.

Out of another I get a lovely view of the bay and a little private wharf belonging to the estate. There is a beautiful shaded lane that runs down there from the house. I always fancy I see people walking in these numerous paths and arbors, but John has cautioned me not to give way to fancy in the least. He says that with my imaginative power and habit of story-making, a nervous weakness like mine is sure to lead to all manner of excited fancies, and that I ought to use my will and good sense to check the tendency. So I try.

I think sometimes that if I were only well enough to write a little it would relieve the press of ideas and rest me.

But I find I get pretty tired when I try.

It is so discouraging not to have any advice and companionship about my work. When I get really well, John says we will ask Cousin Henry and Julia down for a long visit; but he says he would as soon put fireworks in my pillow-case as to let me have those stimulating people about now.

I wish I could get well faster.

But I must not think about that. This paper looks to me as if it *knew* what a vicious influence it had!

There is a recurrent spot where the pattern lolls like a broken neck and two bulbous eyes stare at you upside down.

I get positively angry with the impertinence of it and the everlasting-ness. Up and down and sideways they crawl, and those absurd, unblinking eyes are everywhere. There is one place where two breadths didn't match, and the eyes go all up and down the line, one a little higher than the other.

I never saw so much expression in an inanimate thing before, and we all know how much expression they have! I used to lie awake as a child and get more entertainment and terror out of blank walls and plain furniture than most children could find in a toy-store.

I remember what a kindly wink the knobs of our big, old bureau used to have, and there was one chair that always seemed like a strong friend.

I used to feel that if any of the other things looked too fierce I could always hop into that chair and be safe.

The furniture in this room is no worse than inharmonious, however, for we had to bring it all from downstairs. I suppose when this was used as a playroom they had to take the nursery things out, and no wonder! I never saw such ravages as the children have made here.

The wall-paper, as I said before, is torn off in spots, and it sticketh closer than a brother – they must have had perseverance as well as hatred.

Then the floor is scratched and gouged and splintered, the plaster itself is dug out here and there, and this great heavy bed which is all we found in the room, looks as if it had been through the wars.

But I don't mind it a bit – only the paper.

There comes John's sister. Such a dear girl as she is, and so careful of me! I must not let her find me writing.

She is a perfect and enthusiastic housekeeper, and hopes for no better profession. I verily believe she thinks it is the writing which made me sick!

But I can write when she is out, and see her a long way off from these windows.

There is one that commands the road, a lovely, shaded winding road, and one that just looks off over the country. A lovely country, too, full of great elms and velvet meadows.

This wall-paper has a kind of sub-pattern in a different shade, a particularly irritating one, for you can only see it in certain lights, and not clearly then.

But in the places where it isn't faded and where the sun is just so – I can see a strange, provoking, formless sort of figure, that seems to skulk about behind that silly and conspicuous front design.

There's sister on the stairs!

Well, the Fourth of July is over! The people are all gone and I am tired out. John thought it might do me good to see a little company, so we just had mother and Nellie and the children down for a week.

Of course I didn't do a thing. Jennie sees to everything now.

But it tired me all the same.

John says if I don't pick up faster he shall send me to Weir Mitchell in the fall.

But I don't want to go there at all. I had a friend who was in his hands once, and she says he is just like John and my brother, only more so!

Besides, it is such an undertaking to go so far.

I don't feel as if it was worth while to turn my hand over for anything, and I'm getting dreadfully fretful and querulous.

I cry at nothing, and cry most of the time.

Of course I don't when John is here, or anybody else, but when I am alone.

And I am alone a good deal just now. John is kept in town very often by serious cases, and Jennie is good and lets me alone when I want her to.

So I walk a little in the garden or down that lovely lane, sit on the porch under the roses, and lie down up here a good deal.

I'm getting really fond of the room in spite of the wall-paper. Perhaps *because* of the wall-paper.

It dwells in my mind so!

I lie here on this great immovable bed – it is nailed down, I believe – and follow that pattern about by the hour. It is as good as gymnastics, I assure you. I start, we'll say, at the bottom, down in the corner over there where it has not been touched, and I determine for the thousandth time that I *will* follow that pointless pattern to some sort of a conclusion.

I know a little of the principle of design, and I know that this thing was not arranged on any laws of radiation, or alternation, or repetition, or symmetry, or anything else that I ever heard of.

It is repeated, of course, by the breadths, but not otherwise.

Looked at in one way each breadth stands alone, the bloated curves and flourishes – a kind of "debased Romanesque" with *delirium tremens* – go waddling up and down in isolated columns of fatuity.

But, on the other hand, they connect diagonally, and the sprawling outlines run off in great slanting waves of optic horror, like a lot of wallowing seaweeds in full chase.

The whole thing goes horizontally, too, at least it seems so, and I exhaust myself in trying to distinguish the order of its going in that direction.

They have used a horizontal breadth for a frieze, and that adds wonderfully to the confusion.

There is one end of the room where it is almost intact, and there, when the crosslights fade and the low sun shines directly upon it, I can almost fancy radiation after all, – the interminable grotesques seem to form around a common centre and rush off in headlong plunges of equal distraction.

It makes me tired to follow it. I will take a nap I guess.

I don't know why I should write this.

I don't want to.

I don't feel able.

And I know John would think it absurd. But I *must* say what I feel and think in some way – it is such a relief!

But the effort is getting to be greater than the relief.

Half the time now I am awfully lazy, and lie down ever so much.

John says I mustn't lose my strength, and has me take cod liver oil and lots of tonics and things, to say nothing of ale and wine and rare meat.

Dear John! He loves me very dearly, and hates to have me sick. I tried to have a real earnest reasonable talk with him the other day, and tell him how I wish he would let me go and make a visit to Cousin Henry and Julia.

But he said I wasn't able to go, nor able to stand it after I got there; and I did not make out a very good case for myself, for I was crying before I had finished.

It is getting to be a great effort for me to think straight. Just this nervous weakness I suppose.

And dear John gathered me up in his arms, and just carried me upstairs and laid me on the bed, and sat by me and read to me till it tired my head.

He said I was his darling and his comfort and all he had, and that I must take care of myself for his sake, and keep well.

He says no one but myself can help me out of it, that I must use my will and self-control and not let any silly fancies run away with me.

There's one comfort, the baby is well and happy, and does not have to occupy this nursery with the horrid wall-paper.

If we had not used it, that blessed child would have! What a fortunate escape! Why, I wouldn't have a child of mine, an impressionable little thing, live in such a room for worlds.

I never thought of it before, but it is lucky that John kept me here after all, I can stand it so much easier than a baby, you see.

Of course I never mention it to them any more – I am too wise – but I keep watch of it all the same.

There are things in that paper that nobody knows but me, or ever will.

Behind that outside pattern the dim shapes get clearer every day.

It is always the same shape, only very numerous.

And it is like a woman stooping down and creeping about behind that pattern. I don't like it a bit. I wonder – I begin to think – I wish John would take me away from here.

It is so hard to talk with John about my case, because he is so wise, and because he loves me so.

But I tried it last night.

It was moonlight. The moon shines in all around just as the sun does.

I hate to see it sometimes, it creeps so slowly, and always comes in by one window or another.

John was asleep and I hated to waken him, so I kept still and watched the moonlight on that undulating wall-paper till I felt creepy.

The faint figure behind seemed to shake the pattern, just as if she wanted to get out.

I got up softly and went to feel and see if the paper *did* move, and when I came back John was awake.

"What is it, little girl?" he said. "Don't go walking about like that – you'll get cold."

I thought it was a good time to talk, so I told him that I really was not gaining here, and that l wished he would take me away.

"Why darling!" said he, "our lease will be up in three weeks, and I can't see how to leave before.

"The repairs are not done at home, and I cannot possibly leave town just now. Of course if you were in any danger, I could and would, but you really are better, dear, whether you can see it or not. I am a doctor, dear, and I know. You are gaining flesh and color, your appetite is better, I feel really much easier about you."

"I don't weigh a bit more," said I, "nor as much; and my appetite may be better in the evening when you are here, but it is worse in the morning when you are away!"

"Bless her little heart!" said he with a big hug, "she shall be as sick as she pleases! But now let's improve the shining hours by going to sleep, and talk about it in the morning!"

"And you won't go away?" I asked gloomily.

"Why, how can I, dear? It is only three weeks more and then we will take a nice little trip of a few days while Jennie is getting the house ready. Really dear you are better!"

"Better in body perhaps – " I began, and stopped short, for he sat up straight and looked at me with such a stern, reproachful look that I could not say another word.

"My darling," said he, "I beg of you, for my sake and for our child's sake, as well as for your own, that you will never for one instant let that idea enter your mind! There is nothing so dangerous, so fascinating, to a temperament like yours. It is a false and foolish fancy. Can you not trust me as a physician when I tell you so?"

So of course I said no more on that score, and we went to sleep before long. He thought I was asleep first, but I wasn't, and lay there for hours trying to decide whether that front pattern and the back pattern really did move together or separately.

On a pattern like this, by daylight, there is a lack of sequence, a defiance of law, that is a constant irritant to a normal mind.

The color is hideous enough, and unreliable enough, and infuriating enough, but the pattern is torturing.

You think you have mastered it, but just as you get well underway in following, it turns a back-somersault and there you are. It slaps you in the face, knocks you down, and tramples upon you. It is like a bad dream.

The outside pattern is a florid arabesque, reminding one of a fungus. If you can imagine a toadstool in joints, an interminable string of toadstools, budding and sprouting in endless convolutions – why, that is something like it.

That is, sometimes!

There is one marked peculiarity about this paper, a thing nobody seems to notice but myself, and that is that it changes as the light changes.

When the sun shoots in through the east window – I always watch for that first long, straight ray – it changes so quickly that I never can quite believe it.

That is why I watch it always.

By moonlight – the moon shines in all night when there is a moon – I wouldn't know it was the same paper.

At night in any kind of light, in twilight, candlelight, lamplight, and worst of all by moonlight, it becomes bars! The outside pattern I mean, and the woman behind it is as plain as can be.

I didn't realize for a long time what the thing was that showed behind, that dim sub-pattern, but now I am quite sure it is a woman.

By daylight she is subdued, quiet. I fancy it is the pattern that keeps her so still. It is so puzzling. It keeps me quiet by the hour.

I lie down ever so much now, John says it is good for me, and to sleep all I can.

Indeed he started the habit by making me lie down for an hour after each meal.

It is a very bad habit I am convinced, for you see I don't sleep.

And that cultivates deceit, for I don't tell them I'm awake – O no!

The fact is I am getting a little afraid of John.

He seems very queer sometimes, and even Jennie has an inexplicable look.

It strikes me occasionally, just as a scientific hypothesis, – that perhaps it is the paper!

I have watched John when he did not know I was looking, and come into the room suddenly on the most innocent excuses, and I've caught him several times *looking at the paper*! And Jennie too. I caught Jennie with her hand on it once.

She didn't know I was in the room, and when I asked her in a quiet, a very quiet voice, with the most restrained manner possible, what she was doing with the paper – she turned around as if she had been caught stealing, and looked quite angry – asked me why I should frighten her so!

Then she said that the paper stained everything it touched, that she had found yellow smooches on all my clothes and John's, and she wished we would be more careful!

Did not that sound innocent? But I know she was studying that pattern, and I am determined that nobody shall find it out but myself!

Life is very much more exciting now than it used to be. You see I have something more to expect, to look forward to, to watch. I really do eat better, and am more quiet that I was.

John is so pleased to see me improve! He laughed a little the other day, and said I seemed to be flourishing in spite of my wall-paper.

I turned it off with a laugh. I had no intention of telling him it was *because* of the wall-paper – he would make fun of me. He might even want to take me away.

I don't want to leave now until I have found it out. There is a week more, and I think that will be enough.

I'm feeling ever so much better! I don't sleep much at night, for it is so interesting to watch developments; but I sleep a good deal in the daytime.

In the daytime it is tiresome and perplexing.

There are always new shoots on the fungus, and new shades of yellow all over it. I cannot keep count of them, though I have tried conscientiously.

It is the strangest yellow, that wall-paper! It makes me think of all the yellow things I ever saw – not beautiful ones like buttercups, but old foul, bad yellow things.

But there is something else about that paper – the smell! I noticed it the moment we came into the room, but with so much air and sun it was not bad. Now we have had a week of fog and rain, and whether the windows are open or not, the smell is here.

It creeps all over the house.

I find it hovering in the dining room, skulking in the parlor, hiding in the hall, lying in wait for me on the stairs.

It gets into my hair.

Even when I go to ride, if I turn my head suddenly and surprise it – there is that smell!

Such a peculiar odor, too! I have spent hours in trying to analyze it, to find what it smelled like.

It is not bad – at first, and very gentle, but quite the subtlest, most enduring odor I ever met.

In this damp weather it is awful, I wake up in the night and find it hanging over me.

It used to disturb me at first. I thought seriously of burning the house – to reach the smell.

But now I am used to it. The only thing I can think of that it is like is the *color* of the paper! A yellow smell.

There is a very funny mark on this wall, low down, near the mopboard. A streak that runs round the room. It goes behind every piece of furniture, except the bed, a long, straight, even *smooch,* as if it had been rubbed over and over.

I wonder how it was done and who did it, and what they did it for. Round and round and round – round and round and round – it makes me dizzy!

I really have discovered something at last.

Through watching so much at night, when it changes so, I have finally found out.

The front pattern *does* move – and no wonder! The woman behind shakes it!

Sometimes I think there are a great many women behind, and sometimes only one, and she crawls around fast, and her crawling shakes it all over.

Then in the very bright spots she keeps still, and in the very shady spots she just takes hold of the bars and shakes them hard.

And she is all the time trying to climb through. But nobody could climb through that pattern – it strangles so; I think that is why it has so many heads.

They get through, and then the pattern strangles them off and turns them upside down, and makes their eyes white!

If those heads were covered or taken off it would not be half so bad.

I think that woman gets out in the daytime!

And I'll tell you why – privately – I've seen her!

I can see her out of every one of my windows!

It is the same woman, I know, for she is always creeping, and most women do not creep by daylight.

I see her in that long shaded lane, creeping up and down. I see her in those dark grape arbors, creeping all around the garden.

I see her on that long road under the trees, creeping along, and when a carriage comes she hides under the blackberry vines.

I don't blame her a bit. It must be very humiliating to be caught creeping by daylight!

I always lock the door when I creep by daylight. I can't do it at night, for I know John would suspect something at once.

And John is so queer now, that I don't want to irritate him. I wish he would take another room! Besides, I don't want anybody to get that woman out at night but myself.

I often wonder if I could see her out of all the windows at once.

But, turn as fast as I can, I can only see out of one at one time.

And though I always see her, she *may* be able to creep faster than I can turn!

I have watched her sometimes away off in the open country, creeping as fast as a cloud shadow in a high wind.

If only that top pattern could be gotten off from the under one! I mean to try it, little by little.

I have found out another funny thing, but I shan't tell it this time! It does not do to trust people too much.

There are only two more days to get this paper off, and I believe John is beginning to notice. I don't like the look in his eyes.

And I heard him ask Jennie a lot of professional questions about me. She had a very good report to give.

She said I slept a good deal in the daytime.

John knows I don't sleep very well at night, for all I'm so quiet!

He asked me all sorts of questions, too, and pretended to be very loving and kind.

As if I couldn't see through him!

Still, I don't wonder he acts so, sleeping under this paper for three months.

It only interests me, but I feel sure John and Jennie are secretly affected by it.

Hurrah! This is the last day, but it is enough. John to stay in town over night, and won't be out until this evening.

Jennie wanted to sleep with me – the sly thing! But I told her I should undoubtedly rest better for a night all alone.

That was clever, for really I wasn't alone a bit! As soon as it was moonlight and that poor thing began to crawl and shake the pattern, I got up and ran to help her.

I pulled and she shook, I shook and she pulled, and before morning we had peeled off yards of that paper.

A strip about as high as my head and half around the room.

And then when the sun came and that awful pattern began to laugh at me, I declared I would finish it to-day!

We go away to-morrow, and they are moving all my furniture down again to leave things as they were before.

Jennie looked at the wall in amazement, but I told her merrily that I did it out of pure spite at the vicious thing.

She laughed and said she wouldn't mind doing it herself, but I must not get tired.

How she betrayed herself that time!

But I am here, and no person touches this paper but me, – not *alive!*

She tried to get me out of the room – it was too patent! But I said it was so quiet and empty and clean now that I believed I would lie down again and sleep all I could; and not to wake me even for dinner – I would call when I woke.

So now she is gone, and the servants are gone, and the things are gone, and there is nothing left but that great bedstead nailed down, with the canvas mattress we found on it.

We shall sleep downstairs to-night, and take the boat home to-morrow.

I quite enjoy the room, now it is bare again.

How those children did tear about here!

This bedstead is fairly gnawed!

But I must get to work.

I have locked the door and thrown the key down into the front path.

I don't want to go out, and I don't want to have anybody come in, till John comes.

I want to astonish him.

I've got a rope up here that even Jennie did not find. If that woman does get out, and tries to get away, I can tie her!

But I forgot I could not reach far without anything to stand on!

This bed will *not* move!

I tried to lift and push it until I was lame, and then I got so angry I bit off a little piece at one corner – but it hurt my teeth.

Then I peeled off all the paper I could reach standing on the floor. It sticks horribly and the pattern just enjoys it! All those strangled heads and bulbous eyes and waddling fungus growths just shriek with derision!

I am getting angry enough to do something desperate. To jump out of the window would be admirable exercise, but the bars are too strong even to try.

Besides I wouldn't do it. Of course not. I know well enough that a step like that is improper and might be misconstrued.

I don't like to *look* out of the windows even – there are so many of those creeping women, and they creep so fast.

I wonder if they all come out of that wall-paper as I did?

But I am securely fastened now by my well-hidden rope – you don't get *me* out in the road there!

I suppose I shall have to get back behind the pattern when it comes night, and that is hard!

It is so pleasant to be out in this great room and creep around as I please!

I don't want to go outside. I won't, even if Jennie asks me to.

For outside you have to creep on the ground, and everything is green instead of yellow.

But here I can creep smoothly on the floor, and my shoulder just fits in that long smooch around the wall, so I cannot lose my way.

Why there's John at the door!

It is no use, young man, you can't open it!

How he does call and pound!

Now he's crying for an axe.

It would be a shame to break down that beautiful door!

"John dear!" said I in the gentlest voice, "the key is down by the front steps, under a plantain leaf!"

That silenced him for a few moments.

Then he said – very quietly indeed, "Open the door, my darling!"

"I can't," said I. "The key is down by the front door under a plantain leaf!"

And then I said it again, several times, very gently and slowly, and said it so often that he had to go and see, and he got it of course, and came in. He stopped short by the door.

"What is the matter?" he cried. "For God's sake, what are you doing??"

I kept on creeping just the same, but I looked at him over my shoulder.

"I've got out at last," said I, "in spite of you and Jane. And I've pulled off most of the paper, so you can't put me back!"

Now why should that man have fainted? But he did, and right across my path by the wall, so that I had to creep over him every time!

The Yellow Drawing-Room
by Mona Caird

I approach this episode in my life, which presents itself to my memory thus entitled, with dislike, mingled with fascination. I hate the whole subject, but I can't leave it alone. Those accursed three weeks, spent under the same roof with Vanora Haydon, seem to have deprived me of myself, unhinged me, destroyed the balance of my character. I feel as if I might, perhaps, throw off this absurd spell by calmly smoothing out the ruffled memories and studying them scientifically.

Vanora's aunt, Miss Clementina Thorne, was a nice appreciative old maiden lady, who thought me the most estimable and charming of men. I had long regarded her with warm affection, tempered only by a mild resentment at her perpetual attempts to get me married. In her pressing invitation to come once more to Fairfield, where the fresh air would be so good for me after my dusty and dingy office, I read at sight that another matrimonial scheme was fermenting in that most hymeneal brain. I knew that this time she had destined me for one of her nieces, as she mentioned that they had no visitors at present, and that Vanora would be at home. Though I had hovered about Clara with vague admiration for over a year, I had never yet seen Vanora. Her aunt mentioned, in her much under-lined epistle, that her brother-in-law, since his dear wife's death, had let the girls have too much of their own way, and that Vanora (who had received permission to decorate and furnish the drawing-room at Fairfield exactly as she pleased), had unworthily employed her liberty by producing a room of brilliant yellow.

I had a prejudice against Vanora, and this last freak made me think none the better of her. Evidently she was rather a headstrong and probably affected young person; every one said that she liked to make herself conspicuous, and that you never knew what she was going to do next. I hate that sort of girl. The true woman is retiring, unobtrusive, indistinguishable even until you come to know her well, and then she is very much like what every other true woman would be under the same conditions. I had pronounced views in these matters.

As for the yellow drawing-room —!

I was anxious to see just how far Vanora's mania to be out of the common had carried her in this instance.

Arrived at Fairfield, I was at once shown into the notorious drawing-room. It *was* yellow! The colour had been washed out of the very daffodils, which looked green with jealousy; the sunshine was confronted in a spirit of respectful independence, brotherhood being acknowledged, but the principle of equality uncompromisingly asserted.

Miss Thorne sadly shook her head.

"We want my brother-in-law to have the room done over again, Mr. St. Vincent, but he won't hear of it. We did all we could with Vanora — we told her that *nobody* used such a brilliant colour, but she only said that she found Nobody, when you came to talk to him seriously, was a person quite open to reason. Dear Vanora is so quaint."

"Her taste seems to be rather quaint," I said.

Several visitors were passionately admiring the prospect, the pictures, the chairs and tables, anything to protect themselves against a threatening summons to say something about the general colouring. Miss Thorne seemed to be piteously endeavouring, by her manners, her attire, her sentiments, to atone for that unpardonable drawing-room. The sisters also, Mary and Clara, were doing their best in the same direction. But hopeless was their protest. The room was in a glow of golden light; no ladylike antidote, however strong, could lead one to ignore it. It was radiant, bold, unapologetic, unabashed. It was not the room that my ideal woman would have created. My ideal woman would unfailingly choose a nice tone of grey-blue. Certain suspicions which I had harboured that Clara Haydon was my ideal woman grew stronger as I watched her quiet English face bent over the tea-tray. I liked the straightforward look of the girl, her blue eyes and fair complexion. If I *was* to give up my liberty, the reins should be handed over to a kind, sensible young woman like Clara, who would hate to make herself remarkable, or her drawing-room yellow.

I think the hot afternoon sun, and the unceasing sound of Aunt Clementina's voice, must have made me drowsy, for I was thinking mistily what a wonderfully and conspicuously *clean* girl Clara Haydon was, when the door opened, and I found myself floundering (I cannot do more than describe these dreamy impressions) in an ocean of laughter.

In my efforts to keep my head above water, I discovered rather sharply that I had upset my tea, which Clara's exceedingly clean fingers had just poured out for me. This brought me to my senses.

"I appear to be graduating for an idiot," I exclaimed, furious at my clumsiness and stupidity. Vanora laughed in a friendly manner. "We have all been yearning to get rid of this cup," she said, "and we really feel grateful to you for your opportune assistance."

In the few bewildering moments of apology and re-assurance, I found myself presented emphatically to Vanora, and lightly indicated to a dark and lank young man who followed her into the room. Vanora herself was simply radiant. She had a mass of glistening, golden hair, a colour full, varying, emotional, eyes like the sea (I lose my temper when people ask me to describe their colour). In figure she was robust, erect, pliant, firmly knit. Though her movements were so swift, there was nothing restless about her. A ground-tone of repose sounded up through the surface scintillations. She was vital, not galvanic. That was the revealing word: vital. In the human colour-spectrum, she took the place of the yellow ray.

This was all out of keeping. According to my doctrines it was even impossible. Women ought to take the place of the blue or violet rays. In my scheme of the universe they always did so, except in the case of a distinctly unwomanly woman. But this — in spite of offending against every canon I had ever set up — Vanora certainly was not. She was supremely, overpoweringly womanly. The womanhood of her sisters paled before the exuberant feminine quality which I could not but acknowledge in Vanora. Everything was wrong and contradictory. I seemed to be taking part in some comedy of errors, wherein Vanora played Columbine, and I — the part of fool, I began grimly to suspect. For already (I shrugged my shoulders at myself in contemptuous despair) I found that I hated the lank young man who had been introduced as Mr. George Inglis, simply and solely because I saw that he was head over ears in love with Vanora, and that she treated him with a sort of indescribable good-fellowship, mingled with a peculiar tenderness. I never saw anything to equal Vanora's tenderness when she was moved that way.

"I hear, Miss Vanora," I said, "that the credit of this room is entirely yours."

The lank admirer looked round. Vanora glanced at me alertly.

"You have every reason to be proud," I continued, determined not to spare her; "you must have surprised more people than you could easily count — though I have no wish to impugn your arithmetic. They will all be grateful to you for a new sensation."

"Forgive me for disagreeing with you," she said. "It is so easy to surprise people; they are so amiable; they keep themselves always prepared for astonishment; they are like a sensitised plate which is ready at a moment's notice to be surprised into a photograph. You come with your dogma or your self-evident fact, or simply your pot of yellow paint, and, behold, forth spring the various amazements. Oh, no! (thanking you all the same) I am not proud!"

I raised my eyebrows witheringly. My ideal woman would consider it almost indelicate to play with words in this fantastic fashion. I glanced at my grey-blue goddess. How comfortably certain one felt with *her* of enjoying conversational repose! Dear Clara! With what admirable good taste she carried out one's cherished ideas: she fitted them like a glove. I completely, ardently, approved of Clara. To her I rather ostentatiously devoted myself for the rest of the afternoon, but I was furtively watching her sister.

And now I come to the disagreeable and inexplicable part of my broken and absurd episode. I know not to this day why or wherefore, but Vanora began to exercise over me an extraordinary fascination. If there were any other word I would use it, but I cannot find one. I fell into the strangest and most contradictory state of mind. Vanora's personality seemed to enwrap me as a garment; she was like some great radiating centre of light and warmth; I was penetrated with the glowing atmosphere. I never approved of the girl; I don't believe that I then liked her. I know that I often hated her, and yet I felt miserable out of her sight. She became a necessity to me.

A feeling of misery, which I cannot describe, assailed me in her absence; a sick feeling of senseless despair. I used to pace the terrace among the peacocks (the boys impertinently insisted that they were unable on such occasions to distinguish me from those conceited birds) and as I thus worked off some of my restlessness, I tried to understand what had happened to me.

One morning, before breakfast, Vanora came out on to the terrace. She walked straight up to me and said "Good morning; I think you want to talk to me, don't you?"

I looked at her in despair. If she lived and improved for a thousand years she would never be an ideal woman!

"You disapprove of me," Vanora continued calmly. "I wish you would tell me why."

"You really wish me to be frank?" I said, stopping and facing her.

"I really do," she replied, offering crumbs of bread to a haughty peacock, who eyed them superciliously.

"Well, then, Miss Haydon, your blood be upon your own head (beautiful was that golden head in the morning light). You seem to me to have many qualities and ideas that are not suited to your sex. No doubt, I am old-fashioned about these things, but I confess that I cannot rejoice when I see our beautiful ideas of womanhood set scornfully at naught."

"No?" said Vanora. "Do go on."

"I scarcely know how to approach a subject of which you do not seem to understand the rudiments," I said severely.

"This interests me," cried Vanora. "I particularly desire to be awakened on this drowsy side of me; I can't bear to be blind and stupid. I want very much to be shown at least the gates of realms that are forbidden to me."

"The sacred realms where woman is queen will soon be forbidden to you if you consistently continue to think and act in disharmony with the feminine nature and genius."

"That is what Aunt Clementina and Mr. Barnes so often tell me (Mr. Barnes is our clergyman). But at present the threat of being excluded from the realms you mention does not terrify me. I rather prefer the realms where woman is *not* queen."

"A mistake, a mistake!" I exclaimed. "Yes, so I am told. But often people don't know what is good for them. I have heard of persons of mature judgment who had a chance of going straight off to Heaven to play on golden harps and wear a halo, hanging back and sending for the doctor in a strongly ill-advised manner. Of course we shall all have to go to the realms where woman is queen, but for myself I confess to a weak inclination to postpone, or let us say, not to anticipate, my royalty. The suspicion is clearly blameable, but what if I should happen to get tired of the everlasting harping?"

Vanora's face was perfectly serious.

"Miss Haydon," I said, gravely and sadly, "you may have a brilliant career in the future, but the more brilliant, the more complete will be your failure, the more I shall mourn the loss of a real woman from the spheres where she was intended to create and to maintain those sacred ties and sentiments, without which this world would be a howling wilderness."

Vanora tossed another crumb to the supercilious peacock.

"Do go on," she repeated.

"If women only realised where their true power lay, and how mighty was that power, they would never seek to snatch it in directions where they are inevitably weak, and — if I must say it — inevitably ridiculous."

"I was born to be ridiculous," said Vanora. "My father never sought to arrange a 'sphere' for me, and in my case instinct seems at fault. At one time I used to make a creditable number of antimacassars and sofa-cushions, and to this day my sisters do all that can possibly be required of a well-conducted family, — and what is especially satisfactory from a popular point of view, — they think a baby far more interesting than a grown-up creature with a soul, or even than a child who can think and feel. They are keeping up the feminine traditions admirably. Don't you think it would be a little monotonous if I were to go over exactly the same ground? It seems to me that that ground is getting rather trodden in."

"I am sorry to hear you sneer at your good and charming sisters, and at the true instincts of your sex." Vanora burst out laughing.

"Oh! Mr. St. Vincent, you really are a little stupid sometimes," she said. She turned, and I saw a change come into her face as George Inglis appeared from the wood at the far end of the terrace, and walk towards us. That filled me with unaccountable fury. My critical mood, which I had maintained with no little difficulty, fell off me, and I was swaying as a wind-tossed reed with strange, uncontrollable emotion.

"You don't know what it has cost me to speak to you thus," I said, catching her hand. "You interest me, you — yes, I must say it — you fascinate me, and it distresses me, maddens me to feel myself led away by qualities which ought to repel me — the attraction is morbid — unwholesome. I am angry with myself for even feeling it. Vanora, you must release me."

"Release you," she repeated; "what do you mean?"

"I mean," I replied crazily, "that you must learn to love me and to be a woman in the old sweet sense, for my sake."

"You are very naïf," she said, smiling; "you seem just now to me like a nice, egotistical child."

I turned abruptly away. I knew that George Inglis joined her, and that they walked down the terrace together. I suppose I must have been in love with her, yet all the time I seemed to hate her. I longed to make her yield to me; to love me with a lowly up-looking love. I had a burning desire to subdue her. She seemed to evade me and my theories as if she were a creature from another sphere. I cannot describe the irritation of mind which all this caused me. I set about my wooing as if I had been going to fight a duel.

Shortly after this, to my intense disgust, I found that George Inglis had discovered my accursed secret. I chanced to overhear him saying to Miss Thorne: "The contest is a typical one; if one could imagine the Eighteenth Century as a lover wooing the Nineteenth Century, this is the sort of angular labyrinthine courtship we should have!" I wondered what the chattering fool meant by it!

"She *shall* love me, and she *shall* learn, through love, the sweet lesson of womanly submission," I said to myself, all the dominating instincts of my manhood roused into activity by this hateful experience. I felt that she was utterly wrong, that she had mistaken her own powers and her own noblest impulses. It was for me, through the might of an overwhelming affection, to set alight the true womanly flame within her heart. I would make her proud of her subordination; I would turn the splendid stream of her powers and affection into the true channel.

After a day or two of lover-like devotion, I began to slacken in my pursuit, and to transfer my attentions to Clara. Clara became a new creature. Her expression softened, her eyes brightened, but I was too absorbed in my own little drama to consider what part Clara might be likely to play in it. I watched Vanora secretly. She seemed depressed and restless. My heart bounded. Vanora was jealous; a woman after the old eternal pattern! — therefore to be won! Dear, erratic, foolish, brilliant Vanora, you shall be brought back safe and sound to your true destiny!

I followed her to the garden, whither I knew she had gone to gather flowers. Very lovely she looked in her white dress, with a bunch of daffodils in her belt.

I plunged headlong. "Vanora, I love you; I want to know my fate."

"*Me*," she said, with a gasp of astonishment, "I thought it was Clara!"

I clasped her hands; I protested; I told her how my love for her had overwhelmed and shattered me.

"And Clara?" she repeated in dismay.

Did she not understand. It was out of pique, to make her jealous —

"When I become jealous of my sisters," said Vanora, with a quiet and scornful aloofness, "you can come and preach me your doctrines. I shall understand them then."

"Vanora!"

"At present they seem to me like soap-bubbles; full of emptiness."

"But you don't understand —"

"True," she returned, "they have never before assailed me in this stiff-backed fashion. I offend against them unconsciously. My father never constrained me to move in any particular direction because of my sex. He has perhaps spoiled me. I have hitherto had only a joyous sense of drawing in what was outside, and radiating out what was within me. When you describe your doctrines I seem to see the doors of a dark prison opening out of the sunshine; and strange to say, I feel no divine, unerring instinct prompting me to walk in."

"I offer you no prison but a home," I cried excitedly.

"You would turn all homes into prisons," she returned.

"Prisons whose bars are the golden bars of love and duty."

"Yes, you take a woman's love and duty, and fashion out of them her prison bars. Is that generous? I fancy not, but it is most ingenious. It is Loyalesque. But I don't like even *golden* bars, Mr. St. Vincent."

"You have evidently not a spark of love for me," I cried distractedly.

Her face suddenly changed. "Ah! that is the horrible absurdity of it!" she exclaimed, colouring painfully. "You enthral one part of me and leave the other scornful and indifferent. We have scarcely a thought in common, but I am miserable when you are absent — stop, don't misunderstand. Your Gods and Goddesses are to me creatures of pasteboard; your world of belief seems to me like a realm fashioned out of tissue paper." She spoke with breathless rapidity, and she was quivering from head to foot. "To live with you would be like living in a tomb; I lack the sense of fresh air. And there is no sunshine within miles of you! Yet when I am not with you there is a sort of ache; your personality seems to fascinate me — I wish to Heaven you had never come here. You have disturbed my happiness, destroyed my delight in life, left me miserably dependent on you; yet to the end of time I should continue to shock and irritate you, and you would stifle, depress, and perhaps utterly unhinge me. I wish you would go — to-day, now."

She looked white and distraught. I pleaded like a lunatic, argued, urged; for one supreme moment my arms were round her, and I thought that she would yield. But whether or not a triumph was in store for me I shall never know, for suddenly we both started in dismay. Before us, pausing abruptly as she came round the bend of the laurel shrubberies stood Clara. I shall never forget the look on her face at that moment. It was like that of some gentle animal mortally and wantonly wounded. Without a word Clara turned away, and Vanora and I stood in silence.

At last, slowly moving away, Vanora spoke. "I can forgive you the injury you have done to *me* — that you could not help, and the fault, after all, is my own — but I can never forgive what you have done to Clara."

She passed out of sight, and I stood spellbound.

I never saw Vanora again. I left Fairfield immediately, and I heard that she and her sister had gone abroad. I could not find out where they were, nor had I the temerity to think of following them. I knew that Fate had no reprieve for me.

The episode remains in my mind as a haunting, incomprehensible dream. Ponder as I may, I cannot understand what impulses of our nature Vanora and I had power mutually to set at variance; what irresistible attraction we had for one another, combined with what inevitable antipathy. We could never have lived together; I see that now. Yet, when the memory of those ten days returns to torment me, I feel that neither can we live apart. I have never been the same man since I met Vanora. I am neither my former self, complete and comfortable, nor am I thoroughly a new being. I am a sort of abortive creature, striding between two centuries. The spirit of a coming age has brushed me with his wing, but I resent and resist that which brings havoc into the citadel of my dearest beliefs; and I angrily pluck off the tiny feather which he dropped from those great ploughing pinions of his, that shadow — the firmament of the Future.

The Revolt of 'Mother'
by Mary E. Wilkins

"Father!"

"What is it?"

"What are them men diggin' over there in the field for?"

There was a sudden dropping and enlarging of the lower part of the old man's face, as if some heavy weight had settled therein; he shut his mouth tight, and went on harnessing the great bay mare. He hustled the collar on to her neck with a jerk.

"Father!"

The old man slapped the saddle upon the mare's back.

"Look here, father, I want to know what them men are diggin' over in the field for, an' I'm goin' to know."

"I wish you'd go into the house, mother, an' 'tend to your own affairs," the old man said then. He ran his words together, and his speech was almost as inarticulate as a growl.

But the woman understood; it was her most native tongue. "I ain't goin' into the house till you tell me what them men are doin' over there in the field," said she.

Then she stood waiting. She was a small woman, short and straight-waisted like a child in her brown cotton gown. Her forehead was mild and benevolent between the smooth curves of gray hair; there were meek downward lines about her nose and mouth; but her eyes, fixed upon the old man, looked as if the meekness had been the result of her own will, never of the will of another.

They were in the barn, standing before the wide open doors. The spring air, full of the smell of growing grass and unseen blossoms, came in their faces. The deep yard in front was littered with farm wagons and piles of wood; on the edges, close to the fence and the house, the grass was a vivid green, and there were some dandelions.

The old man glanced doggedly at his wife as he tightened the last buckles on the harness. She looked as immovable to him as one of the rocks in his pasture-land, bound to the earth with generations of blackberry vines. He slapped the reins over the horse, and started forth from the barn.

"*Father!*" said she.

The old man pulled up. "What is it?"

"I want to know what them men are diggin' over there in that field for."

"They're diggin' a cellar, I s'pose, if you've got to know."

"A cellar for what?"

"A barn."

"A barn? You ain't goin' to build a barn over there where we was goin' to have a house, father?"

The old man said not another word. He hurried the horse into the farm wagon, and clattered out of the yard, jouncing as sturdily on his seat as a boy.

The woman stood a moment looking after him, then she went out of the barn across a corner of the yard to the house. The house, standing at right angles with the great barn and a long reach of sheds and out-buildings, was infinitesimal compared with them. It was scarcely as commodious for people as the little boxes under the barn eaves were for doves.

A pretty girl's face, pink and delicate as a flower, was looking out of one of the house windows. She was watching three men who were digging over in the field which bounded the yard near the road line. She turned quietly when the woman entered.

"What are they digging for, mother?" said she. "Did he tell you?"

"They're diggin' for — a cellar for a new barn."

"Oh, mother, he ain't going to build another barn?"

"That's what he says."

A boy stood before the kitchen glass combing his hair. He combed slowly and painstakingly, arranging his brown hair in a smooth hillock over his forehead. He did not seem to pay any attention to the conversation.

"Sammy, did you know father was going to build a new barn?" asked the girl.

The boy combed assiduously.

"Sammy!"

He turned, and showed a face like his father's under his smooth crest of hair. "Yes, I s'pose I did," he said, reluctantly.

"How long have you know it?" asked his mother.

"'Bout three months, I guess."

"Why didn't you tell of it?"

"Didn't think 'twould do no good."

"I don't see what father wants another barn for," said the girl, in her sweet, slow voice. She turned again to the window, and stared out at the digging men in the field. Her tender, sweet face was full of a gentle distress. Her forehead was as bald and innocent as a baby's, with the light hair strained back from it in a row of curl-papers. She was quite large, but her soft curves did not look as if they covered muscles.

Her mother looked sternly at the boy. "Is he goin' to buy more cows?" said she.

The boy did not reply; he was tying his shoes.

"Sammy, I want you to tell me if he's goin' to buy more cows."

"I s'pose he is."

"How many?"

"Four, I guess."

His mother said nothing more. She went into the pantry, and there was a clatter of dishes. The boy got his cap from a nail behind the door, took an old arithmetic from the shelf, and started for school. He was lightly built, but clumsy. He went out of the yard with a curious spring in the hips, that made his loose home-made jacket tilt up in the rear.

The girl went to the sink, and began to wash the dishes that were piled up there. Her mother came promptly out of the pantry, and shoved her aside. "You wipe 'em," said she; "I'll wash. There's a good many this mornin'."

The mother plunged her hands vigorously into the water, the girl wiped the plates slowly and dreamily. "Mother," said she, "don't you think it's too bad father's going to build that new barn, much as we need a decent house to live in?"

Her mother scrubbed a dish fiercely. "You ain't found it out yet we're women-folks, Nanny Penn," said she. "You ain't seen enough of men-folks yet to. One of these days you'll find it out, an' then you'll know that we know only what men-folks think we do, so far as any use of it goes, an' how we'd ought to reckon men-folks in with Providence, an' not complain of what they do any more than we do of the weather."

"I don't care; I don't believe George is anything like that, anyhow," said Nanny. Her delicate face flushed pink, her lips pouted softly, as if she were going to cry.

"You wait an' see. I guess George Eastman ain't no better than other men. You hadn't ought to judge father, though. He can't help it, 'cause he don't look at things jest the way we do. An' we've been pretty comfortable here, after all. The roof don't leak — ain't never but once — that's one thing. Father's kept it shingled right up."

"I do wish we had a parlor."

"I guess it won't hurt George Eastman any to come to see you in a nice clean kitchen. I guess a good many girls don't have as good a place as this. Nobody's ever heard me complain."

"I ain't complained either, mother."

"Well, I don't think you'd better, a good father an' a good home as you've got. S'pose your father made you go out an' work for your livin'? Lots of girls have to that ain't no stronger an' better able to than you be."

Sarah Penn washed the frying-pan with a conclusive air. She scrubbed the outside of it as faithfully as the inside. She was a masterly keeper of her box of a house. Her one living-room never seemed to have in it any of the dust which the friction of life with inanimate matter produces. She swept, and there seemed to be no dirt to go before the broom; she cleaned, and one could see no difference. She was like an artist so perfect that he has apparently no art. To-day she got out a mixing bowl and a board, and rolled some pies, and there was no more flour upon her than upon her daughter who was doing finer work. Nanny was to be married in the fall, and she was sewing on some white cambric and embroidery. She sewed industriously while her mother cooked, her soft milk-white hands and wrists showed whiter than her delicate work.

"We must have the stove moved out in the shed before long," said Mrs. Penn. "Talk about not havin' things, it's been a real blessin' to be able to put a stove up in that shed in hot weather. Father did one good thing when he fixed that stove-pipe out there."

Sarah Penn's face as she rolled her pies had that expression of meek vigor which might have characterized one of the New Testament saints. She was making mince-pies. Her husband, Adoniram Penn, liked them better than any other kind. She baked twice a week. Adoniram often liked a piece of pie between meals. She hurried this morning. It had been later than usual when she began, and she wanted to have a pie baked for dinner. However deep a resentment she might be forced to hold against her husband, she would never fail in sedulous attention to his wants.

Nobility of character manifests itself at loop-holes when it is not provided with large doors. Sarah Penn's showed itself to-day in flaky dishes of pastry. So she made the pies faithfully, while across the table she could see, when she glanced up from her work, the sight that rankled in her patient and steadfast soul — the digging of the cellar of the new barn in the place where Adoniram forty years ago had promised her their new house should stand.

The pies were done for dinner. Adoniram and Sammy were home a few minutes after twelve o'clock. The dinner was eaten with serious haste. There was never much conversation at the table in the Penn family. Adoniram asked a blessing, and they ate promptly, then rosé up and went about their work.

Sammy went back to school, taking soft sly lopes out of the yard like a rabbit. He wanted a game of marbles before school, and feared his father would give him some chores to do. Adoniram hastened to the door and called after him, but he was out of sight.

"I don't see what you let him go for, mother," said he. "I wanted him to help me unload that wood."

Adoniram went to work out in the yard unloading wood from the wagon. Sarah put away the dinner dishes, while Nanny took down her curl-papers and changed her dress. She was going down to the store to buy some more embroidery and thread.

When Nanny was gone, Mrs. Penn went to the door. "Father!" she called.

"Well, what is it!"

"I want to see you jest a minute, father."

"I can't leave this wood nohow. I've got to git it unloaded an' go for a load of gravel afore two o'clock. Sammy had ought to helped me. You hadn't ought to let him go to school so early."

"I want to see you jest a minute."

"I tell ye I can't, nohow, mother."

"Father, you come here." Sarah Penn stood in the door like a queen; she held her head as if it bore a crown; there was that patience which makes authority royal in her voice. Adoniram went.

Mrs. Penn led the way into the kitchen, and pointed to a chair. "Sit down, father," said she; "I've got somethin' I want to say to you."

He sat down heavily; his face was quite stolid, but he looked at her with restive eyes. "Well, what is it, mother?"

"I want to know what you're buildin' that new barn for, father?"

"I ain't got nothin' to say about it."

"It can't be you think you need another barn?"

"I tell ye I ain't got nothin' to say about it, mother; an' I ain't goin' to say nothin'."

"Be you goin' to buy more cows?"

Adoniram did not reply; he shut his mouth tight.

"I know you be, as well as I want to. Now, father, look here" — Sarah Penn had not sat down; she stood before her husband in the humble fashion of a Scripture woman — "I'm goin' to talk real plain to you; I never have sence I married you, but I'm goin' to now. I ain't never complained, an' I ain't goin' to complain now, but I'm goin' to talk plain. You see this room here, father; you look at it well. You see there ain't no carpet on the floor, an' you see the paper is all dirty, an' droppin' off the walls. We ain't had no new paper on it for ten year, an' then I put it on myself, an' it didn't cost but ninepence a roll. You see this room, father; it's all the one I've had to work in an' eat in an' sit in sence we was married. There ain't another woman in the whole town whose husband ain't got half the means you have but what's got better. It's all the room Nanny's got to have her company in; an' there ain't one of her mates but what's got better, an' their fathers not so able as hers is. It's all the room she'll have to be married in. What would you have thought, father, if we had had our weddin' in a room no better than this? I was married in my mother's parlor, with a carpet on the floor, an' stuffed furniture, an' a mahogany card-table. An' this is all the room my daughter will have to be married in. Look here, father!"

Sarah Penn went across the room as though it were a tragic stage. She flung open a door and disclosed a tiny bedroom, only large enough for a bed and bureau, with a path between. "There, father," said she — "there's all the room I've had to sleep in forty year. All my children were born there — the two that died, an' the two that's livin'. I was sick with a fever there."

She stepped to another door and opened it. It led into the small, ill-lighted pantry. "Here," said she, "is all the buttery I've got — every place

I've got for my dishes, to set away my victuals in, an' to keep my milk-pans in. Father, I've been takin' care of the milk of six cows in this place, an' now you're goin' to build a new barn, an' keep more cows, an' give me more to do in it."

She threw open another door. A narrow crooked flight of stairs wound upward from it. "There, father," said she, "I want you to look at the stairs that go up to them two unfinished chambers that are all the places our son an' daughter have had to sleep in all their lives. There ain't a prettier girl in town nor a more ladylike one than Nanny, an' that's the place she has to sleep in. It ain't so good as your horse's stall; it ain't so warm an' tight."

Sarah Penn went back and stood before her husband. "Now, father," said she, "I want to know if you think you're doin' right an' accordin' to what you profess. Here, when we was married, forty year ago, you promised me faithful that we should have a new house built in that lot over in the field before the year was out. You said you had money enough, an' you wouldn't ask me to live in no such place as this. It is forty year now, an' you've been makin' more money, an' I've been savin' of it for you ever since, an' you ain't built no house yet. You've built sheds an' cow-houses an' one new barn, an' now you're goin' to build another. Father, I want to know if you think it's right. You're lodgin' your dumb beasts better than you are your own flesh an' blood. I want to know if you think it's right."

"I ain't got nothin' to say."

"You can't say nothin' without ownin' it ain't right, father. An' there's another thing — I ain't complained; I've got along forty year, an' I s'pose I should forty more, if it wa'n't for that — if we don't have another house. Nanny she can't live with us after she's married. She'll have to go somewheres else to live away from us, an' it don't seem as if I could have it so, noways, father. She wa'n't ever strong. She's got considerable color, but there wa'n't never any backbone to her. I've always took the heft of everything off her, an' she ain't fit to keep house an' do everything herself. She'll be all worn out inside of a year. Think of her doin' all the washin' an' ironin' an' bakin' with them soft white hands an' arms, an' sweepin! I can't have it so, noways, father."

Mrs. Penn's face was burning; her mild eyes gleamed. She had pleaded her little cause like a Webster; she had ranged from severity to pathos; but her opponent employed that obstinate silence which makes eloquence futile with mocking echoes. Adoniram arose clumsily.

"Father, ain't you got nothin' to say?" said Mrs. Penn.

"I've got to go off after that load of gravel. I can't stan' here talkin' all day."

"Father, won't you think it over, an' have a house built there instead of a barn?"

"I ain't got nothin' to say."

Adoniram shuffled out. Mrs. Penn went into her bedroom. When she came out, her eyes were red. She had a roll of unbleached cotton cloth. She spread it out on the kitchen table, and began cutting out some shirts for her husband. The men over in the field had a team to help them this afternoon; she could hear their halloos. She had a scanty pattern for the shirts; she had to plan and piece the sleeves.

Nanny came home with her embroidery, and sat down with her needlework. She had taken down her curl-papers, and there was a soft roll of fair hair like an aureole over her forehead; her face was as delicately fine and clear as porcelain. Suddenly she looked up, and the tender red flamed all over her face and neck. "Mother," said she.

"What say?"

"I've been thinking — I don't see how we're goin' to have any — wedding in this room. I'd be ashamed to have his folks come if we didn't have anybody else."

"Mebbe we can have some new paper before then; I can put it on. I guess you won't have no call to be ashamed of your belongin's."

"We might have the wedding in the new barn," said Nanny, with gentle pettishness. "Why, mother, what makes you look so?"

Mrs. Penn had started, and was staring at her with a curious expression. She turned again to her work, and spread out a pattern carefully on the cloth. "Nothin'," said she.

Presently Adoniram clattered out of the yard in his two-wheeled dump cart, standing as proudly upright as a Roman charioteer. Mrs. Penn opened the door and stood there a minute looking out; the halloos of the men sounded louder.

It seemed to her all through the spring months that she heard nothing but the halloos and the noises of saws and hammers. The new barn grew fast. It was a fine edifice for this little village. Men came on pleasant Sundays, in their meeting suits and clean shirt bosoms, and stood around it admiringly. Mrs. Penn did not speak of it, and Adoniram did not mention it to her, although sometimes, upon a return from inspecting it, he bore himself with injured dignity.

"It's a strange thing how your mother feels about the new barn," he said, confidentially, to Sammy one day.

Sammy only grunted after an odd fashion for a boy; he had learned it from his father.

The barn was all completed ready for use by the third week in July. Adoniram had planned to move his stock in on Wednesday; on Tuesday he received a letter which changed his plans. He came in with it early in the morning. "Sammy's been to the post-office," said he, "an' I've got a letter from Hiram." Hiram was Mrs. Penn's brother, who lived in Vermont.

"Well," said Mrs. Penn, "what does he say about the folks?"

"I guess they're all right. He says he thinks if I come up country right off there's a chance to buy jest the kind of a horse I want." He stared reflectively out of the window at the new barn.

Mrs. Penn was making pies. She went on clapping the rolling-pin into the crust, although she was very pale, and her heart beat loudly.

"I dun' know but what I'd better go," said Adoniram. "I hate to go off jest now, right in the midst of hayin', but the ten-acre lot's cut, an' I guess Rufus an' the others can git along without me three or four days. I can't get a horse round here to suit me, nohow, an' I've got to have another for all that wood-haulin' in the fall. I told Hiram to watch out, an' if he got wind of a good horse to let me know. I guess I'd better go."

"I'll get out your clean shirt an' collar," said Mrs Penn calmly.

She laid out Adoniram's Sunday suit and his clean clothes on the bed in the little bedroom. She got his shaving-water and razor ready. At last she buttoned on his collar and fastened his black cravat.

Adoniram never wore his collar and cravat except on extra occasions. He held his head high, with a rasped dignity. When he was all ready, with his coat and hat brushed, and a lunch of pie and cheese in a paper bag, he hesitated on the threshold of the door. He looked at his wife, and his manner was defiantly apologetic. "*If* them cows come to-day, Sammy can drive 'em into the new barn," said he; "an' when they bring the hay up, they can pitch it in there."

"Well," replied Mrs. Penn.

Adoniram set his shaven face ahead and started. When he had cleared the door-step, he turned and looked back with a kind of nervous solemnity. "I shall be back by Saturday if nothin' happens," said he.

"Do be careful, father," returned his wife.

She stood in the door with Nanny at her elbow and watched him out of sight. Her eyes had a strange, doubtful expression in them; her peaceful forehead was contracted. She went in, and about her baking again. Nanny sat sewing. Her wedding-day was drawing nearer, and she was getting pale and thin with her steady sewing. Her mother kept glancing at her.

"Have you got that pain in your side this mornin'?" she asked.

"A little."

Mrs. Penn's face, as she worked, changed, her perplexed forehead smoothed, her eyes were steady, her lips firmly set. She formed a maxim for herself, although incoherently with her unlettered thoughts. "Unsolicited opportunities are the guide-posts of the Lord to the new roads of life," she repeated in effect, and she made up her mind to her course of action.

"S'posin' I *had* wrote to Hiram," she muttered once, when she was in the pantry — "s'posin' I had wrote, an' asked him if he knew of any horse? But I didn't, an' father's goin' wa'n't none of my doin'. It looks like a providence." Her voice rang out quite loud at the last.

"What you talkin' about, mother?" called Nanny.

"Nothin'."

Mrs. Penn hurried her baking; at eleven o'clock it was all done. The load of hay from the west field came slowly down the cart track, and drew up at the new barn. Mrs. Penn ran out. "Stop!" she screamed — "stop!"

The men stopped and looked; Sammy upreared from the top of the load, and stared at his mother.

"Stop!" she cried out again. "Don't you put the hay in that barn; put it in the old one."

"Why, he said to put it in here," returned one of the hay-makers, wonderingly. He was a young man, a neighbor's son, whom Adoniram hired by the year to help on the farm.

"Don't you put the hay in the new barn; there's room enough in the old one, ain't there?" said Mrs. Penn.

"Room enough," returned the hired man, in his thick, rustic tones. "Didn't need the new barn, nohow, far as room's concerned. Well, I s'pose he changed his mind." He took hold of the horses' bridles.

Mrs. Penn went back to the house. Soon the kitchen windows were darkened, and a fragrance like warm honey came into the room.

Nanny laid down her work. "I thought father wanted them to put the hay into the new barn?" she said, wonderingly.

"It's all right," replied her mother.

Sammy slid down from the load of hay, and came in to see if dinner was ready.

"I ain't goin' to get a regular dinner to-day, as long as father's gone," said his mother. "I've let the fire go out. You can have some bread an' milk an' pie. I thought we could get along." She set out some bowls of milk, some bread, and a pie on the kitchen table. "You'd better eat your dinner now," said she. "You might jest as well get through with it. I want you to help me afterward."

Nanny and Sammy stared at each other. There was something strange in their mother's manner. Mrs. Penn did not eat anything herself. She went into the pantry, and they heard her moving dishes while they ate. Presently she came out with a pile of plates. She got the clothes-basket out of the shed, and packed them in it. Nanny and Sammy watched. She brought out cups and saucers, and put them in with the plates.

"What you goin' to do, mother?" inquired Nanny, in a timid voice. A sense of something unusual made her tremble, as if it were a ghost. Sammy rolled his eyes over his pie.

"You'll see what I'm goin' to do," replied Mrs. Penn. "If you're through, Nanny, I want you to go up-stairs an' pack up your things; an' I want you, Sammy, to help me take down the bed in the bedroom."

"Oh, mother, what for?" gasped Nanny.

"You'll see."

During the next few hours a feat was performed by this simple, pious New England mother which was equal in its way to Wolfe's storming of the Heights of Abraham. It took no more genius and audacity of bravery for Wolfe to cheer his wondering solders up those steep precipices, under the sleeping eyes of the enemy, than for Sarah Penn, at the head of her children, to move all their little household goods into the new barn while her husband was away.

Nanny and Sammy followed their mother's instructions without a murmur; indeed, they were overawed. There is a certain uncanny and superhuman quality about all such purely original undertakings as their mother's was to them. Nanny went back and forth with her light loads, and Sammy tugged with sober energy.

At five o'clock in the afternoon the little house in which the Penns had lived for forty years had emptied itself into the new barn.

Every builder builds somewhat for unknown purposes, and is in a measure a prophet. The architect of Adoniram Penn's barn, while he designed it for the comfort of four-footed animals, had planned better than he knew for the comfort of humans. Sarah Penn saw at a glance its possibilities. Those great box-stalls, with quilts hung before them, would make better bedrooms than the one she had occupied for forty years, and there was a tight carriage-room. The harness-room, with its chimney and shelves, would make a kitchen of her dreams. The great middle space would make a parlor, by-and-by, fit for a palace. Up stairs there was as much room as down. With partitions and windows, what a house would there be! Sarah looked at the row of stanchions before the allotted space for cows, and reflected that she would have her front entry there.

At six o'clock the stove was up in the harness-room, the kettle was boiling, and the table set for tea. It looked almost as home-like as the abandoned house across the yard had ever done. The young hired man milked, and Sarah directed him calmly to bring the milk to the new barn. He came gaping, dropping little blots of foam from the brimming pails on the grass. Before the next morning he had spread the story of Adoniram Penn's wife moving into the new barn all over the little village. Men assembled in the store and talked it over, women with shawls over their heads scuttled into each other's houses before their work was done. Any deviation from the ordinary course of life in this quiet town was enough to stop all progress in it. Everybody paused to look at the staid, independent figure on the side track. There was a difference of opinion with regard to her. Some held her to be insane; some, of a lawless and rebellious spirit.

Friday the minister went to see her. It was in the forenoon, and she was at the barn door shelling pease for dinner. She looked up and returned his salutation with dignity, then she went on with her work. She did not invite him in. The saintly expression of her face remained fixed, but there was an angry flush over it.

The minister stood awkwardly before her, and talked. She handled the pease as if they were bullets. At last she looked up, and her eyes showed the spirit that her meek front had covered for a lifetime.

"There ain't no use talkin', Mr. Hersey," said she. "I've thought it all over an' over, an' I believe I'm doin' what's right. I've made it the subject of prayer, an' it's betwixt me an' the Lord an' Adoniram. There ain't no call for nobody else to worry about it."

"Well, of course, if you have brought it to the Lord in prayer, and feel satisfied that you are doing right, Mrs. Penn," said the minister, helplessly. His thin gray-bearded face was pathetic. He was a sickly man; his youthful confidence had cooled; he had to scourge himself up to some of his pastoral duties as relentlessly as a Catholic ascetic, and then he was prostrated by the smart.

"I think it's right jest as much as I think it was right for our forefathers to come over from the old country 'cause they didn't have what belonged to 'em," said Mrs. Penn. She arose. The barn threshold might have been Plymouth Rock from her bearing. "I don't doubt you mean well, Mr. Hersey," said she, "but there are things people hadn't ought to interfere with. I've been a member of the church for over forty year. I've got my own mind an' my own feet, an' I'm goin' to think my own thoughts an' go my own ways, an' nobody but the Lord is goin' to dictate to me unless I've a mind to have him. Won't you come in an' set down? How is Mis' Hersey?"

"She is well, I thank you," replied the minister. He added some more perplexed apologetic remarks; then he retreated.

He could expound the intricacies of every character study in the Scriptures, he was competent to grasp the Pilgrim Fathers and all historical innovators, but Sarah Penn was beyond him. He could deal with primal cases, but parallel ones worsted him. But, after all, although it was aside from his province, he wondered more how Adoniram Penn would deal with his wife than how the Lord would. Everybody shared the wonder. When Adoniram's four new cows arrived, Sarah ordered three to be put in the old barn, the other in the house shed where the cooking-stove had stood. That added to the excitement. It was whispered that all four cows were domiciled in the house.

Towards sunset on Saturday, when Adoniram was expected home, there was a knot of men in the road near the new barn. The hired man had milked, but he still hung around the premises. Sarah Penn had supper all ready. There were brown-bread and baked beans and a custard pie, it was the supper that Adoniram loved on a Saturday night. She had on a clean calico, and she bore herself imperturbably. Nanny and Sammy kept close at her heels. Their eyes were large, and Nanny was full of nervous tremors. Still there was to them more pleasant excitement than anything else. An inborn confidence in their mother over their father asserted itself.

Sammy looked out of the harness-room window. "There he is," he announced, in an awed whisper. He and Nanny peeped around the casing. Mrs. Penn kept on about her work. The children watched Adoniram leave the new horse standing in the drive while he went to the house door. It was fastened. Then he went around to the shed. That door was seldom locked, even when the family was away. The thought how her father would be confronted by the cow flashed upon Nanny. There was a hysterical sob in her throat. Adoniram emerged from the shed and stood looking about in a dazed fashion. His lips moved; he was saying something, but they could not hear what it was. The hired man was peeping around a corner of the old barn, but nobody saw him.

Adoniram took the new horse by the bridle and led him across the yard to the new barn. Nanny and Sammy slunk close to their mother. The barn doors rolled back, and there stood Adoniram, with the long mild face of the great Canadian farm horse looking over his shoulder.

Nanny kept behind her mother, but Sammy stepped suddenly forward, and stood in front of her.

Adoniram stared at the group. "What on airth you all down here for?" said he. "What's the matter over to the house?"

"We've come here to live, father," said Sammy. His shrill voice quavered out bravely.

"What" — Adoniram sniffed — "what is it smells like cookin?" said he. He stepped forward and looked in the open door of the harness-room. Then he turned to his wife. His old bristling face was pale and frightened. "What on airth does this mean, mother?" he gasped.

"You come in here, father," said Sarah. She led the way into the harness-room and shut the door. "Now, father," said she, "you needn't be scared. I ain't crazy. There ain't nothin' to be upset over. But we've come here to live, an' we're goin' to live here. We've got jest as good a right here as new horses an' cows. The house wa'n't fit for us to live in any longer, an' I made up my mind I wa'n't goin' to stay there. I've done my duty by you forty year, an' I'm goin' to do it now; but I'm goin' to live here. You've got to put in some windows and partitions; an' you'll have to buy some furniture."

"Why, mother!" the old man gasped.

"You'd better take your coat off an' get washed — there's the wash-basin — an' then we'll have supper."

"Why, mother!"

Sammy went past the window, leading the new horse to the old barn. The old man saw him, and shook his head speechlessly. He tried to take off his coat, but his arms seemed to lack the power. His wife helped him. She poured some water into the tin basin, and put in a piece of soap. She got the comb and brush, and smoothed his thin gray hair after he had washed. Then she put the beans, hot bread and tea on the table. Sammy came in, and the family drew up. Adoniram sat looking dazedly at his plate, and they waited.

"Ain't you goin' to ask a blessin', father?" said Sarah.

And the old man bent his head and mumbled.

All through the meal he stopped eating at intervals, and stared furtively at his wife; but he ate well. The home food tasted good to him, and his old frame was too sturdily healthy to be affected by his mind. But after supper he went out, and sat down on the step of the smaller door at the right of the barn, through which he had meant his Jerseys to pass in stately file, but which Sarah designed for her front house door, and he leaned his head on his hands.

After the supper dishes were cleared away and the milk-pans washed, Sarah went out to him. The twilight was deepening. There was a·clear green glow in the sky. Before them stretched the smooth level of field; in the distance was a cluster of hay-stacks like the huts of a village; the air was very cool and calm and sweet. The landscape might have been an ideal one of peace.

Sarah bent over and touched her husband on one of his thin, sinewy shoulders. "Father!"

The old man's shoulders heaved; he was weeping.

"Why, don't do so, father," said Sarah.

"I'll — put up the — partitions, an' — everything you — want, mother."

Sarah put her apron up to her face; she was overcome by her own triumph.

Adoniram was like a fortress whose walls had no active resistance, and went down the instant the right besieging tools were used. "Why, mother," he said, hoarsely, "I hadn't no idee you was so set on't as all this comes to."

The Storm
by Kate Chopin

1

The leaves were so still that even Bibi thought it was going to rain.
Bobinôt, who was accustomed to converse on terms of perfect equality
with his little son, called the child's attention to certain sombre clouds
that were rolling with sinister inattention from the west, accompanied
by a sullen, threatening roar. They were at Friedheimer's store and decided
to remain there till the storm had passed. They sat within the door on
two empty kegs. Bibi was four years old and looked very wise.

"Mama'll be 'fraid, yes," he suggested with blinking eyes.

"She'll shut the house. Maybe she got Silvie helpin' her this evenin',"
Bobinôt responded reassuringly.

"No; she ent got Sylvie. Syvie was helpin' her yistiday," piped Bibi.

Bobinôt arose and going across to the counter purchased a can of
shrimps, of which Calixta was very fond. Then he returned to his perch
on the keg and sat stolidly holding the can of shrimps while the storm
burst. It shook the wooden store and seemed to be ripping great furrows
in the distant field. Bibi laid his little hand on his father's knee and was
not afraid.

2

Calixta, at home, felt no uneasiness for their safety. She sat at a side
window sewing furiously on a sewing machine. She was greatly occupied
and did not notice the approaching storm. But she felt very warm and
often stopped to mop her face on which the perspiration gathered in
beads. She unfastened her white sacque at the throat. It began to grow
dark, and suddenly realising the situation she got up hurriedly and went
about closing windows and doors.

Out on the small front gallery she had hung Bobinôt's Sunday clothes
to air and she hastened out to gather them before the rain fell. As she
stepped outside, Alcée Laballière rode in at the gate. She had not seen
him very often since her marriage, and never alone. She stood there with
Bobinôt's coat in her hands, and the big raindrops began to fall. Alcée
rode his horse under the shelter of a side projection where the chickens
had huddled and there were plough and a harrow piled up in the corner.

"May I come and wait on your gallery till the storm is over, Calixta?"
he asked.

"Come 'long in, M'sieur Alcée."

His voice and her own startled her as if from a trance, and she seized Bobinôt's vest. Alcée, mounting to the porch, grabbed the trousers and snatched Bibi's braided jacket that was about to be carried away by a sudden gust of wind. He expressed an intention to remain outside, but it was soon apparent that he might as well have been out in the open: the water beat in upon the boards in driving sheets, and he went inside, closing the door after him. It was even necessary to put something beneath the door to keep the water out.

"My! what a rain! It's good two years sence it rain' like that," exclaimed Calixta as she rolled up a piece of bagging and Alcée helped her to thrust it beneath the crack.

She was a little fuller of figure than five years before when she married; but she had lost nothing of her vivacity. Her blue eyes still retained their melting quality; and her yellow hair, dishevelled by the wind and rain, kinked more stubbornly than ever about her ears and temples.

The rain beat upon the low, shingled roof with a force and clatter that threatened to break an entrance and deluge them there. They were in the dining-room — the sitting-room — the general utility room. Adjoining was her bedroom, with Bibi's couch along side her own. The door stood open, and the room with its white, monumental bed, its closed shutters, looked dim and mysterious.

Alcée flung himself into a rocker and Calixta nervously began to gather up from the floor the lengths of a cotton sheet which she had been sewing.

"If this keeps up, *Dieu sait* if the levees goin' to stan' it!" she exclaimed.

"What have you got to do with the levees?"

"I got enough to do! An' there's Bobinôt with Bibi out in that storm — if he only didn't left Friedheimer's!"

"Let us hope, Calixta, that Bobinôt's got sense enough to come in out of a cyclone."

She went and stood at the window with a greatly disturbed look on her face. She wiped the frame that was clouded with moisture. It was stiflingly hot. Alcée got up and joined her at the window, looking over her shoulder. The rain was coming down in sheets obscuring the view of far-off cabins and enveloping the distant wood in a grey mist. The playing of the lightning was incessant. A bolt struck a tall chinaberry tree at the edge of the field. It filled all visible space with a blinding glare and the crash seemed to invade the very boards they stood upon.

Calixta put her hands to her eyes, and with a cry, staggered backwards. Alcée's arm encircled her, and for an instant he drew her close and spasmodically to him.

"*Bonté!*" she cried, releasing herself from his encircling arm and retreating from the window. "The house'll go next! If I only knew w'ere Bibi was!" She would not compose herself; she would not be seated.

Alcée clasped her shoulders and looked into her face. The contact of her warm, palpitating body when he had unthinkingly drawn her into his arms, had aroused all the old-time infatuation and desire for her flesh.

"Calixta," he said, "don't be frightened. Nothing can happen. The house is too low to be struck, with so many tall trees standing about. There! aren't you going to be quiet? say, aren't you?" He pushed her hair back from her face that was warm and steaming. Her lips were as red and moist as pomegranate seed. Her white neck and a glimpse of her full, firm bosom disturbed him powerfully. As she glanced up at him the fear in her liquid blue eyes had given place to a drowsy gleam that unconsciously betrayed a sensuous desire. He looked down into her eyes and there was nothing for him to do but to gather her lips in a kiss. It reminded him of Assumption.

"Do you remember — in Assumption, Calixta?" he asked in a low voice broken by passion. Oh! she remembered; for in Assumption he had kissed her and kissed and kissed her; until his senses would well nigh fail, and to save her he would resort to a desperate flight. If she was not an immaculate dove in those days, she was still inviolate, a passionate creature whose very defencelessness had made her defence, against which his honour forbade him to prevail. Now — well, now — her lips seemed in a manner free to be tasted, as well as her round, white throat and her whiter breasts.

They did not heed the crashing torrents, and the roar of the elements made her laugh as she lay in his arms. She was a revelation in that dim, mysterious chamber; as white as the couch she lay upon. Her firm, elastic flesh that was knowing for the first time its birthright, was like a creamy lily that the sun invites to contribute its breath and perfume to the undying life of the world.

The generous abundance of her passion, without guile or trickery, was like a white flame which penetrated and found response in depths of his own sensuous nature that had never yet been reached.

When he touched her breasts they gave themselves up in quivering ecstasy, inviting his lips. Her mouth was a fountain of delight. And when he possessed her, they seemed to swoon together at the very borderland of life's mystery.

He stayed cushioned upon her, breathless, dazed, enervated, with his heart beating like a hammer upon her. With one hand she clasped his head, her lips lightly touching his forehead. The other hand stroked with a soothing rhythm his muscular shoulders.

The growl of the thunder was distant and passing away. The rain beat softly upon the shingles, inviting them to drowsiness and sleep. But they dared not yield.

The rain was over; and the sun was turning the glistening green world into a palace of gems. Calixta, on the gallery, watched Alcée ride away. He turned and smiled at her with a beaming face, and she lifted her pretty chin in the air and laughed aloud.

3

Bobinôt and Bibi, trudging home, stopped without at the cistern to make themselves presentable.

"My! Bibi, w'at will yo' mama say! You ought to be ashame'. You oughtn' put on those good pants. Look at 'em! An' that mud on yo' collar! How you got that mud on yo' collar, Bibi? I never saw such a boy!" Bibi was the picture of pathetic resignation. Bobinôt was the embodiment of serious solicitude as he strove to remove from his own person and his son's the signs of their tramp over heavy roads and through wet fields. He scraped the mud off Bibi's bare legs and feet with a stick and carefully removed all traces from his heavy brogans. Then, prepared for the worst — the meeting with an over-scrupulous housewife, they entered cautiously at the back door.

Calixta was preparing supper. She had set the table and was dripping coffee at the hearth. She sprang up as they came in.

"Oh, Bobinôt! You back! My! but I was uneasy. W'ere you been during the rain? An' Bibi? He ain't wet? He ain't hurt?" She had clasped Bibi and was kissing him effusively. Bobinôt's explanation and apologies which he had been composing all along the way, died on his lips as Calixta felt him to see if he were dry, and seemed to express nothing but satisfaction at their safe return.

"I brought you some shrimps, Calixta," offered Bobinôt, hauling the can from his ample side pocket and laying it on the table.

"Shrimps! Oh, Bobinôt! You too good fo' anything!" and she gave him a smacking kiss on the cheek that resounded. "*J'vous réponds*, we'll have a feas' tonight! Umph–umph!"

Bobinôt and Bibi began to relax and enjoy themselves, and when the three seated themselves at table they laughed much and so loud that anyone might have heard them as far away as Laballière's.

4

Alcée Laballière wrote to his wife, Clarisse, that night. It was a loving letter, full of tender solicitude. He told her not to hurry back, but if she and the babies liked it at Biloxi, to stay a month longer. He was getting on nicely, and though he missed them, he was willing to bear the separation a while longer — realising that their health and pleasure were the first things to be considered.

5

As for Clarisse, she was charmed upon receiving her husband's letter. She and the babies were doing well. The society was agreeable; many of her old friends and acquaintances were at the bay. And the first free breath since her marriage seemed to restore the pleasant liberty of her maiden days. Devoted as she was to her husband, their intimate conjugal life was something which she was more than willing to forgo for a while.

So the storm passed and everyone was happy.

Bro'r Abr'm Jimson's Wedding
A Christmas Story
by Pauline E. Hopkins

It was a Sunday in early spring the first time that Caramel Johnson dawned on the congregation of ——— Church in a populous New England city.

The Afro-Americans of that city are well-to-do, being of a frugal nature, and considering it a lasting disgrace for any man among them, desirous of social standing in the community, not to make himself comfortable in this world's goods against the coming time, when old age creeps on apace and renders him unfit for active business.

Therefore the members of the said church had not waited to be exhorted by reformers to own their unpretentious homes and small farms outside the city limits, but they vied with each other in efforts to accumulate a small competency urged thereto by a realization of what pressing needs the future might bring, or that might have been because of the constant example of white neighbors, and a due respect for the dignity which *their* foresight had brought to the superior race.

Of course, these small Vanderbilts and Astors of a darker hue must have a place of worship in accord with their worldly prosperity, and so it fell out that ——— church was the richest plum in the ecclesiastical pudding, and greatly sought by scholarly divines as a resting place for four years, — the extent of the time-limit allowed by conference to the men who must be provided with suitable charges according to the demands of their energy and scholarship.

The attendance was unusually large for morning service, and a restless movement was noticeable all through the sermon. How strange a thing is nature; the change of the seasons announces itself in all humanity as well as in the trees and flowers, the grass, and in the atmosphere. Something within us responds instantly to the touch of kinship that dwells in all life.

The air, soft and balmy, laden with rich promise for the future, came through the massive, half-open windows, stealing in refreshing waves upon the congregation. The sunlight fell through the colored glass of the windows in prismatic hues, and dancing all over the lofty star-gemmed ceiling, painted the hue of the broad vault of heaven, creeping down in crinkling shadows to touch the deep garnet cushions of the sacred desk, and the rich wood of the altar with a hint of gold.

The offertory was ended. The silvery cadences of a rich soprano voice still lingered on the air, "O, Worship the Lord in the beauty of holiness." There was a suppressed feeling of expectation, but not the faintest rustle as the minister rose in the pulpit, and after a solemn pause, gave the usual invitation:

"If there is anyone in this congregation desiring to unite with this church, either by letter or on probation, please come forward to the altar."

The words had not died upon his lips when a woman started from her seat near the door and passed up the main aisle. There was a sudden commotion on all sides. Many heads were turned — it takes so little to interest a church audience. The girls in the choir-box leaned over the rail, nudged each other and giggled, while the men said to one another, "She's a stunner, and no mistake."

The candidate for membership, meanwhile, had reached the altar railing and stood before the man of God, to whom she had handed her letter from a former Sabbath home, with head decorously bowed as became the time and the holy place. There was no denying the fact that she was a pretty girl; brown of skin, small of feature, with an ever-lurking gleam of laughter in eyes coal black. Her figure was slender and beautifully moulded, with a seductive grace in the undulating walk and erect carriage. But the chief charm of the sparkling dark face lay in its intelligence, and the responsive play of facial expression which was enhanced by two mischievous dimples pressed into the rounded cheeks by the caressing fingers of the god of Love.

The minister whispered to the candidate, coughed, blew his nose on his snowy clerical handkerchief, and, finally, turned to the expectant congregation:

"Sister Chocolate Caramel Johnson—"

He was interrupted by a snicker and a suppressed laugh, again from the choir-box, and an audible whisper which sounded distinctly throughout the quiet church,—

"I'd get the Legislature to change that if it was mine, 'deed I would!" then silence profound caused by the reverend's stern glance of reproval bent on the offenders in the choir-box.

"Such levity will not be allowed among the members of the choir. If it occurs again, I shall ask the choir master for the names of the offenders and have their places taken by those more worthy to be gospel singers."

Thereupon Mrs. Tilly Anderson whispered to Mrs. Nancy Tobias that, "them choir gals is the mos' deceivines' hussies in the church, an' for my part, I'm glad the pastor called 'em down. That sister's too good lookin' for 'em, an' they'll be after her like er pack o' houn's, min' me, Sis' Tobias."

Sister Tobias ducked her head in her lap and shook her fat sides in laughing appreciation of the sister's foresight.

Order being restored the minister proceeded:

"Sister Chocolate Caramel Johnson brings a letter to us from our sister church in Nashville, Tennessee. She has been a member in good standing for ten years, having been received into fellowship at ten years of age. She leaves them now, much to their regret, to pursue the study of music at one of the large conservatories in this city, and they recommend her to our love and care. You know the contents of the letter. All in favor of giving Sister Johnson the right hand of fellowship, please manifest the same by a rising vote." The whole congregation rose.

"Contrary minded? None. The ayes have it. Be seated friends. Sister Johnson, it gives me great pleasure to receive you into this church. I welcome you to its joys and sorrows. May God bless you, Brother Jimson?" (Brother Jimson stepped from his seat to the pastor's side.) "I assign this sister to your class. Sister Johnson, this is Brother Jimson, your future spiritual teacher."

Brother Jimson shook the hand of his new member, warmly, and she returned to her seat. The minister pronounced the benediction over the waiting congregation; the organ burst into richest melody. Slowly the crowd of worshippers dispersed.

Abraham Jimson had made his money as a janitor for the wealthy people of the city. He was a bachelor, and when reproved by some good Christian brother for still dwelling in single blessedness always offered as an excuse that he had been too busy to think of a wife, but that now he was "well fixed," pecuniarily, he would begin to "look over" his lady friends for a suitable companion.

He owned a house in the suburbs and a fine brick dwelling-house in the city proper. He was a trustee of prominence in the church, in fact, its "solid man," and his opinion was sought and his advice acted upon by his associates on the Board. It was felt that any lady in the congregation would be proud to know herself his choice.

When Caramel Johnson received the right hand of fellowship, her aunt, the widow Maria Nash, was ahead in the race for the wealthy class-leader. It had been neck-and-neck for a while between her and Sister Viney Peters, but, finally it had settled down to Sister Maria with a hundred to one, among the sporting members of the Board, that she carried off the prize, for Sister Maria owned a house adjoining Brother Jimson's in the suburbs, and property counts these days.

Sister Nash had "no idea" when she sent for her niece to come to B. that the latter would prove a rival; her son Andy was as good as engaged to Caramel. But it is always the unexpected that happens. Caramel came, and Brother Jimson had no eyes for the charms of other women after he had gazed into her coal black orbs, and watched her dimples come and go.

Caramel decided to accept a position as housemaid in order to help defray the expenses of her tuition at the conservatory, and Brother Jimson interested himself so warmly in her behalf that she soon had a situation in the home of his richest patron where it was handy for him to chat with her about the business of the church, and the welfare of her soul, in general. Things progressed very smoothly until the fall, when one day sister Maria had occasion to call, unexpectedly, on her niece and found Brother Jimson basking in her smiles while he enjoyed a sumptuous dinner of roast chicken and fixings.

To say that Sister Maria was "set way back" would not accurately describe her feelings; but from that time Abraham Jimson knew that he had a secret foe in the Widow Nash.

Before many weeks had passed it was publicly known that Brother Jimson would lead Caramel Johnson to the altar "come Christmas." There was much sly speculation as to the "widder's gittin' left," and how she took it from those who had cast hopeless glances toward the chief man of the church. Great preparations were set on foot for the wedding festivities. The bride's trousseau was a present from the groom and included a white satin wedding gown and a costly gold watch. The town house was refurbished, and a trip to New York was in contemplation.

"Hump!" grunted Sister Nash when told the rumors, "there's no fool like an ol' fool. Car'mel's a han'ful he'll fin', ef he gits her."

"I reckon he'll git her all right, Sis' Nash," laughed the neighbor, who had run in to talk over the news.

"I've said my word an' I ain't goin' change it, Sis'r. Min' me, I says, *ef he gits her*, an' I mean it."

Andy Nash was also a member of Brother Jimson's class; he possessed, too, a strong sweet baritone voice which made him a great value to the choir. He was an immense success in the social life of the city, and had created sad havoc with the hearts of the colored girls; he could have his pick of the best of them because of his graceful figure and fine easy manners. Until Caramel had been dazzled by the wealth of her elderly lover, she had considered herself fortunate as the lady of his choice.

It was Sunday, three weeks before the wedding that Andy resolved to have it out with Caramel.

"She's been hot an' she's been col', an' now she's luke warm, an' today ends it before this gent-man sleeps," he told himself as he stood before the glass and tied his pale blue silk tie in a stunning knot, and settled his glossy tile at a becoming angle.

Brother Jimson's class was a popular one and had a large membership; the hour spent there was much enjoyed, even by visitors. Andy went into the vestry early, resolved to meet Caramel if possible. She was there, at the back of the room sitting alone on a settee. Andy immediately seated himself in the vacant place by her side. There were whispers and much head-shaking among the few early worshippers, all of whom knew the story of the young fellow's romance and his disappointment.

As he dropped into the seat beside her, Caramel turned her large eyes on him intently, speculatively, with a doubtful sort of curiosity suggested in her expression, as to how he took her flagrant desertion.

"Howdy, Car'mel?" was his greeting without a shade of resentment.

"I'm well; no need to ask how you are," was the quick response. There was a mixture of cordiality and coquetry in her manner. Her eyes narrowed and glittered under lowered lids, as she gave him a long side-glance. How could she help showing her admiration for the supple young giant beside her? "Surely," she told herself, "I'll have long time enough to git sick of old rheumatics," her pet name for her elderly lover.

"I ain't sick much," was Andy's surly reply.

He leaned his elbow on the back of the settee and gave his recreant sweetheart a flaming glance of mingled love and hate, oblivious to the presence of the assembled class-members.

"You ain't over friendly these days, Car'mel, but I gits news of your capers 'roun' 'bout some of the members."

"My — Yes?" she answered as she flashed her great eyes at him in pretended surprise. He laughed a laugh not good to hear.

"Yes," he drawled. Then he added with sudden energy, "Are you goin' to tie up to old Rheumatism sure 'nuff, come Chris'mas?"

"Come Chris'mas, Andy, I be. I hate to tell you but I have to do it."

He recoiled as from a blow. As for the girl, she found a keen relish in the situation: it flattered her vanity.

"How comes it you've changed your mind, Car'mel, 'bout you an' me? You've tol' me often that I was your first choice."

"We–ll," she drawled, glancing uneasily about her and avoiding her aunt's gaze, which she knew was bent upon her every movement, "I did reckon once I would. But a man with money suits me best, an' you ain't got a cent."

"No more have you. You ain't no better than other women to work an' help a man along, is you?"

The color flamed an instant in her face turning the dusky skin to a deep, dull red.

"Andy Nash, you always was a fool, an' as ignerunt as a wil' Injun. I mean to have a sure nuff brick house an' plenty of money. That makes people respec' you. Why don' you quit bein' so shifless and save your money. You ain't worth your salt."

"Your head's turned with pianorer-playin' an' livin' up North. Ef you'll turn *him* off an' come back home, I'll turn over a new leaf. Car'mel," his voice was soft and persuasive enough now.

She had risen to her feet; her eyes flashed, her face was full of pride.

"I won't. I've quit likin' you, Andy Nash."

"Are you in earnest?" he asked, also rising from his seat.

"Dead earnes'."

"Then there's no more to be said."

He spoke calmly, not raising his voice above a whisper. She stared at him in surprise. Then he added as he swung on his heel preparatory to leaving her:

"You ain't got him yet, my gal. But remember, I'm waitin' for you when you need me."

While this whispered conference was taking place in the back of the vestry, Brother Jimson had entered, and many an anxious glance he cast in the direction of the couple. Andy made his way slowly to his mother's side as Brother Jimson rose in his place to open the meeting. There was a commotion on all sides as the members rustled down on their knees for prayer. Widow Nash whispered to her son as they knelt side by side:

"How did you make out, Andy?"

"Didn't make out at all, mammy; she's as obstinate as a mule."

"Well, then, there's only one thing mo' to do."

Andy was unpleasant company for the remainder of the day. He sought, but found nothing to palliate Caramel's treachery. He had only surly, bitter words for his companions who ventured to address him, as the outward expression of inward tumult. The more he brooded over his wrongs the worse he felt. When he went to work on Monday morning he was feeling vicious. He had made up his mind to do something desperate. The wedding should not come off. He would be avenged.

Andy went about his work at the hotel in gloomy silence unlike his usual gay hilarity. It happened that all the female help at the great hostelry was white, and on that particular Monday morning was the duty of Bridget McCarthy's watch to clean the floors. Bridget was also not in the best of humors, for Pat McClosky, her special company, had gone to the priest's with her rival, Kate Connerton, on Sunday afternoon, and Bridget had not yet got over the effects of a strong rum punch taken to quiet her nerves after hearing the news.

Bridget had scrubbed a wide swathe of the marble floor when Andy came through with a rush order carried in scientific style high above his head, balanced on one hand. Intent upon satisfying the guest who was princely in his "tips," Andy's unwary feet became entangled in the maelstrom of brooms, scrubbing-brushes and pails. In an instant the "order" was sliding over the floor in a general mix-up.

To say Bridget was mad wouldn't do her state justice. She forgot herself and her surroundings and relieved her feelings in elegant Irish, ending a tirade of abuse by calling Andy a "wall-eyed, bandy-legged nagur."

Andy couldn't stand that from "common, po' white trash," so calling all his science into play he struck out straight from the shoulder with his right, and brought her a swinging blow on the mouth, which seated her neatly in the five-gallon bowl of freshly made lobster salad which happened to be standing on the floor behind her.

There was a wail from the kitchen force that reached to every department. It being the busiest hour of the day when they served dinner, the dish-washers and scrubbers went on a strike against the "nagur who struck Bridget McCarthy, the baste," mingled with cries of "lynch him!" Instantly the great basement floor was a battle ground. Every colored man seized whatever was handiest and ranged himself by Andy's side, and stood ready to receive the onslaught of the Irish brigade. For the sake of peace, and sorely against his inclinations, the proprietor surrendered Andy to the police on a charge of assault and battery.

On Wednesday morning of that eventful week, Brother Jimson wended his way to his house in the suburbs to collect the rent. Unseen by the eye of man, he was wrestling with a problem that had shadowed his life for many years. No one on earth suspected him unless it might be the widow. Brother Jimson boasted of his consistent Christian life — rolled his piety like a sweet morsel beneath his tongue, and had deluded himself into thinking that *he* could do no sin. There were scoffers in the church who doubted the genuineness of his pretentions, and he believed that there was a movement on foot against his power led by Widow Nash.

Brother Jimson groaned in bitterness of spirit. His only fear was that he might be parted from Caramel. If he lost her he felt that all happiness in life was over for him, and anxiety gave him a sickening feeling of unrest. He was tormented, too, by jealousy; and when he was called upon by Andy's anxious mother to rescue her son from the clutches of the law, he had promised her fair enough, but in reality resolved to do nothing but — tell the judge that Andy was a dangerous character whom it was best to quell by severity. The pastor and all the other influential members of the church were at court on Tuesday, but Brother Jimson was conspicuous by his absence.

Today Brother Jimson resolved to call on Sister Nash, and as he had heard nothing of the outcome of the trial, make cautious inquiries concerning that, and also sound her on the subject nearest his heart.

He opened the gate and walked down the side path to the back door. From within came the rhythmic sound of a rubbing board. The brother knocked, and then cleared his throat with a preliminary cough.

"Come," called a voice within. As the door swung open it revealed the spare form of the widow, who with sleeves rolled above her elbows stood at the tub cutting her way through piles of foaming suds.

"Mornin', Sis' Nash! How's all?"

"That you, Bro'r Jimson? How's yourself? Take a cheer an' make yourself to home."

"Cert'nly, Sis' Nash, don' care ef I do," and the good brother scanned the sister with an eagle eye. "Yas'm I'm purty tol'rable these days, thank God. Bleeg'd to you, Sister, I jes' will stop an' res' myself befo' I repair myself back to the city." He seated himself in the most comfortable chair in the room, tilted it on the two back legs against the wall, lit his pipe and with a grunt of satisfaction settled back to watch the white rings of smoke curl about his head.

"These are mighty ticklish times, Sister. How's you continue on the journey? Is you strong in the faith?"

"I've got the faith, my brother, but I ain't on no mountain top this week. I'm way down in the valley; I'm jes' coaxin' the Lord to keep me sweet," and Sister Nash wiped the suds from her hands and prodded the clothes in the boiler with the clothes-stick, added fresh pieces and went on with her work.

"This is a worl' strewed with wrecks an' floatin' with tears. It's the valley of tribulation. May your faith continue. I hear Jim Jinkins has bought a farm up Taunton way."

"Wan'ter know!"

"Doctor tells me Bro'r Waters is comin' after Chris-mus. They do say as how he's stirrin' up things turrible; he's easin' his min' on this lynchin' business, an' it's high time — high time."

"Sho! Don't say so! What you reck'n he's goin' tell us now, Brother Jimson?"

"Suthin' 'stonishin', Sister; it'll stir the country from end to end. Yes'm the Council is powerful strong as an organ'zation."

"Sho! sho!" and the "thrub, thrub" of the board could be heard a mile away.

The conversation flagged. Evidently Widow Nash was not in a talkative mood that morning. The brother was disappointed.

"Well, it's mighty comfort'ble here, but I mus' be goin'."

"What's your hurry, Brother Jimson?"

"Business, Sister, business," and the brother brought his chair forward preparatory to rising. "Where's Andy? How'd he come out of that little difficulty?"

"Locked up."

"You don' mean to say he's in jail?"

"Yes, he's in jail 'tell I git's his bail."

"What might the sentence be, Sister?"

"Twenty dollars fine or six months at the Islan'." There was silence for a moment, broken only by the "thrub, thrub" of the washboard, while the smoke curled upward from Brother Jimson's pipe as he enjoyed a few last puffs.

"These are mighty ticklish times, Sister. Po' Andy, the way of the transgressor is hard."

Sister Nash took her hands out of the tub and stood with arms akimbo, a statue of Justice carved in ebony. Her voice was like the trump of doom.

"Yes; an' men like you is the cause of it. You leadin' men with money an' chances don' do your duty. I arst you, I arst you fair, to go down to the jedge an' bail that po' chile out. Did you go? No; you hard-faced old devil, you lef him be there, an' I had to git the money from my white folks. Yes, an' I'm breakin' my back now, over that pile of clo's to pay that twenty dollars. Um! all the trouble comes to us women."

"That's so, Sister; that's the livin' truth," murmured Brother Jimson furtively watching the rising storm and wondering where the lightning of her speech would strike next.

"I tell you that it is our receiptfulness to each other is the reason we don' prosper an' God's a-punishin' us with fire an' with sward 'cause we's so jealous an' snaky to each other."

"That's so Sister; that's the livin' truth."

"Yes, sir; a nigger's boun' to be a nigger 'tell the trump of doom. You kin skin him, but he's a nigger still. Broad-cloth, biled shirts an' money won' make him more or less, no, Sir."

"That's so, Sister; that's jes' so."

"A nigger can't holp himself. White folks can run agin the law all the time an' they never gits caught, but a nigger! Every time he opens his mouth he puts his foot in it — got to hit that po' white trash gal in the mouth an' git jailed, an' leave his po'r ol' mother to work her fingers to the secon' jint to get him out. Um!"

"These are might ticklish times, Sister. Man's boun' to sin; it's his nat'ral state. I hope this will teach Andy humility of the sperit."

"A little humility'd be good for yourself, Abra'm Jimson." Sister Nash ceased her sobs and set her teeth hard.

"Lord, Sister Nash, what compar'son is there 'twixt me an' a worthless nigger like Andy? My business is with the salt of the earth, an' so I have dwelt ever since I was consecrated."

"Salt of the earth! But ef the salt has los' its saver how you goin' salt it ergin'? No, sir, you cain't do it; it mus' be cas' out an' trodded under foot of men. That's who's goin' happen you Abe Jimson, hyar me? An' I'd like to trod on you with my foot, an' every ol' good fer nuthin' bag o' salt like you," shouted Sister Nash. "You're a snake in the grass; you done stole the boy's gal an' then try to git him sent to the Islan'. You cain't deny it, fer the jedge done tol' me all you said, you ol' rhinoceros-hided hypercrite. Salt of the earth! You!"

Brother Jimson regretted that Widow Nash had found him out. Slowly he turned, settling his hat on the back of his head.

"Good mornin', Sister Nash. I ain't no hard feelin's agains' you. I too near to the kingdom to let trifles jar me. My bowels of compassion yearns over you, Sister, a pilgrim an' a stranger in this unfriendly worl'."

No answer from Sister Nash. Brother Jimson lingered.

"Good mornin', Sister," still no answer.

"I hope to see you at the weddin', Sister."

"Keep on hopin', I'll be there. That gal's my own sister's chile. What in time she wants of a rheumatic ol' sap-head like you for, beats me. I wouldn't marry you for no money, myself; no, sir; it's my belief that you've done goophered her."

"Yes, Sister; I've hearn tell of people refusin' befor' they was ask'd," he retorted, giving her a sly look.

For answer the widow grabbed the clothes-stick and flung it at him in speechless rage.

"My, what a temper it's got," remarked Brother Jimson soothingly as he dodged the shovel, the broom, the coal-hod and the stove-covers. But he sighed with relief as he turned into the street and caught the faint sound of the washboard now resumed.

To a New Englander the season of snow and ice with its clear biting atmosphere, is the ideal time for the great festival. Christmas morning dawned in royal splendor; the sun kissed the snowy streets and turned the icicles into brilliant stalactites. The bells rang a joyous call from every steeple, and soon the churches were crowded with eager worshippers — eager to hear again the oft-repeated, the wonderful story on which the heart of the whole Christian world feeds its faith and hope. Words of tender faith, marvellous in their simplicity fell from the lips of a world-renowned preacher, and touched the hearts of the listening multitude: "The winter sunshine is not more bright and clear than the atmosphere of living joy, which stretching back between our eyes and that picture of Bethlehem, shows us its beauty in unstained freshness. And as we open once again those chapters of the gospel in which the ever fresh and living picture stands, there seems from year to year always to come some newer, brighter meaning into the words that tell the tale.

St. Matthew says that when Jesus was born in Bethlehem the wise men came from the East to Jerusalem. The East means man's search after God; Jerusalem means God's search after man. The East means the religion of the devout soul; Jerusalem means the religion of the merciful God. The East means Job's cry, 'Oh, that I knew where I might find him!' Jerusalem means 'Immanuel — God with us.'"

Then the deep-toned organ joined the grand chorus of human voices in a fervent hymn of praise and thanksgiving:

> Lo! the Morning Star appeareth,
>   O'er the world His beams are cast;
> He the Alpha and Omega,
>   He, the Great, the First the Last!
> Hallelujah! hallelujah!
>   Let the heavenly portal ring!
> Christ is born, the Prince of glory!
>   Christ the Lord, Messiah, King!

Everyone of the prominence in church circles had been bidden to the Jimson wedding. The presents were many and costly. Early after service on Christmas morning the vestry room was taken in hand by leading sisters to prepare the tables for the supper, for on account of the host of friends bidden to the feast, the reception was to be held in the vestry.

The tables groaned beneath their loads of turkey, salads, pies, puddings, cakes and fancy ices.

Yards and yards of evergreen wreaths encircled the granite pillars; the altar was banked with potted plants and cut flowers. It was a beautiful sight. The main aisle was roped off for the invited guests with white satin ribbons.

Brother Jimson's patrons were to be present in a body, and they had sent the bride a solid silver service, so magnificent that the sisters could only sigh with envy.

The ceremony was to take place at seven sharp. Long before that hour the ushers in full evening dress were ready to receive the guests. Sister Maria Nash was among the first to arrive, and even the Queen of Sheba was not arrayed like unto her. At fifteen minutes before the hour, the organist began an elaborate instrumental performance. There was an expectant hush and much head-turning when the music changed to the familiar strains of the "Wedding March." The minister took his place inside the railing ready to receive the party. The groom waited at the altar.

First came the ushers, then the maids of honor, then the flower girl — daughter of a prominent member — carrying a basket of flowers which she scattered before the bride, who was on the arm of the best man. In the bustle and confusion incident to the entrance of the wedding party no one noticed a group of strangers accompanied by Andy Nash enter and occupy seats near the door.

The service began. All was quiet. The pastor's words fell clearly upon the listening ears. He had reached the words:

"If any man can show just cause, etc.," when like a thunder-clap came a voice from the back part of the house — an angry, excited voice, and a woman of ponderous avoirdupois advanced up the aisle.

"Hol' on thar, pastor, hol' on! A man cain't have but one wife 'cause it's agin' the law. I'm Abe Jimson's lawful wife, an' hyars his six children — all boys — to pint out their daddy." In an instant the assembly was in confusion.

"My soul," exclaimed Viney Peters, "the ol' sarpan'! An' to think how near I come to takin' up with him. I'm glad I ain't Car'mel."

Sis'r Maria said nothing, but a smile of triumph lit her countenance.

"Brother Jimson, is this true?" demanded the minister, sternly. But Abraham Jimson was past answering. His face was ashen, his teeth chattering, his hair standing on end. His shaking limbs refused to uphold his weight; he sank upon his knees on the steps of the altar.

But now a hand was laid upon his shoulder and Mrs. Jimson hauled him upon his feet with a jerk.

"Abe Jimson, you know me. You run'd 'way from me up North fifteen year ago, an' you hid yourself like a groun' hog in a hole, but I've got you. There'll be no new wife in the Jimson family this week. I'm yer fus' wife and I'll be yer las' one. Git up hyar now, you mis'able sinner an' tell the pastor who I be." Brother Jimson meekly obeyed the clarion voice. His sanctified air had vanished; his pride humbled into the dust.

"Pastor," came in trembling tones from his quivering lips. "These are mighty ticklish times." He paused. A deep silence followed his words. "I'm a weak-kneed, mis'able sinner. I have fallen under temptation. This is Ma' Jane, my wife, an' these hyar boys is my sons, God forgive me."

The bride, who had been forgotten now, broke in:

"Abraham Jimson, you ought to be hung. I'm going to sue you for breach of promise." It was a fatal remark. Mrs. Jimson turned upon her.

"You will, will you? Sue him, will you? I'll make a choc'late Car'mel of you befo' I'm done with you, you 'ceitful hussy, hoodooin' hones' men from thar wives."

She sprang upon the girl, tearing, biting, rendering. The satin gown and gossamer veil were reduced to rags. Caramel emitted a series of ear-splitting shrieks, but the biting and tearing went on. How it might have ended no one can tell if Andy had not sprang over the backs of the pews and grappled with the infuriated woman.

The excitement was intense. Men and women struggled to get out of the church. Some jumped from the windows and others crawled under the pews, where they were secure from violence. In the midst of the melee, Brother Jimson disappeared and was never seen again, and Mrs. Jimson came into possession of his property by due process of law.

In the church Abraham Jimson's wedding and his fall from grace is still spoken of in eloquent whispers.

In the home of Mrs. Andy Nash a motto adorns the parlor walls worked in scarlet wool and handsomely framed in gilt. The text reads: "Ye are the salt of the earth; there is nothing hidden that shall not be revealed."

The Game that wasn't Cricket
by Evelyn Sharp

Down the alley where I happen to live, play-time draws a sharp line between the sexes. It is not so noticeable during working hours, when girls and boys, banded together by the common grievance of compulsory education, trot off to school almost as allies, even hand-in-hand in those cases where protection is sought from the little girl by the little boy who raced her into the world and lost — or won — by half a length. But when school is over, sex antagonism, largely fostered by the parent, immediately sets in. Knowing the size of the average back yard in my neighbourhood, I have plenty of sympathy for the mother who wishes to keep it clear of children. But I always want to know why, in order to secure this privacy, she gives the boy a piece of bread-and-dripping and a ball, while the girl is given a piece of bread-and-dripping and a baby. And I have not yet decided which of the two toys is the more destructive of my peace.

Every evening during the summer, cricket is played just below my window in the hour preceding sunset. Cricket, as played in my alley, is less noisy than football, in which anything that comes handy as a substitute for the ball may be used, preferably an old, jagged salmon-tin. But cricket lasts longer, the nerves of the parents whose windows overlook the cricket-ground being able to stand it better. As the best working hour of my day is destroyed equally by both, I have no feeling either way, except that the cricket, as showing a more masterly evasion of difficulties, appeals to me rather more. It is comparatively easy to achieve some resemblance to a game of football even in a narrow strip of pavement bordered by houses, where you can place one goal in the porch of the model dwellings at the blind end of the alley, and the other goal among the motor traffic at the street end. But first-class cricket is more difficult of attainment when the field is so crowded as to make it hard to decide which player out of three or four has caught you out, while your only chance of not being run out first ball is to take the wicket with you — always a possibility when the wicket is somebody's coat that has a way of getting mixed up with the batsman's feet.

In spite of obstacles, however, the cricket goes on every evening before sunset; and all the while, the little girl who tripped to school on such a gay basis of equality with her brother only a few hours back, sits on the doorstep minding the baby. I do not say that she actively objects to this; I only know with acute certainty that the baby objects to it, and for a long time I felt that it would be at least interesting to see what would happen if the little girl were to stand up at the wicket for a change while her brother dealt with the baby.

And the other evening this did happen. A mother, making one of those sorties from the domestic stronghold, that in my alley always have the effect of bringing a look of guilt into the faces of the innocent, shouted something I did not hear, picked up the wicket, cuffed somebody's head with it and made him put it on, gave the baby to a brother, and sent his sister off to the oil-shop with a jar in one hand and a penny tightly clasped in the other. The interruption over, the scattered field re-formed automatically, somebody else's jacket was made into a mound, and cricket was resumed with the loss of one player, who, by the way, showed an astonishing talent for minding the baby.

Then the little girl came back from the oil-shop. I know not what spirit of revolt entered suddenly her small, subdued soul; perhaps the sight of a boy minding the baby suggested an upheaval of the universe that demanded her instant co-operation; perhaps she had no distinct idea in her mind beyond a wish to rebel. Whatever her reasons, there she stood, bat in hand, waiting for the ball, while the baby crowed delightedly in the unusual embrace of a boy who, by all the laws of custom, was unsexing himself.

Another instant, and the air was rent with sound and fury. In front of the wicket stood the Spirit of Revolt, with tumbled hair and defiant eyes, breathless with much running, intoxicated with success; around her, an outraged cricket team, strong in the conventions of a lifetime, was protesting fiercely.

What had happened was quite simple. Grasping in an instant of time the only possible way of eluding the crowd of fielders in the narrow space, the little impromptu batswoman had done the obvious thing and struck the ball against the wall high over their heads, whence it bounded into the open street and got lost in the traffic. Then she ran till she could run no more. Why wasn't it fair? she wanted to know.

"'Cause it ain't — there!" was one illuminating reply.

"'Cause we don't never play that way," was another upon which she was quick to pounce.

"You never thought of it, that's why!" she retorted shrewdly.

She was desperately outnumbered. It was magnificent, but it wasn't cricket; moreover, her place was the doorstep, as she was speedily reminded when the door reopened and avenging motherhood once more swooped down upon the scene. A shake here, a push there — and the boy was back again at the wicket, while a weeping baby lay unheeded on the lap of a weeping Spirit of Revolt.

And the queer thing is that the innovation made by the small batswoman in her one instant of wild rebellion has now been adopted by the team that plays cricket down my alley, every evening before sunset.

A Bird on its Journey
by Beatrice Harraden

It was about four in the afternoon when a young girl came into the salon of the little hotel at C. in Switzerland, and drew her chair up to the fire.

"You are soaked through," said an elderly lady, who was herself trying to get roasted. "You ought to lose no time in changing your clothes."

"I have not anything to change," said the young girl, laughing. "Oh, I shall soon be dry!"

"Have you lost all your luggage?" asked the lady, sympathetically.

"No," said the young girl, "I had none to lose." And she smiled a little mischievously, as though she knew by instinct that her companion's sympathy would at once degenerate into suspicion!

"I don't mean to say that I have not a knapsack," she added, considerately. "I have walked a long distance — in fact from Z."

"And where did you leave your companions?" asked the lady, with a touch of forgiveness in her voice.

"I am without companions, just as I am without luggage," laughed the girl.

And then she opened the piano, and struck a few notes. There was something caressing in the way in which she touched the keys: whoever she was, she knew how to make sweet music: sad music too, full of that undefinable longing, like the holding out of one's arms to one's friends in the hopeless distance.

The lady bending over the fire looked up at the little girl, and forgot that she had brought neither friends nor luggage with her. She hesitated for one moment, and then she took the childish face between her hands and kissed it.

"Thank you, dear, for your music," she said, gently.

"The piano is terribly out of tune," said the little girl suddenly, and she ran out of the room and came back carrying her knapsack.

"What are you going to do?" asked her companion.

"I am going to tune the piano," the little girl said; and she took a tuning-hammer out of her knapsack, and began her work in real earnest. She evidently knew what she was about, and pegged away at the notes as though her whole life depended on the result.

The lady by the fire was lost in amazement. Who could she be? Without luggage and without friends, and with a tuning-hammer!

Meanwhile one of the gentlemen had strolled into the salon; but hearing the sound of tuning, and being in secret possession of nerves, he fled, saying, "The tuner, by Jove!"

A few minutes afterwards, Miss Blake, whose nerves were no secret possession, hastened into the salon, and in her usual imperious fashion demanded instant silence.

"I have just done," said the little girl. "The piano was so terribly out of tune; I could not resist the temptation."

Miss Blake, who never listened to what any one said, took it for granted that the little girl was the tuner, for whom M. le Propriétaire had promised to send; and having bestowed on her a condescending nod, passed out into the garden, where she told some of the visitors that the piano had been tuned at last, and that the tuner was a young woman of rather eccentric appearance.

"Really it is quite abominable how women thrust themselves into every profession," she remarked, in her masculine voice. "It is so unfeminine, so unseemly."

There was nothing of the feminine about Miss Blake: her horse-cloth dress, her waistcoat and high collar, and her billy-cock hat were of the masculine genus; even her nerves could not be called feminine, since we learn from two or three doctors (taken off their guard) that nerves are neither feminine nor masculine, but common.

"I should like to see this tuner," said one of the tennis-players, leaning against a tree.

"Here she comes," said Miss Blake, as the little girl was seen sauntering into the garden.

The men put up their eye-glasses, and saw a little lady with a childish face and soft brown hair, of strictly feminine appearance and bearing. The goat came towards her and began nibbling at her frock. She seemed to understand the manner of goats, and played with him to his heart's content. One of the tennis-players, Oswald Everard by name, strolled down to the bank where she was having her frolic.

"Good afternoon," he said, raising his cap. "I hope the goat is not worrying you. Poor little fellow! This is his last day of play. He is to be killed tomorrow for table d'hôte."

"What a shame!" she said. "Fancy to be killed, and then grumbled at!"

"That is precisely what we do here," he said, laughing. "We grumble at everything we eat. And I own to being one of the grumpiest; though the lady in the horse-cloth dress yonder follows close upon my heels."

"She was the lady who was annoyed at me because I tuned the piano," the little girl said. "Still it had to be done. It was plainly my duty. I seemed to have come for that purpose."

"It has been confoundedly annoying having it out of tune," he said. "I've had to give up singing altogether. But what a strange profession you have chosen! Very unusual, isn't it?"

"Why, surely not," she answered, amused. "It seems to me that every other woman has taken to it. The wonder to me is that any one ever scores a success. Nowadays, however, no one could amass a huge fortune out of it."

"No one, indeed!" replied Oswald Everard, laughing. "What on earth made you take to it?"

"It took to me," she said, simply. "It wrapt me round with enthusiasm. I could think of nothing else. I vowed that I would rise to the top of my profession. I worked day and night. But it means incessant toil for years if one wants to make any headway."

"Good gracious! I thought it was merely a matter of a few months," he said, smiling at the little girl.

"A few months!" she repeated, scornfully. "You are speaking the language of an amateur. No: one has to work faithfully year after year; to grasp the possibilities and pass on to greater possibilities. You imagine what it must feel like to touch the notes, and know that you are keeping the listeners spellbound; that you are taking them into a fairyland of sound, where petty personality is lost in vague longing and regret."

"I confess I had not thought of it in that way," he said, humbly. "I have only regarded it as a necessary everyday evil; and to be quite honest with you, I fail to see now how it can inspire enthusiasm. I wish I could see," he added, looking up at the engaging little figure before him.

"Never mind," she said, laughing at his distress; "I forgive you. And after all, you are not the only person who looks upon it as a necessary evil. My poor old guardian abominated it. He made many sacrifices to come and listen to me. He knew I liked to see his kind old face, and that the presence of a real friend inspired me with confidence."

"I should not have thought it was nervous work," he said.

"Try it and see," she answered. "But surely you spoke of singing. Are you not nervous when you sing?"

"Sometimes," he replied, rather stiffly. "But that is slightly different." (He was very proud of his singing, and made a great fuss about it.) "Your profession, as I remarked before, is an unavoidable nuisance. When I think what I have suffered from the gentlemen of your profession, I only wonder that I have any brains left. But I am uncourteous."

"No, no," she said. "Let me hear about your sufferings."

"Whenever I have specially wanted to be quiet," he said; and then he glanced at her childish little face, and he hesitated. "It seems so rude of me," he added. He was the soul of courtesy, although he was an amateur tenor singer.

"Please tell me," the little girl said, in her winning way.

"Well," he said, gathering himself together, "it is the one subject on which I can be eloquent. Ever since I can remember, I have been worried and tortured by those rascals. I have tried in every way to escape from them, but there is no hope for me. Yes; I believe that all the tuners in the universe are in league against me, and have marked me out for their special prey."

"*All the what?*" asked the little girl, with a jerk in her voice.

"All the tuners, of course," he replied, rather snappishly. "I know that we cannot do without them; but, good heavens! they have no tact, no consideration, no mercy. Whenever I've wanted to write or read quietly, that fatal knock has come at the door, and I've known by instinct that all chance of peace was over. Whenever I've been giving a luncheon-party, the tuner has arrived, with his abominable black bag, and his abominable card, which has to be signed at once. On one occasion I was just proposing to a girl in her father's library, when the tuner struck up in the drawing-room. I left off suddenly, and fled from the house. But there is no escape from these fiends: I believe they are swarming about in the air like so many bacteria. And how, in the name of goodness, you should deliberately choose to be one of them, and should be so enthusiastic over your work, puzzles me beyond all words. Don't say that you carry a black bag, and present cards which have to be filled up at the most inconvenient time: don't—"

He stopped suddenly, for the little girl was convulsed with laughter. She laughed until the tears rolled down her cheeks; and then she dried her eyes and laughed again.

"Excuse me," she said, "I can't help myself; it's so funny."

"It may be funny to you," he said, laughing in spite of himself; "but it is not funny to me."

"Of course it isn't," she replied, making a desperate effort to be serious. "Well, tell me something more about these tuners."

"Not another word," he said, gallantly. "I am ashamed of myself as it is. Come to the end of the garden, and let me show you the view down into the valley."

She had conquered her fit of merriment, but her face wore a settled look of mischief, and she was evidently the possessor of some secret joke. She seemed in capital health and spirits, and had so much to say that was bright and interesting, that Oswald Everard found himself becoming reconciled to the whole race of tuners. He was amazed to learn that she had walked all the way from Z, and quite alone too.

"Oh, I don't think anything of that," she said; "I had a splendid time, and I caught four rare butterflies. I would not have missed those for anything. As for the going about by myself, that is a second nature. Besides, I do not belong to any one. That has its advantages, and I suppose its disadvantages; but at present I have only discovered the advantages. The disadvantages will discover themselves!"

"I believe you are what the novels call an advanced young woman," he said. "Perhaps you give lectures on Woman's Suffrage or something of that sort?"

"I have very often mounted the platform," she answered. "In fact, I am never so happy as when addressing an immense audience. A most unfeminine thing to do, isn't it? What would the lady yonder in the horse-cloth dress and billy-cock hat say? Don't you think you ought to go and help her to drive away the goat? She looks so frightened. She interests me deeply. I wonder whether she has written an essay on the Feminine in Woman. I should like to read it: it would do me so much good."

"You are at least a true woman," he said, laughing, "for I see you can be spiteful. The tuning has not driven that away."

"Ah, I had forgotten about the tuning," she answered, brightly; "but now you remind me, I have been seized with a great idea."

"Won't you tell it to me?" he asked.

"No," she answered. "I keep my great ideas for myself, and work them out in secret. And this one is particularly amusing. What fun I shall have!"

"But why keep the fun to yourself?" he said. "We all want to be amused here; we all want to be stirred up: a little fun would be a charity."

"Very well, since you wish it, you shall be stirred up," she answered; "but you must give me time to work out my great idea. I do not hurry about things, not even about my professional duties. For I have a strong feeling that it is vulgar to be always amassing riches! As I have neither a husband nor a brother to support, I have chosen less wealth, and more leisure to enjoy all the loveliness of life! So you see I take my time about everything. And to-morrow I shall catch butterflies at my leisure, and lie amongst the dear old pines, and work at my great idea."

"I shall catch butterflies," said her companion. "And I too shall lie amongst the dear old pines."

"Just as you please," she said; and at that moment the table d'hôte bell rang.

The little girl hastened to the bureau and spoke rapidly in German to the cashier.

"Ach, Fräulein!" he said. "You are not really serious?"

"Yes, I am," she said. "I don't want them to know my name. It will only worry me. Say I am the young lady who tuned the piano."

She had scarcely given these directions and mounted to her room, when Oswald Everard, who was much interested in his mysterious companion, came to the bureau and asked for the name of the little lady.

"Es ist das Fräulein welches das Piano gestimmt hat," answered the man, returning with unusual quickness to his account-book.

No one spoke to the little girl at table d'hôte; but for all that, she enjoyed her dinner, and gave her serious attention to all the courses. Being thus solidly occupied, she had not much leisure to bestow on the conversation of the other guests. Nor was it specially original; it treated of the shortcomings of the chef, the tastelessness of the soup, the toughness of the beef, and all the many failings which go to complete a mountain-hotel dinner. But suddenly, so it seemed to the little girl, this time-honoured talk passed into another phase: she heard the word music mentioned, and she became at once interested to learn what these people had to say on a subject which was dearer to her than any other.

"For my own part," said a stern-looking old man, "I have no words to describe what a gracious comfort music has been to me all my life. It is the noblest language which man may understand and speak. And I sometimes think that those who know it, or know something of it, are able at rare moments to find an answer to life's perplexing problems."

The little girl looked up from her plate. Robert Browning's words rose to her lips, but she did not give them utterance:

> "God has a few of us whom He whispers in the ear;
> The rest may reason, and welcome; 'tis we musicians know."

"I have lived through a long life," said another elderly man, "and have therefore had my share of trouble; but the grief of being obliged to give up music was the grief which held me longest, or which perhaps has never left me. I still crave for the gracious pleasure of touching once more the strings of a violoncello, and hearing the dear tender voice singing and throbbing and answering even to such poor skill as mine. I still yearn to take my part in concerted music, and be one of those privileged to play Beethoven's string quartettes. But that will have to be in another incarnation, I think."

He glanced at his shrunken arm, and then, as though ashamed of this allusion to his own personal infirmity, he added hastily:

"But when the first pang of such a pain is over, there remains the comfort of being a listener. At first one does not think it a comfort; but as time goes on, there is no resisting its magic influence. And Lowell said rightly, 'that one of God's great charities is music.'"

"I did not know you were musical, Mr Keith," said an English lady. "You have never before spoken of music."

"Perhaps not, madam," he answered. "One does not often speak of what one cares for most of all. But when I am in London, I rarely miss hearing our best players."

At this point others joined in, and the various merits of eminent pianists were warmly discussed.

"What a wonderful name that little English lady has made for herself!" said the Major, who was considered an authority on all subjects. "I would go anywhere to hear Miss Thyra Flowerdew. We all ought to be very proud of her. She has taken even the German musical world by storm, and they say her recitals at Paris have been brilliantly successful. I myself have heard her at New York, Leipsic, London, Berlin, and even Chicago."

The little girl stirred uneasily in her chair.

"I don't think Miss Flowerdew has ever been to Chicago," she said.

There was a dead silence. The admirer of Miss Thyra Flowerdew looked much annoyed, and twiddled his watch-chain. He had meant to say Philadelphia, but he did not think it necessary to own to his mistake.

"What impertinence!" said one of the ladies to Miss Blake. "What can she know about it? Is she not the young person who tuned the piano?"

"Perhaps she tunes Miss Thyra Flowerdew's piano!" suggested Miss Blake in a loud whisper.

"You are right, madam," said the little girl, quietly. "I have often tuned Miss Flowerdew's piano."

There was another embarrassing silence; and then a lovely old lady, whom every one reverenced, came to the rescue.

"I think her playing is simply superb," she said. "Nothing that I ever hear satisfies me so entirely. She has all the tenderness of an angel's touch."

"Listening to her," said the Major, who had now recovered from his annoyance at being interrupted, "one becomes unconscious of her presence, for she *is the music itself*. And that is rare. It is but seldom nowadays that we are allowed to forget the personality of the player. And yet her personality is an unusual one: having once seen her, it would not be easy to forget her. I should recognise her anywhere."

As he spoke, he glanced at the little tuner, and could not help admiring her dignified composure under circumstances which might have been distressing to any one; and when she rose with the others, he followed her, and said stiffly:

"I regret that I was the indirect cause of putting you in an awkward position."

"It is really of no consequence," she said, brightly. "If you think I was impertinent, I ask your forgiveness. I did not mean to be officious. The words were spoken before I was aware of them."

She passed into the salon, where she found a quiet corner for herself, and read some of the newspapers. No one took the slightest notice of her: not a word was spoken to her; but when she relieved the company of her presence, her impertinence was commented on.

"I am sorry that she heard what I said," remarked Miss Blake. "But she did not seem to mind. These young women who go out into the world lose the edge of their sensitiveness and femininity. I have always observed that."

"How much they are spared then!" answered some one.

Meanwhile the little girl slept soundly. She had merry dreams, and finally woke up laughing. She hurried over her breakfast, and then stood ready to go for a butterfly-hunt. She looked thoroughly happy, and evidently had found, and was holding tightly the key to life's enjoyment.

Oswald Everard was waiting on the balcony, and he reminded her that he intended to go with her.

"Come along, then," she answered; "we must not lose a moment."

They caught butterflies, they picked flowers, they ran; they lingered by the wayside, they sang; they climbed, and he marvelled at her easy speed. Nothing seemed to tire her, and everything seemed to delight her: the flowers, the birds, the clouds, the grasses, and the fragrance of the pine-woods.

"Is it not good to live?" she cried. "Is it not splendid to take in this scented air? Draw in as many long breaths as you can. Isn't it good? Don't you feel now as though you were ready to move mountains? I do. What a dear old nurse Nature is! How she pets us, and gives us the best of her treasures!"

Her happiness invaded Oswald Everard's soul, and he felt like a schoolboy once more, rejoicing in a fine day and his liberty; with nothing to spoil the freshness of the air, and nothing to threaten the freedom of the moment.

"Is it not good to live?" he cried. "Yes, indeed it is, if we know how to enjoy."

They had come upon some haymakers, and the little girl hastened up to help them. There she was in the midst of them, laughing and talking to the women, and helping them to pile up the hay on the shoulders of a broad-backed man, who then conveyed his burden to a pear-shaped stack. Oswald Everard watched his companion for a moment, and then, quite forgetting his dignity as an amateur tenor singer, he too lent his aid, and did not leave off until his companion sank exhausted on the ground.

"Oh," she laughed, "what delightful work for a very short time! Come along; let us go into that brown châlet yonder and ask for some milk. I am simply parched with thirst. Thank you, but I prefer to carry my own flowers."

"What an independent little lady you are!" he said.

"It is quite necessary in our profession, I can assure you," she said, with a tone of mischief in her voice. "That reminds me that my profession is evidently not looked upon with any favour by the visitors at the hotel. I am heartbroken to think that I have not won the esteem of that lady in the billy-cock hat. What will she say to you for coming out with me? And what will she say of me for allowing you to come? I wonder whether she will say, 'How unfeminine!' I wish I could hear her!"

"I don't suppose you care," he said. "You seem to be a wild little bird."

"I don't care what a person of that description says," replied his companion.

"What on earth made you contradict the Major at dinner last night?" he asked. "I was not at the table, but some one told me of the incident; and I felt very sorry about it. What could you know of Miss Thyra Flowerdew?"

"Well, considering that she is in my profession, of course I know something about her," said the little girl.

"Confound it all!" he said, rather rudely. "Surely there is some difference between the bellows-blower and the organist."

"Absolutely none," she answered — "merely a variation of the original theme!"

As she spoke she knocked at the door of the châlet, and asked the old dame to give them some milk. They sat in the *Stube*, and the little girl looked about, and admired the spinning-wheel, and the quaint chairs, and the queer old jugs, and the pictures on the walls.

"Ah, but you shall see the other room," the old peasant woman said, and she led them into a small apartment, which was evidently intended for a study. It bore evidences of unusual taste and care, and one could see that some loving hand had been trying to make it a real sanctum of refinement. There was even a small piano. A carved book-rack was fastened to the wall.

The old dame did not speak at first; she gave her guests time to recover from the astonishment which she felt they must be experiencing; then she pointed proudly to the piano.

"I bought that for my daughters," she said, with a strange mixture of sadness and triumph. "I wanted to keep them at home with me, and I saved and saved and got enough money to buy the piano. They had always wanted to have one, and I thought they would then stay with me. They liked music and books, and I knew they would be glad to have a room of their own where they might read and play and study; and so I gave them this corner."

"Well, mother," asked the little girl, "and where are they this afternoon?"

"Ah!" she answered, sadly, "they did not care to stay. But it was natural enough; and I was foolish to grieve. Besides, they come to see me."

"And then they play to you?" asked the little girl, gently.

"They say the piano is out of tune," the old dame said. "I don't know. Perhaps you can tell."

The little girl sat down to the piano, and struck a few chords.

"Yes," she said. "It is badly out of tune. Give me the tuning-hammer. I am sorry," she added, smiling at Oswald Everard, "but I cannot neglect my duty. Don't wait for me."

"I will wait for you," he said, sullenly; and he went into the balcony and smoked his pipe, and tried to possess his soul in patience.

When she had faithfully done her work, she played a few simple melodies, such as she knew the old woman would love and understand; and she turned away when she saw that the listener's eyes were moist.

"Play once again," the old woman whispered. "I am dreaming of beautiful things."

So the little tuner touched the keys again with all the tenderness of an angel.

"Tell your daughters," she said, as she rose to say good-bye. "that the piano is now in good tune. Then they will play to you the next time they come."

"I shall always remember you, mademoiselle," the old woman said; and, almost unconsciously, she too took the childish face and kissed it.

Oswald Everard was waiting in the hay-field for his companion; and when she apologised to him for this little professional intermezzo, as she called it, he recovered from his sulkiness and readjusted his nerves, which the noise of the tuning had somewhat disturbed.

"It was very good of you to tune the old dame's piano," he said, looking at her with renewed interest.

"Some one had to do it, of course," she answered, brightly, "and I am glad the chance fell to me. What a comfort it is to think that the next time those daughters come to see her, they will play to her, and make her happy! Poor old dear!"

"You puzzle me greatly," he said. "I cannot for the life of me think what made you choose your calling. You must have many gifts; any one who talks with you must see that at once. And you play quite nicely too."

"I am sorry that my profession sticks in your throat," she answered. "Do be thankful that I am nothing worse than a tuner. For I might be something worse — a snob, for instance."

And so speaking, she dashed after a butterfly, and left him to recover from her words. He was conscious of having deserved a reproof; and when at last he overtook her, he said as much, and asked for her kind indulgence.

"I forgive you," she said, laughing. "You and I are not looking at things from the same point of view; but we have had a splendid morning together, and I have enjoyed every minute of it. And to-morrow I go on my way."

"And to-morrow you go," he repeated. "Can it not be the day after to-morrow?"

"I am a bird of passage," she said, shaking her head. "You must not seek to detain me. I have taken my rest, and off I go to other climes."

They had arrived at the hotel, and Oswald Everard saw no more of his companion until the evening, when she came down rather late for table d'hôte. She hurried over her dinner and went into the salon. She closed the door and sat down to the piano, and lingered there without touching the keys: once or twice she raised her hands, and then she let them rest on the notes, and half-unconsciously they began to move and make sweet music, and then they drifted into Schumann's *Abendlied,* and then the little girl played some of his *Kinderscenen,* and some of his *Fantasie Stücke,* and some of his songs.

Her touch and feeling were exquisite; and her phrasing betrayed the true musician. The strains of music reached the dining-room, and one by one the guests came creeping in, moved by the music, and anxious to see the musician.

The little girl did not look up: she was in a Schumann mood that evening; and only the players of Schumann know what enthralling possession he takes of their very spirit. All the passion and pathos and wildness and longing had found an inspired interpreter; and those who listened to her were held by the magic which was her own secret, and which had won for her such honour as comes only to the few. She understood Schumann's music, and was at her best with him.

Had she, perhaps, chosen to play his music this evening because she wished to be at her best? Or was she merely being impelled by an overwhelming force within her? Perhaps it was something of both.

Was she wishing to humiliate these people who had received her so coldly? This little girl was only human: perhaps there was something of that feeling too. Who can tell? But she played as she had never played in London, or Paris, or Berlin, or New York, or Philadelphia.

As last she arrived at the Carnéval, and those who heard her, declared afterwards that they had never listened to a more magnificent rendering: the tenderness was so restrained, the vigour was so refined. When the last notes of that spirited *Marche des Davidsbündler contre les Philistins* had died away, she glanced at Oswald Everard, who was standing near her, almost dazed.

"And now my favourite piece of all," she said; and she at once began the Second Novellette, the finest of the eight, but seldom played in public.

What can one say of the wild rush of the leading theme, and the pathetic longing of the Intermezzo?

"... The murmuring dying notes,
     That fall as soft as Snow on the sea;"
and

"The passionate strain that deeply going,
     Refines the bosom it trembles through."

What can one say of those vague aspirations and finest thoughts which possess the very dullest amongst us when such music as that which the little girl had chosen, catches us and keeps us, if only for a passing moment, but that moment of the rarest worth and loveliness in our unlovely lives?

What can one say of the highest music, except that, like death, it is the great leveller: it gathers us all to its tender keeping — and we rest.

The little girl ceased playing. There was not a sound to be heard; the magic was still holding her listeners. When at last they had freed themselves with a sigh, they pressed forward to greet her.

"There is only one person who can play like that," cried the Major, with sudden inspiration: "she is Miss Thyra Flowerdew."

The little girl smiled.

"That is my name," she said, simply; and she slipped out of the room.

The next morning, at an early hour, the Bird of Passage took her flight onwards, but she was not destined to go off unobserved. Oswald Everard saw the little figure swinging along the road, and he overtook her.

"You little wild bird!" he said. "And so this was your great idea: to have your fun out of us all, and then play to us and make us feel, I don't know how — and then to go."

"You said the company wanted stirring up," she answered; "and I rather fancy I have stirred them up."

"And what do you suppose you have done for me?" he asked.

"I hope I have proved to you that the bellows-blower and the organist are sometimes identical," she answered.

But he shook his head.

"Little wild bird," he said, "you have given me a great idea, and I will tell you what it is: *to tame you*. So good-bye for the present."

"Good-bye," she said. "But wild birds are not so easily tamed."

Then she waved her hand over her head, and went on her way singing.

Biographical Notes

MONA CAIRD (1854–1932)

Alice Mona Alison was born in the Isle of Wight. In 1877 she married a Scottish farmer, James Alexander Henryson-Caird, and their only child, Alister James, was born in 1884. Caird is remembered primarily for her role in initiating a major debate with her article "Marriage" in the *Westminster Review* (August 1888). She declared that marriage was "a vexatious failure", condemned the "legalized injustice" of England's social system, and proposed a new ideal of true equality in which a key element would be economic independence for women. Further discussion was fuelled when the *Daily Telegraph* posed the question "Is Marriage a Failure?" Around 27,000 letters were written to the newspaper. *Whom Nature Leadeth* and *One That Wins*, Caird's early novels, were published under the male pseudonym of G. Noel Hatton. Her other fictional works appeared under the name Mona Caird, her most famous being *The Daughters of Danaus*. Caird studied a wide variety of subjects: sociology, history, ethnology, economics, philosophy, feminist thought and science. She was a freethinker, with the reputation of being a radical, subversive reformer. She wrote a sympathetic introduction to the memoirs of the Russian Nihilist Sophie Wassilieff, and was one of the two female members of the Free Press Defence Committee established to help George Bedborough, secretary of the Legitimation League, during his trial in 1898. Caird became President of the Independent Anti-Vivisection League and was also committed to the Personal Rights Association. Her concern for feminist issues is reflected in her published articles; however she did not join the militant suffragists.

KATE CHOPIN (1850–1904)

Kate O'Flaherty was born in St Louis, Missouri. Her mother was a Creole; her father, who was of Irish descent, died in 1855. Chopin studied at the Sacred Heart Academy; but she was also educated by her great-grandmother, who helped her with her French and music and encouraged her storytelling. At the age of twenty Chopin married Oscar Chopin. They lived in New Orleans and Cloutierville, and had five sons and a daughter. Oscar died from malaria in 1882. Chopin found herself in financial difficulties, but set about managing her husband's business interests. She had a scandalous affair with a neighbouring landowner before returning to St Louis in 1884. She tried her hand at writing "local color" fiction, focusing on life in Louisiana. Initially her work appeared in local journals, but the vogue for regional writing led to her stories being taken up by some of the national magazines such as the *Atlantic* and the *Century*. Chopin was wary about being pigeonholed, as she did not fit snugly into the same mould as many of the other "local colorists". She was a prolific writer, producing over one hundred stories in fourteen years, as well as essays, novels, plays, poems and reviews. Her collections of stories include: *Bayou Folk* (1894) and *A Night in Acadie* (1897), but the volume entitled *A Vocation and a Voice* was turned down in 1900 following controversy over her novel *The Awakening* (1899). Chopin died of a cerebral haemorrhage.

ELLA D'ARCY (185?–1939)

Ella D'Arcy was a British short-story writer, novelist and translator. Her birth-date has been given variously as 1851, 1856 and 1857. She was born in London, to Irish parents, grew up in the Channel Islands, and received some of her schooling in France and Germany. D'Arcy was an art student at the Slade School in London, but unfortunately her eyesight deteriorated to such an extent that she had to leave. Instead she turned her talents to writing. D'Arcy is remembered mainly for her connection with the *Yellow Book*. She assisted the editors, Henry Harland and John Lane, who welcomed items from female contributors. Lane was eager to publish unusual, innovative fiction, and encouraged authors to experiment with both the form and content of their work. D'Arcy's own short stories were printed in ten of the thirteen issues of the *Yellow Book*. Later they were collected in two volumes: *Monochromes* (1895) and *Modern Instances* (1898). D'Arcy also published a novel, *The Bishop's Dilemma*, in 1898. The novelist and playwright Netta Syrett was one of D'Arcy's friends. As part of the "*Yellow Book* set" they attended parties at the home of Henry and Aline Harland on Saturday evenings. In her autobiography, *The Sheltering Tree*, Syrett observed that D'Arcy received an astonishing amount of praise for her writing, considering that her literary output was so small: "though her prose was indeed distinguished, and she herself very clever and amusing, she was the laziest woman I ever met". She described D'Arcy's behaviour as erratic, and claimed that she was not dependable; nevertheless she was an amusing and genial companion. In 1924 D'Arcy published a translation of *Ariel*, André Maurois's fictionalised biography of Shelley. She also wrote a biography of Rimbaud, but it was never published. D'Arcy did not marry. Most of her later life was spent in Paris; however she died in Kent.

ELLA HEPWORTH DIXON (1855–1932)

Ella Nora Hepworth Dixon was born in London, the seventh of eight children. Her father was William Hepworth Dixon, the editor of the *Athenaeum*, and her mother, Marion, was also a journalist. Dixon was educated privately at home, before attending school in Heidelberg and then studying art in Paris. She was art critic on the *Westminster Gazette* for five years, and contributed articles, short stories and travel items to a range of newspapers and periodicals, including the *Daily Mail, Daily Telegraph, Ladies' Field, Ladies' Pictorial, Pall Mall Gazette, St James's Gazette,* the *Yellow Book, Woman* and *Woman's World.* In 1892 Dixon published *My Flirtations,* a series of amusing sketches, under the pseudonym "Margaret Wynman". The alias was also used for her volume of short stories in 1904, *One Doubtful Hour, and Other Sidelights on the Feminine Temperament.* She is remembered mainly for her extremely successful novel *The Story of a Modern Woman* (1894). From 1895-1900 Dixon edited the *Englishwoman.* The magazine featured its own version of an employment bureau. People seeking work could advertise themselves in the journal, which displayed their photographs along with summaries of their employment needs. In 1930 Dixon published *As I Knew Them: Sketches of People I Have Met Along the Way,* in which she referred to Robert Browning, Henry James, George Meredith and Oscar Wilde.

MÉNIE MURIEL DOWIE (1866–1945)

Ménie Muriel Dowie was a travel writer and novelist. She was educated in her home city, Liverpool, but also in Stuttgart and France. Dowie was an intrepid traveller. In *A Girl in the Karpathians,* published in 1891, she urged: "Give your whims a loose rein, follow the promptings of that queer live soul in you which always retains its affinity to simpleness and green-growing things, and be prepared to be thought very odd when you come back." Dowie edited *Women Adventurers: The Lives of Madame Velazquez, Hannah Snell, Maryanne Talbot and Mrs Christian Davies* (1893). Her best known book is the New Woman novel *Gallia* (1895), which is regarded as a feminist classic. It highlights the importance of eugenic theory at the *fin-de-siècle*: Gallia does not choose to marry for love, but selects "a fine, strong, manly man, full of health and strength." Dowie's contributions to *The Yellow Book* are included in a volume of five short stories entitled *Some Whims of Fate* (1897). She also wrote *The Crook of the Bough* (1898), a satirical novel describing contemporary attitudes to women in Turkey; *Love and His Mask* (1901), about the Boer War, and *Things About Our Neighbourhood* (1903), a compilation of her pieces in *Country Life.* In 1891 Dowie married Sir Henry Norman, M.P., but they divorced twelve years later. She lived in India with her second husband, Major Edward Fitzgerald. Versions of her later life differ: it has been said that she returned to England to breed cattle and sheep; but another account states that she became a society hostess.

'GEORGE EGERTON' (1859–1945)

Mary Chavelita Dunne was born in Melbourne, to an Irish father and a Welsh mother. During her childhood she lived in New Zealand, Chile, Wales, Ireland and Germany.

She taught and studied in Germany, then worked in New York, Dublin and London. After eloping with her employer's husband – a bigamist – she settled with him in Norway. There she was introduced to the work of Bjornsen, Hamsun, Hansson, Ibsen, Nietzsche and Strindberg, and was heavily influenced by the Scandinavian realists. In 1891 she married George Egerton Clairmonte, and they had a son, George, in 1895. Financial hardship induced her to become an author. Her volume of stories, *Keynotes* (1893), swiftly gained notoriety and gave rise to John Lane's Keynote Series. *Punch* parodied the work as "She-Notes" by "Borgia Smudgiton", including "Japanese Fan-de-Siecle" (sic) illustrations by "Mortarthurio Whiskersly" to mock Aubrey Beardsley's cover design. Egerton's stories appeared in the *Yellow Book*, and her other volumes were *Discords* (1894), *Symphonies* (1897), *Fantasias* (1898) and *Flies in Amber* (1905). *Young Ofeg's Ditties* (1895) was her translation of a book by Ola Hansson, and she also translated Hamsun's *Hunger* (1899). She wrote a semi-autobiographical novel, *The Wheel of God* (1898). At the turn of the century Egerton fell in love with a Norwegian called Ole. *Rosa Amorosa* (1901) contains a version of her letters to him. She divorced her husband in 1901, and married a theatrical agent called Reginald Golding Bright. Increasingly she turned her attention to the stage, writing plays and translating or adapting others.

CHARLOTTE PERKINS GILMAN (1860–1935)

Charlotte Anna Perkins was born in Hartford, Connecticut. When her parents separated she moved repeatedly with her mother and brother, and was mainly self-educated. From 1878-1880 Charlotte attended the Rhode Island School of Design, after which she was employed as an art teacher, governess, decorative artist and greetings card designer. She was interested in physical fitness, exercising regularly, and was an advocate of dress reform. In 1884 she married Charles Walter Stetson. They had one daughter, Katharine, in 1885, but Charlotte suffered from severe depression and was prescribed the "rest cure" by Silas Weir Mitchell. This experience inspired her most famous work, the short story "The Yellow Wall-paper" (1892). A volume of satiric poems, *In This Our World*, came out in 1893. She and Stetson were divorced the following year. Charlotte travelled widely, lecturing on socialism and women's issues. *Women and Economics* (1898) brought her international recognition. She married her cousin, George Houghton Gilman, in 1900. Works from this period include: *Concerning Children* (1900), *The Home: Its Work and Influence* (1903) and *Human Work* (1904). In 1909 she founded *The Forerunner*, a monthly magazine focusing on contemporary topics, which she wrote by herself right up until 1916. Charlotte was diagnosed with breast cancer in 1932. Her husband died in 1934, and the next year she committed suicide explaining: "I have preferred chloroform to cancer". Gilman's other writings include: *What Diantha Did* (1910), *The Man-Made World; or, Our Androcentric Culture* and *The Crux* (1911), *Moving the Mountain* and *Mag-Marjorie* (1912), *Won Over* (1913) and *Benigna Machiavelli* (1914). *Herland* (1915) describes a feminist utopian community of women, and was followed by *With Her in Ourland* (1916). *His Religion and Hers* came out in 1923, and her autobiography, *The Living of Charlotte Perkins Gilman*, in 1935. Gilman was an optimistic reformer, maintaining that mankind can change for the better.

SARAH GRAND (1854–1943)

Sarah Grand was born Frances Elizabeth Bellenden Clarke. As a teenager she was asked to leave school after supporting Josephine Butler's campaign against the Contagious Diseases Acts. At sixteen she married a thirty-nine year old widower with two boys, and they had a son together. They lived in Kent, the Far East, Malta, Norwich and Warrington. Frances published her novel *Ideala* anonymously in 1888. Aged thirty-six she left her husband, moved to London and changed her name to Sarah Grand. Her controversial novel *The Heavenly Twins* (1893) warned of the dangers of venereal disease. It was a stunning success and facilitated more open discussion of a previously taboo subject. Grand moved to Tunbridge Wells in 1898, where she was in demand as a lecturer and was a member of many suffrage societies. In 1920 she moved to Bath, and served as Mayoress. Ironically the notorious, vilified authoress of the 1890s came to be regarded as a pillar of respectability. Her other works include the novels *A Domestic Experiment* (1891), *Singularly Deluded* (1893), *The Beth Book* (1897), *Babs the Impossible* (1901), *Adnam's Orchard* (1912) and *The Winged Victory* (1916); a pamphlet, *The Modern Man and Maid* (1898), and the volumes of short stories *Our Manifold Nature* (1894), *Emotional Moments* (1908) and *Variety* (1922).

BEATRICE HARRADEN (1864–1936)

Beatrice Harraden was born in London, the youngest daughter of an importer of musical instruments. She became the ward of the novelist and journalist Eliza Lynn Linton. Harraden was educated in Dresden, and at Cheltenham Ladies' College, Queen's College and Bedford College, qualifying with a BA from London University. Some of her short stories appeared in *Blackwood's Magazine*, but her first significant publication was a children's book called *Things Will Take a Turn* (1889). In 1893 she produced an extremely popular novel, *Ships that Pass in the Night*, set in a Swiss sanatorium. Her other novels include *Hilda Strafford* (1897), *The Fowler* (1899), *Katharine Frensham* (1903), *The Scholar's Daughter* (1906), *Interplay* (1908) and *Out of the Wreck I Rise* (1912). The volume of short stories, *In Varying Moods*, came out in 1894, and some of her short stories for children were gathered in *Untold Tales of the Past* (1897). With Dr William Edwards she brought out a guide entitled *Two Health Seekers in Southern California*. She lived there for a while, but for many years was based in Hampstead. Harraden was a keen advocate of the suffrage movement. She supported the Women's Social and Political

Union and the Women Writers' Suffrage League, and was a vice-president of the United Suffragists. In her forties she wrote her first play, and her short comic dialogue *Lady Geraldine's Speech* was performed by the Actresses' Franchise League. She also wrote a book about suffrage, *Our Warrior Women* (1916). Mildred Robertson Nicoll described Harraden thus: "Small, dark, vivacious, with one of the first 'bobbed' heads to be seen in London, and charmingly dressed by Liberty." Apparently Harraden was very well-liked. In the *Vote* (11 November 1909) Ethel Hill observed: "To know Miss Beatrice Harraden is to love her." During the war she gave her services to the Belgian relief effort, and went to visit refugees in their camps.

PAULINE ELIZABETH HOPKINS (1859–1930)

Pauline Elizabeth Hopkins was an African-American actress, author, biographer, dramatist, journalist and singer. She was born in Portland, Maine, but spent most of her life in Boston, Massachusetts. In 1880 she performed in her own musical play, *Slaves Escape: Or the Underground Railroad*, which also starred her mother and stepfather. They were billed as "The Hopkins Colored Troubadours", and when touring Pauline was described as "Boston's Favorite Soprano". Hopkins was a founder of the *Colored American Magazine*, serving as Women's Editor then Literary Editor. She travelled widely, giving lectures and promoting sales. Her other novels were serialized in the magazine: *Hagar's Daughter* (1901: published under her mother's name Sarah A. Allen); *A Dash For Liberty* (also 1901); *Winona* and *Of One Blood* (both 1902). Hopkins penned biographical sketches of famous men and women "of the Negro Race" in *Colored American*. In 1905 her work on "The Dark Races of the Twentieth Century" was printed in *Voice of the Negro*. She championed the cause of independence for black writers, although she resigned from the *Colored American Magazine* when there was a battle between W.E.B. Du Bois and Booker T. Washington to control the Negro press. In later years Hopkins edited *New Era*, which published her novella *Topsy Templeton* (1916). She was also employed as a stenographer for the Bureau of Statistics at the Massachusetts Institute of Technology. Following an accidental fire, she died from burns. Her papers are held at Fisk University Library, Nashville, Tennessee.

ANNA KINGSFORD (1846–1888)

Annie Bonus was born in Stratford, Essex. She was educated by tutors, then attended a finishing school in Brighton. In 1867 she married her cousin Algernon Kingsford, the vicar of Atcham in Shropshire; but after three years she rejected both her husband and Anglicanism, converting to Catholicism. Kingsford wrote stories for magazines, using her married name and also the name Ninon Kingsford. She published *Rosamunda the Princess* in 1875. From 1872-1873 she owned and edited *The Lady's Own Paper*. At that time she was a suffrage campaigner, but gradually she chose to concentrate on other pressing issues. Kingsford was a vegetarian, and a vociferous opponent of blood sports and vivisection. She studied medicine in Paris from 1874-1880, determined to demonstrate that it was possible to qualify as a doctor without seeing or participating in animal experimentation. She shared a home with her fellow-theosophist Edward Maitland, who later wrote her biography. They collaborated in writing *The Perfect Way* (1882). In 1883 Kingsford became President of the Theosophical Society's London lodge, and also founded an anti-vivisection society in Geneva. The following year she and Maitland established the Hermetic Society. Her volume *Dreams and Dream Stories* was published in 1888. Kingsford caught a cold after visiting Pasteur's laboratory, and died of consumption.

CHARLOTTE MEW (1869–1928)

Charlotte Mary Mew was born in Bloomsbury, London. She was educated at Lucy Harrison's School for Girls in Gower Street, where she dedicated herself specifically to the subjects that appealed to her: art, literature and music. Later she attended lectures at University College, London. When Mew was twenty-nine her father died, leaving the family in poor circumstances. A brother and a sister had to be confined to institutions because they became insane. Mew lived with her mother and sister, Anne, and the two girls took the decision never to marry and have children because of the taint of madness in the family. Mew's literary career began with the publication of her story 'Passed' in the second issue of the *Yellow Book* in 1894. She used to attend the Saturday evening parties at Henry Harland's home. She liked visiting Paris and Brittany, and some of her writing has French settings. As time went on, however, her life-style became increasingly secluded. Her essays, poems and stories were printed in the *Egoist*, the *Englishwoman*, the *Nation*, the *New Statesman* and *Temple Bar*. Mew wrote a play, *The China Bowl*, but is mainly acclaimed for her verse. *The Farmer's Bride*, a compilation of sixteen poems, came out in 1916. Her early poems were published posthumously in *The Rambling Sailor* (1929). In 1923 Mew was awarded a Civil List pension of £75 per annum. Her mother passed away that year, then Anne died of cancer in 1927. Mew was inconsolable. She became convinced that Anne might have been buried alive, and that her belongings and room were infected with the "germ" that had killed her sister. In 1928 she was admitted to a nursing home to receive treatment for neurasthenia, but committed suicide by drinking Lysol. Mew's writing was highly praised by de la Mare, Hardy, Masefield, Pound, Sassoon and Woolf, among others. Stylistically she is viewed as a significant transitional figure, poised between the old and the new.

OLIVE SCHREINER (1855–1920)

Olive Emilie Albertina Schreiner was born in South Africa, the child of missionaries. She worked as a governess before travelling to England, where her successful novel *The Story of an African Farm* paved the way for the New Woman fiction of the 1890s. Schreiner mixed with eminent intellectuals, including Havelock Ellis and Karl Pearson. Late in 1886, after a traumatic episode with Pearson, she retreated to Europe. During this period she wrote many moving allegories. Published in *Dreams* (1890) and *Dream Life and Real Life* (1893), they had a powerful impact upon the public and inspired the suffragettes. In 1889 Schreiner returned to South Africa, where she married Samuel Cronwright in 1894. Their only daughter died shortly after her birth. Schreiner spoke out against the government's imperialist and racist policies. She also supported suffrage organizations, and was vice-president of the Women's Enfranchisement League, but as a pacifist she did not advocate militant tactics. *Woman and Labour* (1911) warned women of the dangers of "sex-parasitism". Schreiner called for more career opportunities for women, and financial independence. She left her husband and lived in England during World War I, but died in South Africa after travelling back there in 1920. Schreiner's other works include: *The Political Situation* (co-authored with her husband in 1896); a novella, *Trooper Peter Halket of Mashonaland* (1897); *An English South African's View of the Situation* (1899); *Thoughts on South Africa* and *Stories, Dreams and Allegories* (1923), and the novels *From Man to Man* (1926) and *Undine* (1929).

EVELYN SHARP (1869–1955)
Evelyn Sharp was born in London, the youngest of nine children of a slate merchant. One of her brothers, Cecil Sharp, is remembered for his attempts to revive and preserve English folk dancing songs. Sharp was educated at home by her sisters before attending Strathallan House School, then attending boarding school in Kensington. Having finished her studies at the age of sixteen, to please her parents, she was unhappy with her "purposeless existence" and went to London in 1894. She supported herself by teaching private pupils. During the course of that year Sharp had the first of six stories accepted for publication in *The Yellow Book*, and became part of its circle. She was a journalist, novelist and short story writer. *Nicolette* came out in 1907, and then in 1910 the volume of short stories *Rebel Women*. These fictionalize some of her own experiences. Sharp also wrote children's books. She was an important figure in the suffragette movement, joining the Women's Social and Political Union in 1906. Her militant activities resulted in imprisonment, and she went on hunger strike in 1913. She was Vice-President of the Women Writers' Suffrage League and a founder member of the United Suffragists in 1914. When the war broke out, Sharp did not undertake war work as most other suffrage campaigners did. She declared herself to be a pacifist, and was a founder of the Women's League for Peace and Freedom. After the vote had been won, she did relief work for the Society of Friends in Germany and Russia. Sharp was an active campaigner for

many human rights and pacifist organizations. In 1933 she published a partial autobiography entitled *An Unfinished Adventure: Selected Reminiscences*. During that year she married her old friend Henry Nevinson. As well as having a way with words, she had musical talents: she wrote the libretto for Ralph Vaughan Williams's opera "The Poisoned Kiss". Her papers are in the Bodleian Library in Oxford.

EDITH WHARTON (1862–1937)

Edith Newbold Jones was born in New York, to a wealthy aristocratic family. From 1866-72 they travelled or resided in England, France, Germany, Italy and Spain, where Edith was schooled in the countries' languages and literatures. She wrote poetry at a young age, and had some verse published privately in 1878. Her parents introduced her into society at seventeen, but after marrying Theodore Wharton in 1885 Edith showed early and persistent signs of depression. She suffered from asthma, exhaustion and nausea, and underwent Silas Weir Mitchell's rest cure. The couple divorced in 1913. In collaboration with an architect Wharton published *The Decoration of Houses* in 1897, then she produced a series of articles on Italian villas and gardens. A volume of collected fiction, *The Greater Inclination*, came out in 1899, and a major novel, *The House of Mirth*, in 1905. Eventually she settled in France, returning to America only once to receive an honorary degree. During World War I Wharton opened a workroom in Paris for seamstresses, providing much-needed employment, and assisted civilian refugees by opening American Hostels. She set up The Children of Flanders Rescue Committee and established a cure programme for French soldiers who had contracted TB in the trenches. The French President made Wharton a Chevalier of the Legion of Honour in 1916. Altogether she wrote 46 books, including the novels *Ethan Frome* (1911) and the Pulitzer Prize winner *The Age of Innocence* (1920); stories, travel writing and her autobiography *A Backward Glance* (1934). She died in France, following a stroke.

MARY E. WILKINS (FREEMAN) (1852–1930)

Mary Eleanor Wilkins was born in Randolph, Massachusetts, the daughter of a carpenter. The family moved to Brattleboro, Vermont, when Mary was fifteen, but suffered financial misfortune. Her education was at Brattleboro High School, Mount Holyoke Female Seminary and Mrs Hosford's Glenwood Seminary. Initially Wilkins published children's poems, then won a prize from the Boston *Sunday Budget* for a story for adults. After her parents died she returned in 1884 to Randolph, where she lived for eighteen years with a childhood friend, Mary John Wales. The editor of *Harper's Bazaar* urged her to write about New England, and her "local color" stories proved to be highly successful. Wilkins's regional tales were compiled in fourteen volumes, such as *A Humble Romance and Other Stories* (1887), *A New England Nun and Other Stories*

(1891) and *Edgewater People* (1918). She penned thirteen novels, including *Jane Field* (1893), *Jerome, A Poor Man* (1897), *The Heart's Highway* (1900) and *The Portion of Labor* (1901). Her most acclaimed novel is *Pembroke* (1894). She also wrote children's books, and a play, *Giles Corey, Yeoman* (1893), about the Salem witch trials. From 1895 Wilkins began to travel, visiting Boston, Chicago and Paris. In 1902, after a long engagement, she married Charles M. Freeman, and they moved to Metuchen, New Jersey. Freeman was institutionalized in 1919 because of alcoholism, and the couple were legally separated in 1921. Mary Wilkins Freeman won great acclaim in her own lifetime, receiving the William Dean Howells gold medal for fiction and attaining recognition from the American Academy of Arts and Letters.

MABEL E. WOTTON (1863–1927)

Mabel Emily Wotton was born in Lambeth, London. A volume of her tales, entitled *A Pretty Radical and Other Stories*, was published in 1889. Her novel *A Girl Diplomatist* (1892) received unfavourable criticism. In 1896 a compilation of four of her stories formed part of the "Keynotes" series for John Lane's The Bodley Head. It was called *Day-Books*, but the author enlarged upon this with the explanatory phrase: "... chronicles of good and evil". The volume opens with a poem dedicated to Mrs Wilfrid Meynell (the poet Alice Meynell), reflecting Wotton's gratitude for her friendship and support. The Meynells were known for their kindness to a number of writers who were down on their luck, and welcomed young artists into their home in Palace Court. Wotton published another book of stories, *On Music's Wings* (1898). She died at home in London.

SOURCES

In 1891 Mona Caird published a volume called *A Romance of the Moors*, which contained "The Yellow Drawing-Room". The first edition is rare; the one used was published in 1892 by The English Library, No. 94. (Leipzig: Heinemann and Balestier Ltd. London).

"The Storm" was not published in its author's lifetime, but appeared posthumously in *The Complete Works of Kate Chopin* (ed. Per Seyerstad, Baton Rouge: Louisiana State University, 1969).

Ella D'Arcy's "An Engagement" is from *Modern Instances* (London: John Lane, 1898).

" 'The World's Slow Stain' " by Ella Hepworth Dixon is taken from *One Doubtful Hour and Other Side-Lights on the Feminine Temperament* (London: Grant Richards, 1904).

Ménie Muriel Dowie's "A Cowl in Cracow" was in *Some Whims of Fate* (London and New York: John Lane, The Bodley Head, 1897).

George Egerton's "The Mandrake Venus" was published in *Fantasias* (London: John Lane, 1898).

"The Yellow Wall-paper" by Charlotte Perkins Gilman was written in 1890, but was first published in the *New England Magazine*, New Series, vol.5, no.5, January 1892 (by Charlotte Perkins Stetson as she was then).

Sarah Grand "The Man in the Scented Coat" was printed in *Emotional Moments* (London: Hurst and Blackett, 1908).

"A Bird on its Journey" by Beatrice Harraden was published in *Blackwood's Magazine*, then in the volume *In Varying Moods* (Edinburgh and London: William Blackwood and Sons, 1894).

"Bro'r Abr'm Jimson's Wedding" by Pauline E. Hopkins was in the *Colored American Magazine*, December 1901, pp. 103–12.

Anna Kingsford's "The City of Blood" is dated 1877. It was published in *Dreams and Dream Stories* (London: John M. Watkins, 1908).

Charlotte Mew's "A White Night" came out in *Temple Bar*, CXXVII, May 1903, pp. 625–39.

Olive Schreiner's "Dream Life and Real Life: a Little African Story" was written for *The New College Magazine* in 1881, then published in the volume *Dream Life and Real Life* (London: T. Fisher Unwin, 1893).

Evelyn Sharp's "The Game that wasn't Cricket" was in *Rebel Women* (London: A.C. Fifield, 1910).

Edith Wharton's "The Quicksand" was published in *The Descent of Man and Other Stories* (London: Macmillan and Co., Ltd, 1904).

"The Revolt of 'Mother' " featured in *A New England Nun and Other Stories* by Mary E. Wilkins (published by Harper & Brothers in 1891, then in London by Osgood, McIlvaine & Co., 1894).

Mabel E. Wotton's "The Hour of Her Life" appeared in *Day-Books* (London: John Lane, 1896).

Printed in the United Kingdom
by Lightning Source UK Ltd.
9706400001BA